D0482352

TEMPERAMENT IN CLINICAL PRACTICE

TEMPERAMENT IN CLINICAL PRACTICE

STELLA CHESS, MD
ALEXANDER THOMAS, MD
New York University Medical Center

FOREWORD BY MELVIN LEWIS, MD

THE GUILFORD PRESS
New York London

LIBRARY OF CONGRESS CATALOGING IN PUBLICATION DATA

Chess, Stella.
  Temperament in clinical practice.

  Includes bibliographies and index.
  1. Temperament—Longitudinal studies.   2. Temperament in children—Longitudinal studies.   3. Psychiatry.
4. Child psychiatry.   I. Thomas, Alexander, 1914–
II. Title. [DNLM: 1. Personality.   2. Psychotherapy.
BF 798 C542t]
RC455.4.T45C44   1986   616.89′14   85-17733
ISBN 0-89862-669-2

Foreword

This book is rooted in the concern of two gifted clinician–investigators, Stella Chess and Alexander Thomas, for the clinician who is committed to as full an understanding as possible of the human nature of the child and family. This understanding requires a balanced perspective that not only includes the role of the environment and the individual contribution of the child, but most importantly, recognizes their interweaving, complex dynamic interactions over time.

In the course of their clinical observations and research, Chess and Thomas became fascinated with what they perceived as the individual styles that characterized each child—or rather, the peculiar shaping and reshaping of these styles as the child and his or her family develop. This phenomenon came to be known as the temperament of the child, and subsequently Chess and Thomas, together with the late Dr. Herbert Birch, launched their now famous New York Longitudinal Study in 1956.

The New York Longitudinal Study is an exemplary study of the enormous complexity of an interactional model. It shows, among other things, that the consistency of the interactional process constitutes a kind of continuity. This kind of continuity provides for a great deal of plasticity in development. While this plasticity makes prediction uncertain, it also suggests that early parental errors and even specific emotional trauma to the child do not necessarily have fixed, inevitable consequences, and that therapeutic intervention can help at any stage of development. Indeed, it suggests that improved subsequent experiences in themselves often have a therapeutic effect.

I think it is fair to say that these ideas challenged some previously held views on the causes of various developmental and clinical phenomena. Until the 1950s the prevailing explanations, when there was not actual organic brain damage present, were largely based on either psychoanalytic assumptions and inferences or behavioral and learning theory notions. Both approaches still serve us well. However, Thomas,

Chess, and Birch changed the balance when they added the important idea that the child, far from being a passive recipient, or simply a responder to various stimuli, was an active initiator and contributor to his or her own experience and development. They found too that this activity on the part of the child was determined to an extent by the child's temperament, and that the child's particular developmental characteristics contributed in important ways to some of the behavior disorders we see in children.

Numerous studies throughout the world have shown that temperament, which in itself derives in part from genetic influences, is associated with such observable phenomena as different levels of activity, varying degrees of sociability (including different reactions to the strange and the unfamiliar), school performance, differences in mother–child interactions, and accident rates in children. These findings suggested the possibility of therapeutic intervention and led to the search for clinical applications.

The idea of the child as an active person had of course been promulgated in some form by others. Rousseau, for example, in his book *Emile* in 1762, conceived of the child as a separate person who actively discovered the world and constructed his or her own knowledge—a forerunner, if you will, of modern Piagetian views of the construction of reality in the child. Rousseau was in fact probably the first to introduce the ideas of development and developmental stages. (The term "maturation" was later introduced by Gesell in the 1930s and 40s.) Freud too had laid the framework for an understanding of the active internal processes at work within the mind of the child. What is new here is not only the child's active contribution to his or her own actual life experiences and conflicts in the course of the child's interaction with parents and other individuals, but the notion of genotypical variations in style originating in the genotype of an individual and brought out and modified by the individual child's active interaction with his or her environment. In other words, here, as in breeds found in some other species, we can see a variety of strains among human beings (such as fearful, shy, and timid; or bold, outgoing, and aggressive), with each strain modified and capable of being shaped by experience, teaching, and learning. (Interestingly, such "strains" have been suggested by previous investigators—Jung, for example, suggested two types, the introvert and the extravert; however, the scientific data for such strains were hitherto found lacking.)

Over and over again, Chess and Thomas found possible clinical uses for their findings. These clinical applications soon came to the attention of pediatricians, educators, mental health professionals, and nurses, as well as of those parents who at times felt baffled by their children's behavior.

All of us are aware of an individual who attacks a new experience with gusto and enthusiasm, or one who very cautiously, perhaps fearfully, dips but one toe at a time to test the water. The goal for the child is, or should be, mastery. How does a particular child go about achieving this goal, what may interfere with the accomplishment of the task, and how may the child be helped in this endeavor? The central concept Chess and Thomas devised to study and understand these questions was that of the "goodness of fit" in the complex interactions over time between the child's temperament and the environment.

These two concepts, temperament and goodness of fit, were found to give clinicians an additional general way of understanding the various and varying difficulties children of the same family have with their parents (and vice versa), and specifically offered clinicians the opportunity to identify certain particular temperamental characteristics that predict to some degree the possibility of a "poor fit" between the child and his or her caretakers. Here then was a practical approach that added to our way of assessing behavior and the difficulties that may arise between child and parent.

In their study, about one in ten children was found to have a so-called "difficult" temperament, and about one in six was in the "slow-to-warm-up" group. About two-fifths of the children studied were found to have an "easy" temperament. Parents worry a great deal about their children, especially the difficult child. They may also feel guilty and believe that they have caused the difficulty. Often this is far from the truth, and the parents can be reassured and helped to learn better ways of handling the child with a difficult temperament.

None of us, least of all Chess and Thomas, is so naive as to think that children and parents can be so easily and simply categorized, advised, and reassured, once and for all time. The matter is more complicated; hence the need for this book. Here Chess and Thomas trace the intricate weavings of life's vicissitudes in the myriad of stresses and circumstances that impinge on individuals within a family, making full use of the goodness of fit model as a framework through which they analyze and demonstrate some of the causes of difficulties between child and parent.

Temperament, of course, is not confined to children, and neither is development. Chess and Thomas recognize this in their descriptions of temperament and adult development, and in the even greater complexity of "fits" that may occur.

Temperament is not a theory of development; rather it is but one attribute of an individual—albeit an important one. Similarly, the therapist does not confine his or her approach to treatment primarily to issues of temperament: most treatments in child psychiatry now include multiple approaches. However, this book focuses on the treatment of individuals in whom temperamental issues are prominent and important in the development of the behavioral difficulties that bring such an individual to the attention of the teacher, nurse, pediatrician, or child psychiatrist.

This book represents a sound, almost commonsense approach to understanding and managing the difficult child. But it is more than that: it is the distillation of years of careful observations and compassionate work with children and their parents over their lifetimes. The rare wisdom imparted in this volume is worth our attention. We are not so advanced in our understanding and success in treatment that we can afford to overlook this contribution to our professional armamentarium. We, like the children and parents so thoughtfully described in this book, need all the help we can get. Chess and Thomas offer such help.

Melvin Lewis, MD

Preface

We have written this volume to formulate in practical usable form the clinical application of the concept of temperament. This was the primary reason we committed ourselves in 1956 to start the New York Longitudinal Study (NYLS) and carry it forward for 30 years. Thus, both our research studies and the preparation of this volume have been motivated by a similar professional concern. The longitudinal study was initiated in 1956 because we had become aware as clinicians that an important aspect of the human nature of infants, children, adolescents, and adults was being ignored by the dominant concepts that shaped the clinical assessments and therapeutic intervention of that period. And now, both our research and that of others, as well as our continuing clinical experience, have come to a point where it is possible to take stock and offer substantial information in a form that other clinicians can utilize in their professional work.

Our interest in the study of temperament arose primarily from our experiences in clinical psychiatric practice in the 1940s and early 1950s. During those decades, the dominant theoretical formulations gave exclusive etiologic importance for both healthy and pathologic psychological development to environmental forces—first and foremost the influence of the mother or other primary caretaker. Also included, to varying degrees, depending on one's particular conceptual viewpoint, were other intra- and extrafamilial environmental factors. The significance for the developmental process of individual differences in behavioral style, a phenomenon evident even in the neonate and young infant, was, with few exceptions, either ignored, minimized, or categorized as secondary reactive effects of the caretakers' attitudes and practices.

However, as clinicians we saw too many cases in which this one-sided environmentalist approach could not, at least to our satisfaction, explain adequately the child or adult's developmental course or personality structure. As important as the influence of family and the larger social environment was, there was something missing. It was our hypothesis that at least one significant gap in our clinical evaluations resulted from assigning the child only a secondary reactive role, rather than an active one. Development then would reflect the continuous dynamic interaction between the individual and the environment at all sequential age-periods.

We first explored the possible usefulness of our hypothesis by formulating impressionistic judgments as to the child's own behavioral characteristics from the clinical data we obtained in individual cases. It was exciting to find that even these simplified and impressionistic evaluations widened significantly our understanding of the dynamics of the origins and evolution of these children's behavior problems. The implications for prevention and treatment were apparent and significant.

These clinical experiences encouraged us to make the commitment to a systematic study of individual behavioral styles and their functional significance for psychological development. A search of the literature revealed a number of pertinent reports of specific aspects of behavioral individuality, but none that had attempted a systematic comprehensive study of this phenomenon, nor provided a methodology adequate for such an endeavor. It was clear to us that a prospective longitudinal study was required, in which data of sufficient scope and pertinence could be gathered and analyzed to test our hypothesis. With this commitment to test our clinically based hypothesis of the significance of individual behavioral styles for the process of development, we launched the New York Longitudinal Study in 1956.

Our clinical judgment shaped our decisions as to the kind of data we should gather, and the data then provided us with clues as to the categories of individuality that seemed functionally significant. But these clinical evaluations were not adequate to the development of a comprehensive identification of the categories of behavioral individuality, nor to the formulation of a quantitative scheme of rating these categories. This task was brilliantly accomplished by Dr. Herbert Birch, who became our coworker until his untimely death in 1973. Dr. Michael Rutter also contributed significantly to the progress of our study in its early years by his incisive critique of our methods and concepts. He also pointed out that the term "temperament" was a more fitting characterization for the qualities of individuality we were studying than the awkward and rather inaccurate label of "primary reaction pattern" that we had been using.

Our findings have been reported in a number of research articles and volumes over the years. These have highlighted the results of the quantitative and statistical analyses of our data, a complex and demanding task that Drs. Jack Cohen and Sam Korn accomplished for us. These quantitative studies have been vital in elucidating many issues and in identifying correlations and connections for which qualitative analysis alone would have been inadequate.

At the same time, we have always simultaneously searched for the clinical significance of our findings. For us, the most important goal of our studies has remained unchanged from our original incentive to undertake this work. How can our findings on the functional significance of temperament be useful to the mental health professional, the pediatrician, the nurse, and the educator in the prevention and treatment of behavior disorders? We have discussed various aspects of this fundamental question in a number of our publications, and an increasing number of clinical research workers have taken up this issue in recent years. In this volume, we have attempted to bring together the accumulated knowledge from our own longitudinal studies, from our clinical experience, and from the work of other clinicians, in a form that will be useful to professionals responsible for advising and treating families and individual children and adults. Parents may also find a number of sections of this volume helpful in managing their day-by-day caretaking responsibilities with their children.

We are fortunate that Dr. William Carey consented to write Chapter 14, "Temperament and Pediatric Practice." Dr. Carey has not only pioneered in the application of our knowledge of temperament to the clinical practice of pediatrics, but has also made important theoretical, clinical, and methodological contributions to the fields of temperament research and behavioral pediatrics. Dr. Carey likes to refer to himself as "just a country doctor." In return, we remind him how many "country doctors" have made basic contributions to clinical theory and practice in all fields of medicine.

We have organized this volume into three sections. The first reviews the findings on the functional significance of temperament, in which the primary importance of the interaction of the individual's temperament with pertinent environmental factors is emphasized. For the child, this means first of all the interaction with parents, and this is discussed in Chapters 2 and 3. The importance of temperament can never be viewed in the abstract, but only with regard to the individual's developmental level and the environmental context. The succeeding chapters of this first section, therefore, focus the discussion on the role of temperament at succeeding age-stage developmental levels.

Although this first section constitutes a general overview of temperament, we have tried to make the discussion directly applicable to the clinician's interest.

The second section deals with direct clinical applications for diagnosis, prevention, and treatment. It is not our intent to try to give any kind of overall comprehensive survey of these clinical issues as such. This attempt would take several volumes. Rather, we have kept our focus on the issue of temperament as it involves diagnostic procedures, and as it provides an important tool for prevention and treatment.

The third section focuses on the role of temperament in special areas of interest to clinicians and educators: school functioning, pediatric practice, nursing practice, and the handicapped child. The final chapter of the volume provides a summary and overview, and looks to the perspective for future research in issues of temperament.

Inasmuch as many of our readers will be familiar with our categories of temperament and their definitions, we have placed this information in Appendix A. Readers unfamiliar with this material might find it helpful to go through this Appendix before starting Chapter 1. The issue of consistency and change in temperament over time is of great theoretical and practical significance, but in the main does not bear directly on clinical practice. We have therefore included a discussion of this question in Appendix B rather than in the text itself.

Throughout the volume, we have relied on our "goodness of fit" model in analyzing the interaction between temperament and environment, and in providing the theoretical basis for the approach to prevention and treatment. This has involved rephrasing of this concept as we have applied it in the different sections and chapters. Inevitably, therefore, there are overlappings and repetitions in different chapters. This was unavoidable, otherwise each chapter could not have constituted an integrated unit.

We express our appreciation to Dr. Carey and to Dr. Margaret Hertzig for their careful review of the entire manuscript of this volume, and for their many helpful suggestions which have significantly enhanced its quality.

Contents

TEMPERAMENT IN CLINICAL PRACTICE

PART ONE

The Functional Significance of Temperament

CHAPTER 1

The Significance of Temperament

Whether we are mental health professionals, pediatricians, nurses, or educators, we are concerned with the individual differences in the behavioral patterns of children, adolescents, and adults. Why does the management of one 6-month-old infant go smoothly and easily, while another is so difficult that the parents are chronically exhausted, and, to boot, often guilty or angry at the child, or both? Why does one 3-year-old take cheerfully and quickly to any new situation, while another is inhibited and shy, and literally clings to her mother's skirts? Why does one 5-year-old with a bad cold and fever become very quiet, while another fusses and cries continuously? Why does one 6-year-old find the visit to the pediatrician's office a pleasant experience in which she cooperates peacefully with the examination and treatment procedures, while another cries and struggles from beginning to end with the same pediatrician? Why does one well-functioning adult respond to a new challenge at work with immediate interest and zest, while another equally competent worker approaches a similar challenge cautiously, with initial resistance and even distress?

As clinicians we are concerned with these differences, which produce smooth and effective mastery of the usual environmental expectations and demands in some, and even in most children, adolescents, and adults. Yet, in others, who are not suffering from any major psychiatric disorder, these same environmental challenges, whether in the home, in school, with peers, or at work, are mastered only with difficulty, or not at all. What factors are responsible for these behavioral differences? How can we intervene most effectively to change or at least ameliorate the problems in functioning and coping that this latter group of individuals experience?

Thirty years ago, most professionals had a simple answer to these questions. Deviant and maladaptive behavior was presumed to derive primarily and directly from the influence of the family, especially the mother, in the early years of life (Chess, 1964). We now know, from a number of long-term developmental studies, that the child's early life does not fix decisively the course of his subsequent psychological development. Behavioral patterns can change at any age-period, and even change qualitatively, if a significant change in the individual or the environment alters the dynamics of the developmental process (Kagan, 1984; Murphy & Moriarty, 1976; Thomas & Chess, 1980; Vaillant, 1977; Werner & Smith, 1982). Furthermore, the influence of the parents in the first years of the child's life is only one of a number of biological and environmental variables, albeit an important one, which interact with each other over time in shaping the course of psychological development.

Among these functionally significant variables is the individual's temperament, that is, *how* she behaves, as contrasted to *why* the individual does what she does (motivation), and to how *well* she does it (abilities).[1] The extensive studies of temperament in recent years from our own research unit, as well as from a number of other centers (see Porter & Collins, 1982), have provided specific and detailed data on the theoretical and practical importance of temperament. As summarized by Rutter (1982) in a recent international conference on temperament research: "The last decade has seen a burgeoning of interest in temperament. There has been an accompanying substantial growth in our knowledge and understanding of the importance of temperamental differences. Temperament constitutes a variable of considerable predictive power in developmental psychopathology, a power with both practical and theoretical implications" (p. 14).

While emphasizing the functional importance of temperament, in no way do we advocate a temperament-based theory of personality. As we put it in one of our earlier volumes:

> As in the case when any significant influencing variable is identified, there is an understandable temptation to make temperament the heart and body of a general theory. To do so would be to repeat a frequent approach in psychiatry, which, over the years, has been beset by general theories of behavior based upon fragments rather than the totality of influencing mechanisms. A one-sided emphasis on temperament would merely repeat and perpetuate such a tendency and would be antithetical

---

1. We presume that most readers will be familiar with our categories of temperament and their definition. For those readers who are unfamiliar with this material, we have included Appendix A, which summarizes this information.

to our viewpoint, which insists that we recognize temperament as only one attribute of the organism . . . the relevance of the concept of temperament to general psychiatric theory lies neither in its sole pertinence for behavior disorders, nor in its displacement of other conceptualizations, but in the fact that it must be incorporated into any general theory of normal and aberrant behavioral development if the theory is to be complete. (Thomas, Chess, & Birch, 1968, pp. 182–183)

Behavioral issues in which temperamental characteristics play a significant role may come to the clinician's attention in a number of ways; (1) extremes of one or another temperamental traits or constellations which are within the normal range, but appear deviant and abnormal to the parents or others, and may be creating some problems of mastery and adaptation; (2) an unfavorable interaction between the individual and the environment so that one or another temperamental characteristic becomes exaggerated to the point where it is pathologic; (3) a more extensive unfavorable temperament–environment interaction so that a more generalized behavior disorder develops; and (4) the presence of a psychiatric disorder or physical handicap, such as organic brain disorder, mental retardation, deafness, and so forth, in which one or another temperamental trait intensifies and/or modifies the symptomatology.

A NORMAL EXTREME OF TEMPERAMENT

This is perhaps most often seen in children with a marked pattern of difficult temperament. Such a youngster's irregularity, intense negative responses to new situations or demands, and slow adaptability usually makes the process of socialization—establishment of regular sleep and feeding patterns, positive peer relations, adaptation to school—relatively arduous and prolonged, especially when compared to the temperamentally easy child. This may even lead to the judgment that the child is actually suffering from a psychiatric disorder, and the child may be given a clinical diagnosis such as adjustment disorder or "minimal brain dysfunction." Some child psychiatrists have even raised the question as to whether difficult temperament in fact represents a mild stage of behavior problem (Stevenson & Graham, 1982). Several considerations, however, militate against this position. First, if difficult temperament, as we have defined it, represented a mild pattern of psychopathology, then we would have to find a cause for this pathology, either in the form of brain damage or an excessively stressful environment, or both. Yet, our detailed New York Longitudinal Study records show a number of instances in which no such pathogenic factor was evident in the infancy period, at which time the difficult temperament constellation was already clearly evident. Where a behavior disorder did develop in this group, and this did occur more frequently than with any other temperamental pattern, it was most often the case that the excessively stressful parental functioning, or other pathogenic environmental factors, developed *after*, and not *before* the child's difficult temperament pattern was already evident. Second, when a behavior disorder did develop in a child with difficult temperament, the symptoms and areas of disturbed functioning varied from one child to another. If difficult temperament represented the first stage of such a disorder, why should the "symptoms" be so uniform at this "first stage," and so different at a more severe stage? Third, some, though not all, children with difficult temperament who did not develop a behavior disorder, continued to show this temperamental pattern into adult life, though they functioned well and were symptom-free throughout.

This issue is by no means academic, but has great clinical significance. Difficult temperament is infrequent (about 10% in our longitudinal sample). Easy temperament is much more frequent (about 40% in our sample), the slow-to-warm-up group makes up about 15%, and the remainder cannot be easily categorized in one of these three constellations. Parents of a temperamentally difficult child often worry that their child's irregular sleep, frequent fussing and crying, and slowness of adaptation to the new, as compared to other children they know, might mean that they are "bad" parents. If the clinician labels this behavioral style as evidence of a behavior disorder, he will inevitably look for the cause in the parents' child-care attitudes and practices. This can only reinforce the parents' worry that they must be bad parents, intensify the anxiety and guilt over this fear, and convince the clinician that these are disturbed parents who are the cause of the child's presumed deviant behavior. If, on the other hand, the clinician identifies the pattern as difficult temperament for which the parents are not responsible, he can reassure them and advise them as to the optimal methods of child care for such a child.

Other extremes of temperament can also be mistaken for pathology. The slow-to-warm-up child may be labeled as timid and anxious because she stands at the periphery of any new group. The highly active child may be called hyperactive; the low-active child may be considered to be sluggish or developmentally retarded. The highly distractible child may come under suspicion for brain damage, especially if he is also highly active. Moralistic judgments may also be made. One father in our longitudinal study sample, himself a very persistent individual, had a son with high distractibility and low persistence. The father interpreted his boy's inability to stick with a task without breaks or distractions as a character defect. He labeled his son as "lacking will-power" and "character," and persisted in this judgment in spite of all our discussions with him. Finally, these labels became self-fulfilling prophecies, as the son came to believe his father's pronouncements and lost all his motivation for independent achievement in adolescence and adult life.

EXAGGERATION OF A TEMPERAMENTAL CHARACTERISTIC

If the expectations and demands made upon a child are excessive because of one or another temperamental characteristic, the result may be a pathologic exaggeration of that particular temperamental trait or constellation. Thus, slow-to-warm-up children may be pressured by parents or teachers to adapt quickly and even immediately to a new play group or school setting, instead of allowing them first to stand at the edge of the group, and then move in gradually. Such a demand is unrealistic and stressful for such youngsters, and may only lead to an intensification of their initial withdrawal response to the point where they do not adapt adequately at all to the new situation. A highly active child may be expected to sit quietly for several hours or more at her school desk, during long automobile rides, or at protracted family dinners, without giving the child breaks in which to expend harmlessly at least some of her pent-up motoric energy. Such an expectation is all too likely to lead to fidgety and restless behavior as the child is made to sit still, and overactive and uncontrolled motor activity once she is released. Persistent children who are pulled away abruptly and without notice from an activity in which they are absorbed, may react by a prolonged insistence on returning to the activity, which ends in a destructive battle with parent, teacher, or nurse. The temperamentally difficult youngster who is expected to adapt immediately and cheerfully to new places and new people may very well respond by an exaggeration of her intense negative reactions which makes the child an unwelcome guest and a trial to the family. A child with mild intensity of expressiveness may be scolded repeatedly by the parents for not showing the kind of happy appreciative responses to special treats and occasions they consider appropriate. The stress and anxiety occasioned by these criticisms might cause an emotional inhibition that would make it harder for the youngster to even express her normal mild level of positive mood.

These are not hypothetical examples, but rather case instances, among many others, that we have documented among the subjects in our longitudinal study. Such pathologic exaggeration of a temperamental characteristic was harmful to the child first of all by its direct consequences on her self-image, social relationships, and activities. Beyond this, such a pathologic exaggeration, unless identified quickly and corrected, usually led to a snowballing interaction with the environment which had further unhealthy consequences. Pressured slow-to-warm-up children began to consider themselves socially deficient, and this became a self-fulfilling prophecy as they began to avoid new situations in which they couldn't meet parents' standards of quick adaptation. The restrained highly active youngster who became impulsively overactive when the opportunity arose, began to have the problems of adjustment and functioning of the truly hyperactive child. The destructive battles of the overly persistent child led to reactions of condemnation and punishment by teachers and others which eventually eroded seriously the child's sense of self-worth. The irritation and anger engendered in others by the temperamentally difficult child led to defensive responses that created new and more serious symptoms of behavioral disturbance. The emotional inhibition of the child with mild intensity of expressiveness led to further devaluation by the parents, unfavorable comparisons with their other children, so that the child became the family scapegoat.

Clinically, the pathologic exaggeration of a temperamental characteristic may resemble symptoms that are the result of other types of psychopathology. Thus, extreme temperamental persistence must be differentiated from the perseveration of an organic brain syndrome, extreme high activity from the hyperactivity of the so-called attention deficit disorder, and the emotional and social inhibition of the pressured slow-to-warm-up child from the social unawareness and inability to relate to other people of the autistic child. The clinical criteria for the differential diagnosis of temperament-related behavioral symptoms and other psychopathology will be discussed in Chapter 9 of the present volume.

BEHAVIOR DISORDER DEVELOPMENT

Basically, a psychologically determined behavior disorder in a child or adult develops out of a substantial incompatibility between the individual's capacities and coping abilities and the expectations and demands of the environment. (We have called this concept "a poorness of fit," as contrasted with "a goodness of fit" when there is compatibility, and this will be discussed in Chapter 2.) Such incompatibility may result from many different patterns of interaction between the individual and the environment, and the consequences of the incompatibility may take many different forms. The role of temperament in such a pathogenic developmental process can be very varied, as illustrated in the previous section of this chapter—the slow-to-warm-up child who is pressured to adjust to a new group quickly, the highly active youngster who is expected to sit still without interruption for long periods of time, and so forth. In some children, a behavior disorder begins and evolves in the manner described in this previous section: first a pathologic exaggeration of a temperamental characteristic or constellation, followed by a snowballing interaction with the environment that leads to further unhealthy consequences. In other individuals, the incompatibility and poorness of fit leads to a behavior disorder with one or another pattern of symptoms without an initial stage of temperamental exaggeration.

In no way are we saying that temperament *always* plays a significant role in the development of a behavior disorder. Environmental demands can become excessive for many reasons, such as an unrecognized mental retardation or dyslexia, a severe physical handicap whose consequences are minimized or exaggerated by parents, teachers, or others, or a biological disturbance that leads to an endogenous depression, schizophrenia, or an organic brain syndrome. In rare cases, a special environmental trauma may be an overwhelming stress in itself and in its direct consequences (K. Erikson, 1976; Terr, 1981).

TEMPERAMENT AND PHYSICAL HANDICAP

Individuals with a serious physical handicap, such as blindness, deafness, cerebral palsy, or functionally significant congenital defects, necessarily find the adaptation to the new and the mastery of routines of living more difficult and stressful than do nonhandicapped persons.

For the handicapped child or adult, his temperamental characteristics may make these necessary adaptations less difficult, more difficult, or, in some cases, even impossible (Chess, Fernandez, & Korn, 1980). The highly persistent handicapped child may succeed in many efforts where the less persistent youngster may have given up. The child with a tendency to intense negative mood reactions may develop trantrums or other severe frustration responses as she struggles with the tasks her handicap makes so difficult. Such intense frustrations all too often interfere further with the child's coping abilities. Another child with the same handicap, but with predominantly mild positive mood responses, may experience only minor feelings of frustration, which do not interfere significantly with the ability to master the same tasks.

For handicapped children, therefore, their temperamental individuality may be even more important in influencing their developmental course than for nonhandicapped children. Here, again, we are not saying that temperament is the all-decisive factor. The handicapped child's ability to master the routines of living and to pursue her own goals effectively is influenced by a number of other factors as well—the presence of special talents, how the parents and teachers handle the problems created by the child's handicap, whether the school and community are structured so as to facilitate or hinder the child's own efforts, whether a new age-period, such as adolescence, brings a new more complex environment that proves especially difficult for the child to master (Chess et al., 1980).

This overview of temperament and its functional significance for normal and deviant psychological development raises a number of issues for the clinician and educator. How can I identify my patient or student's temperament in the office, hospital, or classroom? How can I distinguish a temperamental characteristic that is normal from one that is a pathologic exaggeration? How can I tease out the specific influence of temperament in a case of behavior disorder or physical handicap? How can I apply my knowledge of the individual's temperament to map out an appropriate strategy of prevention and treatment? These are the questions with which this volume is concerned. But, first, in the next chapters, it is desirable to discuss a number of general concepts, which will provide a theoretical framework for the specific clinical discussions to follow.

CHAPTER 2

Goodness of Fit: Control and Mastery versus the Controlling Parent or Child

As we have emphasized in Chapter 1, in no way do we advocate a temperament-based theory of personality. So many factors influence the course of normal and deviant psychologic development, that any theory based on one set of determinants, whether these are genes, neurochemical structures, instinctual drives, temperament, conditioned reflex patterns, early life experience, or the impact of the extra-familial social environment, is bound to be simplistic and inadequate. Thus, Marmor, after enumerating the many variables that have to be considered in the study of personality, concludes that "we begin to get a glimpse of how difficult it is to accurately trace the origins of specific personality patterns at all, let alone to try to derive them from just one or two variables" (1983, p. 856).

Furthermore, the characteristics of the individual and the environment also interact continuously with each other, so that the influence on development of any one factor may be modified or changed at sequential age-periods. Also, the nature of the interplay among these variables may be different from one person to another, or at different ages in the same person. These complexities and variabilities of the process of psychologic development have been increasingly high-lighted by the research findings of recent years in developmental psychology and psychiatry (Thomas, 1981), and have brought to the forefront of current theory a number of related conceptualizations, including the interactional model (Thomas & Chess, 1980), the trans-

11

actional model (Sameroff, 1975), the life-span developmental perspective (Baltes, Reese, & Lipsitt, 1980), the biopsychosocial model (Engel, 1977), and systems theory (Marmor, 1983). These various formulations, though they may differ in their specific emphases and terminologies, all agree on the need for interacting multidimensional approaches to the study of both normal and pathological development. Such an orientation also indicates, as Rutter has put it, that "attention must be paid to the specificities of person–situation interactions . . . it may be suggested that it is preferable to take an idiographic approach which explicitly focuses on the individuality of human beings—not just in the degree to which they show particular traits or even in terms of the traits which are relevant to them, but more generally in terms of the idiosyncrasies which make each person uniquely different from all others" (1980, p. 5).

THE "GOODNESS OF FIT" MODEL

In our own studies of normal and pathologic development, we have found the goodness of fit model to be a most useful conceptual framework and analytic strategy for the implementation of an interactionist approach that focuses on the specific characteristics of the developmental process in each specific person. This model postulates that healthy functioning and development occurs when there is a goodness of fit (what we have called "compatibility" in Chapter 1) between the capacities and characteristics of the individual and the demands and expectations of the environment. If, on the other hand, there is a poorness of fit (what we have called "incompatibility" in Chapter 1) between individual and environment, psychologic functioning is impaired, with the risk of behavior disorder development (Thomas & Chess, 1980; Thomas, Chess, & Birch, 1968). Poorness of fit in specific cases can arise in a number of different ways, can involve different psychologic and environmental factors in different individuals, and can express itself in different interactional processes and sequences (Chess & Thomas, 1984). It is of interest that the goodness of fit concept has been utilized in recent years by a number of other investigators of normal and pathologic child development (Greenspan, 1981; Kagan, 1971; Murphy, 1981; Stern, 1977). A similar formulation has also been applied by Dubos as a measure of physical health: "Health can be regarded as an expression of fitness to the environment, as a state of adaptedness. . . . The words health and disease are meaningful only when defined in terms of a given person functioning in a given physical and social environment" (1965, pp. 350–351). In a larger sense, the goodness of fit model is also consonant with the Darwinian concept of natural selection. In this basic formulation of evolutionary theory, those organisms whose characteristics are most adaptive to their environment, that is, who show a goodness of fit with their environment, have the best chance to survive and flourish. Similarly, for human beings on the psychologic level, those persons whose characteristics are most adaptive to their environment, that is, who show a goodness of fit with environmental demands and expectations, have the best chance to flourish in their psychologic development. Also, the concept of natural selection does not specify only one or two or three ways in which favorable or unfavorable adaptation to the environment can occur, but includes the possibility of multiple and varied types of species–environment interaction that can be adaptive or maladaptive. The goodness of fit concept also does not specify that any one pattern of species–environment interaction is required for favorable psychologic development to occur. As with natural selection, goodness or poorness of fit includes the possiblility that multiple, varied, and unpredictable types of interactional patterns may produce either adaptive or maladaptive functioning.

It is our responsibility as clinicians to promote such a goodness of fit, to do our best to change a poorness of fit to a goodness of fit. This involves first the attempt to modify or change those environmental demands and expectations, whether within the family or outside it, that are incompatible with the person's capacities. Secondly, it requires the effort, wherever possible, to help the individual mobilize, and, if necessary, to modify his behavioral patterns to achieve an optimal goodness of fit with the environment. In this volume, we are concerned with temperament, and its role in promoting either a goodness or poorness of fit in specific person–environment interactions. This concern is not academic, but focuses on the strategies that can be employed to change a temperament–environment poorness of fit to a goodness of fit. This in no way implies a judgment that temperament is always a prominent factor in a poorness of fit that leads to a behavior disorder. Other characteristics of the person, such as motivation, pathogenic defense mechanisms, and handicaps or illnesses, may also play important roles in the evolution of a poorness of fit. In some individuals these factors may be dominant, and temperament may play a relatively minor or even insignificant part in the development of a behavior disorder. In other persons, as will be documented in subsequent chapters of this volume (especially Chapters 3–8), even when these other characteristics are influential, temperament may also contribute significantly to the evolution of a pathologic developmental course.

The proposal that parents should shape the expectations and demands they make on their children to be compatible with their youngsters' temperaments, raises two opposite questions. If a parent learns how to influence effectively a child's functioning through a knowledge of the youngster's temperament, are we not in danger of aiding and abetting the development of a manipulative, controlling parent? And, conversely, if the parent should modify his or her behavior to fit a youngster's temperament, are we not in danger of fostering the creation of a child tyrant? These concerns raise the issue of differentiating healthy control and mastery by parent and child from the undesirable and potentially pathogenic pattern of the controlling parent or child.

CONTROL AND MASTERY VERSUS
THE CONTROLLING PARENT OR CHILD

The parents, or their surrogates, are the primary caretakers, and as such have the major responsibility for the health and welfare of their children. But responsibility must be accompanied by authority. Specifically, the parent must be able to excercise substantial control over the child's environment, and make those demands that are essential for the youngster's healthy functioning and development.

The term "control" has contradictory connotations. On the one hand, it is used in a positive sense, as when we speak of self-control, control of a machine's operation, or control of one's daily schedule. On the other hand, we use the term negatively when we speak of a despot's control of his or her subjects' actions, or thought control, or a controlling parent. Mastery, by contrast, has unambiguous connotations. People are masters of their fate; one masters a subject or task; an actor or musician performs in a masterly fashion.

The issue with parents is whether they use their authority and control for the child's benefit or whether the control is exercised to satisfy some self-centered desire. Parental control that promotes children's progressive mastery of environmental expectations and their own goals and impulses is not only desirable, but essential. Parental control that serves the parent's goals at the expense of the child, such as a neurotic need for domination or for creating a perfect child, makes for a controlling parent whose influence on the youngster's development is likely to be pathologic. It is also true that the parent who is unable to exercise authority and control will be ineffective, with consequences for the child that may be as unfavorable as those created by a controlling parent. Thus, the parent who fails to exercise the necessary controls in enforcing safety rules, and the parent who insists on excessive restriction of the child's activities because of his or her own anxieties, are both endangering their youngster's welfare, though in opposite ways.

PARENTAL CONTROL VERSUS THE CONTROLLING PARENT

The need to differentiate parental control from the controlling parent is evident in evaluating the significance of the parent's reactions to the child's temperament.

The child with a high activity level provides a clear illustration. For a child of high activity level, even in early infancy, the caretaker must be especially on guard lest the child give a sudden wiggle or twist and fall off a table or bed while diapers or clothing are being changed. For an infant of low activity level, content to lie quietly while safety precautions must always be taken, the caretaker need not be alert for such swift movement. As the infant grows older, changing diapers and clothing can be done with ease for a quiet baby, with some ingenuity for a moderately active child, but for a youngster with a high activity level the caretaker must be swift, deft, and often mobile as this squirming, moving body is being dressed, played with, or bathed. Such measures are clearly necessary for safety and should not be considered to be signs of "controlling" caretaker behavior. Later, when the child is at the toddler stage, restrictions on freedom of movement will also be varied, depending upon the child's activity level. A quiet toddler who is happily sitting tearing up paper, might safely be left for a moment while some action takes the caretaker out of the room briefly. With moderate, and especially high activity as a child characteristic, it is more prudent to organize the other task so as not to leave the child alone, even for a moment, unless the room has been thoroughly childproofed and all potentially dangerous objects are out of reach. What is considered out of reach may prove not to be—the highly active youngster may be able to climb and reach an object that has been placed on a shelf thought to be beyond reach—and in the attempt to climb up, the child may topple over the book shelf or chest he was attempting to climb. Rearranging rooms, closing doors that give onto stairs, and fixing barricades may be overcontrolling for one child but may be merely prudent precaution-taking for another.

Once the child is of school age, another set of decisions arise that constitute parental control, but do not merit the negative title of "controlling." One set of parents with a highly active and very agile boy of 7 years, and with a number of trees on their land, made a rule as to which trees the child was allowed to climb. Their reasoning was that, if the child were forbidden to climb trees at all, he would do so unobserved and indiscriminately. The trees they prohibited were those with no limbs for many feet from the ground, while those they permitted had low branches that might break the boy's fall were his grip to fail. Since his parents were aware of the child's penchant for going higher than any of his friends, this rule allowed him to join in their games with at least some degree of parental assurance that, if he fell, while he might break an arm or leg, he would be less likely to sustain a skull fracture. As a child increases in age, parents have less and less control to specify actions that are off limits, but they can expect that, if their early rules had been reasonable and consistent, older children and adolescents will continue to set reasonable and consistent limits for themselves when they are on their own.

In the Puerto Rican working-class sample of the NYLS, by contrast to our middle-class families, parental restriction of high-activity children was more extreme and even harmful, but still represented necessary control and not controlling behavior. These working-class parents lived in the East Harlem area of Manhattan, where the streets were unsafe, and where there were no nearby neighborhood children's recreational facilities available. Because the streets were dangerous, the younger children were cooped-up in their small apartments. This did not represent an excessively stressful poorness of fit for the low-activity children, but did so for the high-activity children. If anything, the latter group of children had more restrictions imposed on them as to playing outside the home, because the parents rightfully feared that their high activity level put them at higher risk for dangerous accidents in the unsafe streets. As a result, in this sample, children's high activity became a significant factor in the production of a behavior disorder. By contrast, in the middle-class families who mostly lived in the areas where the streets were safe, or if not so, had adequate recreational facilities available to their children, in no case did high activity enter into a pathogenic poorness of fit.

The controlling parent, on the other hand, would unnecessarily restrict the movements of the high-activity child. Typically, such parents would demand that their children sit still for long periods of time and expect that the youngsters should be able to play quietly without moving, so as not to inconvenience or bother them. These parents would basically not be concerned with finding safe and reasonable outlets for the child's physical energies, but rather would be demanding conformity to their own a priori standards and desires.

The issue of parental control can also be illustrated with the temperamental traits of distractibility and persistence. A highly distractible infant can ease many of the caretaker's responsibilities. When diapering or changing the infants, should he turn in a position that makes for difficulty of handling, a toy placed in the proper direction will distract the infant so that he turns in a convenient manner. If the infant, as a crawling baby, comes across a sharp object, it can be removed easily if a substitute is offered to engage the infant's interest elsewhere. As a toddler, with longer cruising range and greater possibilities for danger, the ability to obtain the infant's attention through distraction can make for safety without conflict. In middle childhood, should he begin to discuss a topic loudly that may not be socially acceptable or convenient in public, the child can be diverted and the discussion deferred to a more suitable time and place. In all of these instances, the parent is in control, but unlikely to be deemed "controlling."

However, high distractibility can be less convenient for the caretaker under some other circumstances. When feeding such an infant, for example, any sight or sound may pull the child away from completing the meal. Not only does the child's glance follow the person coming into the room in which the child is being fed, but he may stop eating and give full attention to the distracting stimulus. The meal will be protracted, unless the caretaker makes certain that competing stimuli are kept to a minimum. The toddler starts to play with one toy, is soon distracted by the sight of another and changes gears; the appearance of still another toy produces similar results. Soon the room is strewn with push toys, blocks, jig-saw puzzle pieces, stackable toy pieces, and more. When asked to clean up, the child starts to do so with good will, but is similarly distracted so that not only is there a double task for the caretaker, but the social lesson of tidiness is lost.

At school age, when the child is asked to return home for a doctor's appointment, he meets a friend who suggests that they go to the neighborhood playground where a game of basketball is planned.

Arriving home in good spirits and clear conscience, the youngster is contrite when faced with his forgetfulness, but the high distractibility has indeed been not only an inconvenience, but has also interfered with the child's health care and wasted the time of the parent and doctor. Should the parents assume that such behavior is deliberate disobedience, parental control is likely to be lost if a confrontation is made with the child. If such youngsters just as often forget plans they have themselves made and desired, it should be clear that the issue is not a tug of wills but a temperamental trait. Parents who are in control will attempt to ally themselves with the child's dismay at being so forgetful by trying to work out maneuvers to help the child remember, such parents will give as much attention in this respect to the child's own plans as to carrying out the parentally arranged schedule.

The highly distractible youngster may, on the way to brush his teeth, be sidetracked by noting a chess game puzzle left in mid-action, and may sit down and work on it. Or this type of child may suddenly recall that he has a test on the morrow and has forgotten to study for it. To respond to such events with long lectures can end in selective blocking out of parental admonitions by the child. Some forgetting can be funny; some requires mutual concern and planning—as in deciding that some studying can still be done before going to bed, and the rest had best be achieved by early rising. Whatever the solutions arrived at, if parents are to be in control, they will best do so by taking as a temperamental trait the high distractibility and refraining from demanding from the child that which is excessively stressful, namely, maintaining a constant alertness regarding plans and commitments. True, it may be annoying to work out the keeping of lists, only to find that the child has forgotten to consult them. But parents are not in control if, in addition to failing to channel productively the expression of their child's temperamental makeup, they also create mutual animosity.

A parental program to help a child learn to cope with the undesirable aspects of high distractibility is usually not easy or quickly successful. But it can be effective if pursued patiently, and of enormous value to the child when he grows up. Otherwise, as an adult, unreliability in the fulfillment of obligations because of high distractibility can have serious consequences.

Low distractibility, especially when combined with high persistence, also has its convenient and inconvenient aspects. In infancy, the child whose attention is difficult to sidetrack may have to be restrained, picked up and placed elsewhere, or simply allowed to cry in order to protect his safety and get necessary things done. At the toddler stage, it may be a matter of pride that one's daughter works on the puzzle to completion even if interesting activities are going on nearby. Sometimes the child's self-selected project may be constructive, such as helping with cooking or gardening, but may interfere with the parent's quick and efficient completion of the task. In such instances the parent may have to invoke the motto that, when a child helps, if you get half as much done in twice the time, you are ahead. And should the child's self-selected task be dangerous, as in sticking fingers into an electric outlet, or socially outrageous, as in persistently asking personal questions about a fellow passenger in a piercing voice on a public bus, the pleasure in the child's low distractibility and high persistence may be much diminished.

At school age, it is commendable that such a child remembers to do homework assignments faithfully and carries them through persistently, no matter how difficult they may be. However, it is less than desirable that this same conscientious child is equally persistent about trying to convince his parents that he needs new shoes because his friend has just acquired ones of a particular style. Parents in control, in dealing with a child with low distractibility and high persistence, need techniques of daily management that are different from those required for the child with high distractibility. However, it is equally true that the task of helping the child to modify the undesirable aspects of low distractibility and high persistence must be undertaken as a long-range project. Again, the parents need to assist the child to overcome behaviors that he finds distressing, joining this motivation to the overcoming of behaviors that distress them. While an outrageous expression of persistence may merit sharp and even punitive measures, these lose effectiveness if employed frequently, even if one leaves out the question of the pros and cons of types of punishment, or the virtues of punishment as compared with reasoning. Certainly the parent in control can and ought to identify for the child those behaviors that are merely inconvenient, and differentiate them from those that are unacceptable. And certainly, confrontation may be unavoidable at times, or may even be deliberately selected to emphasize the importance to the issue at hand. It would be incorrect to characterize such parents as "controlling."

It is only when parents are intent on constantly shaping the child's behavior to suit their own convenience and preferences, rather than the youngster's short-range and long-range needs, that we can label these parents as controlling, rather than as being constructively in control. This differential judgment is pertinent to all the variations in temperamental traits and patterns, and not just to high activity and low or high distractibility or persistence. Beyond this, the same criteria for distinguishing constructive parental control from unhealthy controlling attitudes and behavior apply to the parental approach to other characteristics of the child, whether they be special talents and abilites, moral standards, interests and ambitions, social functioning, or physical appearance.

MASTERY BY THE CHILD VERSUS THE CHILD TYRANT

When we have discussed the goodness of fit concept before professional groups, occasionally a question will be raised, "If you tell parents to accept their child's temperament and not try to change it, aren't you in danger of creating a child tyrant?" But goodness of fit is not the same as the extreme permissiveness that has characterized the child-care advice of some experts, especially in the 1950s and 1960s. While it is essential that parents should not make demands that the child cannot fulfill because of his temperament, this does not mean that the child should become the piper to whose tune the parents dance. Thus, for example, is a child tends to withdraw from new situations and adapts slowly to them, it is a poorness of fit and excessively stressful to expect him to move rapidly into a new recreational group. But, if participation in this group would be a desirable social experience, it would also be a poorness of fit for the parents to abandon the effort because of the child's initial negative reaction. Such an action would deprive the youngster of the opportunity to master the rules and routines of peer group social situations.

Rather than the one extreme of excessive demand or the other extreme of no demand, the parents should excercise their ability for control so that the child can gradually achieve a postitive adaptation to the new group. A first contact could be arranged in which the child has an opportunity to watch from the sidelines without the pressure to participate immediately and actively. Several such warm-up experiences will usually be required. It is not unusual for such slow-to-warm-up youngster, whose initial contact with the new group would suggest dislike and even anxiety, to talk afterward of his enjoyment of the experience. After this initial period, in which the child has had the opportunity to watch and become familiar with the new setting and the nature of the group's program, he can then be drawn in gradually and positively, finally becoming an active and even enthusiastic member of the group. In this way, an initially negative experience will have been mastered and transformed into its opposite, with an enhancement of social competence and self-confidence.

The greatest danger of creating a child tyrant is usually with the temperamentally difficult child. The youngster's intense negative reactions to new situations may intimidate parents and lead them to appease the younster to gain some peace and quiet in the household. In this process, the parents lose control, the child is denied the experiences of sucessful mastery of the new situation, and a child tyrant is created. Food preferences provide a good example. Children with high withdrawal often reject a new food on the first introduction. The child may require several opportunities to taste the new food before a genuine preference for or against it can emerge. Should the parent refrain from further attempts to offer a new food because there has been an initial withdrawal response accompanied by screaming and kicking, the child may build up only a very limited diet repertoire. By toddler age, when table foods are generally the rule, this youngster refuses what the rest of the family has, and, because of the commotion, a special meal is prepared. Capriciousness may become evident, so that even the special meal may be rejected with the expectation that still another dish will be made available. By middle childhood it will have become well established that this child's limited tastes either dictate the family's menu or that two meals be prepared. And on visits, the child either refuses to eat or, by advance arrangement, the entire meal is determined by the child's food preferences. Enlarge this script to take in not only food, but family excursions, games played by the child with sibs, or the selection of television programs, and we are indeed dealing with a child tyrant. This is *not* a goodness of fit. A goodness of fit consists of an approach that takes into account the child's temperamental attributes, and, utilizing this knowledge, introduces the child to the social rules of fairness and sharing that will help in the development of social ease with those situations that will, in the child's culture, be part of his life. By achieving these ends, the child will be in a good position to develop his intellectual capacities, talents, and social graces, and become a functioning and welcome member of society.

INSIGHT INTO ONE'S OWN TEMPERAMENT

Thus far, we have discussed the importance of the parents' insight into their child's temperament. In the same way, such insight will be valuable to other caretakers, to mental health professionals, to pediatricians and nurses in the care of their patients, and to teachers in the education of their students. For youngsters themselves, insight into their own temperament, as they develop into adolescence and adult life, is of equal or even greater importance. This is especially true for those temperamental traits that can be strengths in certain situations, but potential handicaps in other settings. Thus, for example, it can make a great difference in social functioning and task mastery for an individual to know when the characteristics of high activity, or high intensity or expressiveness, or nondistractibility are assets and should be given free play, and when they may have unfavorable consequences and should be kept under control.

Some youngsters develop this kind of insight on their own as they grow up. One young woman told us "I'm shy, but I'm not timid." What she was saying was that she was temperamentally slow-to-warm-up, but that she did not mean that she lacked self-assurance. This she had figured out for herself, and accurately, without help from her parents or others.

Parents can be very influential in guiding their children to understand their own temperament, as well as their other psychologic and physical characteristics. This process can be initiated at least by middle childhood and extended as youngsters enter their teens. One set of parents, when their intellectually gifted but temperamentally difficult 13-year-old daughter began to worry about her impending transition to high school, said to her "It's the first grade again." With this phrase they reminded her that when she started elementary school she was intensely distressed at first. But then she gradually adapted, and after a few months she was relaxed and school became a happy and stimulating experience. They had used the same phrase "It's the first grade again" whenever she had a negative first reaction to a new situation, and it had become an effective reassuring slogan for the girl. Hopefully, and predictably, as she matures she will be able to identify and understand any initial feelings of distress to a new experience, and instead of withdrawing, tell herself "It's the first grade again."

In a sense, the goodness of fit model suggests the parents use their control first of all to achieve the best possible match between their child's characteristics and capacities and the demands of the environment. But, then, as the child matures and gains progressively the capacity for self-awareness, this control can be gradually relinquished in favor of the younster's insight and self-control of the expression of his or her temperament.

CONTINUITY OF TEMPERAMENT

The examples used in this chapter to illustrate the concepts of goodness of fit, parental control, and child mastery and insight, have relied primarily on instances where one or another extreme temperamental characterisitc is consistent over time. These are the cases in which the clinical usefulness of the goodness of fit model is most evident. However, even a youngster with a medium level of temperament may experience excessive stress if the parents or others demand an extreme level of activity or persistence or emotional expressiveness.

As to continuity of temperament, this is evident, even dramatically so, in some children, as they grow older. In other instances, such continuity is not striking, and change in temperament over time may even be apparent. This should be no surprise. So many variables can influence psychologic development and the interaction among these factors may vary so much from one age-period to another, that immutability over time cannot be expected for temperament or any other attribute of an individual. The developmental process is thus characterized by a complex interplay of continuity and change. We have included a discussion of this issue, "Consistency and Change in Temperament over Time," as Appendix B.

The clinician has to deal with the patient's current temperament in planning a strategy of prevention and treatment. Also important, however, is an assessment, however tentative and partial, of the patient's past temperament, so that the dynamics of the developmental process can be identified. It is also essential to recognize that, even if temperament does not change, different life situations may bring different aspects of temperament to the fore, with different consequences for the individual's functioning. For example, a person with difficult temperament may have reactions of discomfort and tension in new situations. However, when this individual has adapted positively, his high intensity may lead to involvement with zest and enthusiasm in the new situation. This is desirable, but does create the danger of overinvolvement and the resulting problem of overcommitment.

These issues of assessment of current and past temperament will be considered in Chapter 9 of the current volume.

CHAPTER 3

Parental Reactions to the Child's Temperament

Currently a consensus has been achieved among developmental psychiatrists and psychologists that the child's own attributes play an active role, in interaction with environmental factors, in shaping the course of psychological development (Lerner & Busch-Rossnagel, 1981). Thus, temperament, perceptual and cognitive characteristics, special talents or handicaps, physical attractiveness, and certain motivational patterns—all these, while they may be modified by the environment over time, are influential variables that are not determined exclusively by the environment.

This consensus, however, did not exist in the 1950s, when we began the New York Longitudinal Study (NYLS). Quite the contrary. While it was accepted that certain psychologic characteristics, such as perceptual and cognitive abilities, were not exclusively shaped by the environment, the dominant concepts with regard to the child's behavioral patterns were quite different. Here, there was agreement among most psychiatrists and psychologists that the child's behavior was determined entirely by environmental factors—first and foremost the parents, then other family members, such as brothers and sisters, as well as the larger sociocultural environment. In effect, the neonate was considered to be a *tabula rasa*, as the 17-century British philosopher John Locke had put it in his essay concerning human understanding (Gough, 1973), a clean slate on which the environment would inscribe its influence until the adult personality was etched to completion. This concept was not limited to any one school of thought. It was manifest in the formulations derived from psychoanalytic theory, behaviorism, and various other positions in academic psychology.

This environmentalist bias resulted from a rejection of the static mechanical beliefs of past centuries, which conceived of development as the mere unfolding and elaboration of fixed characteristics already present in the newborn infant (Allport, 1961). A host of scientific and empirical studies had also made it evident that differences in environmental stimuli and life experiences were highly influential in the origin and evolution of individual differences in both healthy and pathologic psychologic development (Rose, 1955). However, highly influential is not the same as an *exclusive* determinant. And by the 1950s, a number of specific studies and reviews of the literature suggested considerable skepticism of this exclusively environmentalist view. A number of reports had also appeared that described observations of individual differences in infants and young childen that could not be correlated with differences in their environment (see Thomas & Chess, 1977, Chapter 1, for a summary of this literature). Beyond these doubts, we and a number of other mental health professionals (Bruch, 1954) were concerned over the burden of guilt imposed on so many parents, who were automatically blamed for any deviant or pathologic behavior on their children's part, no matter how meager the evidence for such a judgment might be.

It was with these considerations in mind that we launched the NYLS in 1956. This study of temperament and its functional significance has been the first systematic exploration of the active influence of the child's own characteristics on the parents, as well as on other influential persons in the child's environment. The data from the NYLS have confirmed abundantly our original hypothesis (Thomas & Chess, 1957) that the parent–child interaction is a two-way street: The child's behavioral style influences parental attitudes and practices, and the parents' attitudes and practices influences the child. It is with this first issue, the parental reactions to the child's temperament, that this chapter is concerned. However, inasmuch as the parent–child relationship is a mutually interactional process at all times, the child's influence on the parent must be considered in the context of the simultaneous influence of the parent on the child. This interplay between child and parent will be evident in the following discussion.

GENERAL COMMENTS

The reactions of the parent to the child's temperament are not determined by whether or not there is a similarity between parent and child in their temperaments. We have seen all kinds of combinations. In some cases parents may be pleased with their youngster's temperament because it is similar to their own; in other instances they may be pleased because the child is different from them. The two parents may have similar reactions to the child, or they may differ markedly. Thus, for example, one father, who was himself mild-mannered and low-keyed in his emotional expressiveness, had a son who showed an extreme of difficult temperament from the first few months of life onward. The father appreciated that the child would adapt slowly to any new situation, but would eventually achieve a positive adaptation. At the same time, he took delight in the youngster's intense expressiveness, so different from his own style, and called the boy "lusty." By contrast, the mother could not reach this same objective appraisal as her husband did, and judged her son's intense negative responses to the new and his slow adaptation as evidence that she was a bad mother. Here the father's response to the child's temperament was patient acceptance and pleasure, while the mother's reaction was one of guilt and anxiety.

A different parent–child pattern was exemplified by the family in which both parents were quick-moving and had lively expressiveness of feelings and ideas. One daughter had similar temperamental characteristics, and easily gained her parents' understanding and approval. Another daughter, by contrast, was slow-moving, and also had a low level of intensity of mood expression. With this girl, the parents were often bewildered and exasperated. By their standards, her low-keyed expressions of pleasure even with special treats meant that she had not enjoyed herself, which they could not understand. And when she moved slowly to comply with a request, both parents were annoyed at what they considered her reluctant obedience. In this case, the parents looked for similarity in temperament, and misjudged with disapproval the meaning of their daughter's differences in activity and expressiveness.

As the instance of the mild-mannered father and his "lusty" son cited above indicates, a goodness of fit between parent and child does not necessarily involve similarity of temperament between the two. This father recognized that the youngster, even as a 2-month-old infant, with his intense negative reactions to the new and slow adaptability, was very different from himself, and that the boy's behavior pattern did make caretaking strenuous and difficult. But the father also knew, without any coaching from us, that with patient, quiet, and consistent handling of each new situation, his son not only did adapt finally, but also that this positive adaptation had a vigor and ebullience that was very attractive. The father was also able to be supportive of his wife in her anxious and guilty moments, and a true goodness of fit was achieved in their handling of the boy. As a result, the youngster's developmental course was strongly positive.

As discussed earlier in this chapter, the infant is not a *tabula rasa*, but brings her own characteristics actively to the interaction with parental attitudes and practices. The parents, on their part, also bring their own psychologic attributes—their temperament, cognitive characteristics, standards and values, and special personality traits and vulnerabilities—to bear in their reactions to their child's temperament. The different patterns of parental reactions can be best considered in relationship to the specific temperamental patterns of the child.

THE EASY CHILD

For the vast majority of parents, the easy child is a delight. This child's positive responses to the first bath, to most new foods, to new places and people, and her regular sleep and feeding patterns lighten the burden of caretaking routines. The easy child's quick and frequent smile evokes a pleasurable response from the parents, older children, and other adults. The parents are pleased when family, friends, and strangers praise their cheerful and adaptable child as "cute" and "nice." As such children grow older, their positive responses to the new and their quick adaptability make the adjustment to babysitters, to school, to a new home, and to social activities easy in most if not all instances. Again, this makes the parents' caretaking responsibilities easier and more pleasurable.

For these reasons, the development of affectionate and emotional closeness by the parents usually goes smoothly with a temperamentally easy child. Sometimes, having an easy child may even be crucial for the development of a positive parental attachment. For example, one young woman delayed having a child because of her sense that this would conflict with her career goals. She had entered a highly competitive professional field and was gradually achieving recognition and success. She worried that the burdens and responsibilities of caring for a baby, even with her husband's assurance that he would be equally involved, would take so much of her time and energy that she would not be able to pursue her career effectively. But she did want a child, and so did her husband, and finally, with much trepidation, she became pregnant. Fortunately, her pregnancy was uncomplicated, and her baby turned out to have an easy temperament. Within a few months the child was on a regular sleep schedule with very little night awakening; he fussed very little and smiled easily. There were no problems taking him on car rides or visiting, and excellent babysitting arrangements were expedited by this child's easy adaptability. The mother found him a delight, her positive maternal feelings flourished rapidly, and she was able to return to full-time work without strain. It is reasonable to estimate that the outcome would have been very different if she had had a temperamentally difficult child who cried a great deal, interrupted her sleep at night, was unpredictable as to sleep and feeding schedules, and whose slow adaptability and fussing would have created problems in arriving at a satisfactory baby-sitting arrangement. In such a situation, with her energies drained by the care-taking difficulties, returning to full-time work would have been a great strain, and the mother's conflict, instead of being resolved favorably, would undoubtedly have been intensified.

Some parents of easy children recognize that they did not create these desirable attributes. Other parents will feel that they had shaped their child's behavior and take credit for the youngster's positive responses, easy adaptability, and regular sleep and feeding schedules. Should we go along with thir self-congratulation, or should we try to point out that the baby also had, on her own, contributed to this favorable state of affairs? Actually, the answer is not categorically one or the other. Easy temperament does not by itself guarantee desirable adaptations. Even easy children will get frustrated and protest if denied something they want to do, such as poking at electrical outlets, or trying to use the telephone in imitation of their parents. If the parents feel guilty at depriving their child, especially since she is so reasonable in general, they may be on the road to creating a child tyrant, who has learned quickly, as a temperamentally easy child will, that all that need be done is to fuss or cry and her parents will give in. As a simple example of this sequence, one easy child in the NYLS had an upper respiratory infection when she was 2 years old. Instead of sleeping through the night, as she had been doing, she began waking up and crying with discomfort because of a stuffed nose. Her mother picked her up, comforted her, cleared her nose, and put her back to bed. The infection disappeared after a week, but the child now had learned a new sleep pattern and continued to awaken crying several times a night, expecting her mother to continue coming in and to pick her up. This the mother did, feeling guilty if she didn't, and hoping that the girl would give up this night awakening on her own. When this didn't happen after several weeks, she consulted us and was ready to follow our advice to let her daughter cry it out. It only took several nights before the youngster was sleeping peacefully through the night again, to her own and her parents' greater comfort.

What we can tell the parents of an easy child who is doing well is that both they and their child deserve the credit. The youngster's temperament makes for the easy achievement of desirable behavioral patterns, but this occurs only if the parents handle the issues of child-care appropriately, so that a goodness of fit is achieved.

Occasionally, an easy child adapts too well to parental expectations and demands. This happens when the rules, mores, and manners the child has learned at home, with the parents' approval, come in conflict with the standards and expectations of the peer group or the school setting outside the home. In such instances, some easy children can adapt to functioning one way at home, and differently in the outside world. Others cannot make this flexible adjustment, especially if the contradiction between parental and extrafamilial standards of acceptable behavior is extreme and acute, and such children find themselves the object of unexpected and bewildering criticism, punishment, teasing, or ridicule. A case in point was Hal, one of the NYLS subjects with easy temperament. His parents consulted us when he was 4 years old because he had become the butt of ridicule of his peer group. When other children took his toys, he did not defend himself, but instead came home crying. When then seen in a clinical playroom session, the striking finding was Hal's formalistic polite manners, which were a caricature of the good manners expected of an adult. Inquiry of his parents quickly revealed that they set great store by politeness and its formal expression. They had brought Hal up to behave according to these standards, and he had learned all too well, becoming in effect a "stuffed shirt" by age 4. Inevitably, this made him the butt of his peer group, which he could not understand and could not cope with. This issue was spelled out to the parents, who then realized the problem they were creating for their son, and they made substantial efforts to modify their demands on Hal. With this, the boy was able to change his behavior sufficiently so that he was no longer scapegoated by his playmates and school mates.

Rarely, parents will worry that their easily adaptable and cheerful child will become a "pushover," who will give in too easily to others and let them take advantage of her. Such parents can be reassured that this does not necessarily have to happen. Easy children can learn to stand up for themselves when necessary, just as they can learn other necessities of social behavior. They will assert themselves in their own style, quietly rather than loudly, but this can be as effective as any other style of self-assertion.

THE DIFFICULT CHILD

In sharp contrast to the easy child, nurturing a temperamentally difficult child places special demands on parents and acts as a stress for them. Some parents are capable of coping objectively and patiently with such a youngster, knowing that she will eventually adapt positively to the succession of new situations and experiences she has to master. Many others, however, are bewildered, overwhelmed or angered by the caretaking difficulties they face day by day, especially as they contrast their problems to the ease of management of their other children or the easy children of relatives or friends. As a result, the parent–child interaction is often less than optimal, with frequent behavior disorder development. Thus, of the 10% of subjects in the NYLS who showed clear-cut difficult temperament, 70% developed a behavior disorder during childhood.

The maladaptive reactions of parents to a difficult child can take a number of different forms. Essentially, though, these are variations on the theme of whether the parents blame themselves or blame the child. Also, the maladaptive reactions differ as to whether they are caused by parental ignorance and confusion over the meaning of their child's behavior, or whether they are the result of parental personality patterns such as competitiveness, the need to control, or self-derogation.

Parents who blame themselves for the turmoil and stress involved in taking care of a difficult child most often do so on the basis of the thesis asserted by many mental health professionals that all behavioral difficulties shown by a child must be the direct result of parental, and especially maternal mishandling. And if there is no overt evidence that the mother is inept or disturbed in her child-care practices, this can only mean, so the argument goes, that the mother is harboring unconscious pathologic attitudes toward the child that are affecting the child subtly but deeply. Such an automatic reproach of the mother all too often becomes a self-fulfilling prophecy. The mother accepts this critical judgment as valid and becomes anxious and guilty, which in turn then does interfere with her ability to handle the child properly. This outcome is then used as evidence to justify the original assertion that it must be the mother's fault.

While this "blame the mother" ideology is not as prevalent among mental health professionals as it was 30 years ago, it continues to crop up in a number of different forms (see Chess & Thomas, 1982, for a fuller discussion of this issue). And many young mothers, especially if they are working mothers, are still vulnerable to judgments as to their adequacy in fulfilling the maternal role.

The anxious and guilty mother often will try to minimize her difficult child's episodes of loud crying by appeasing her and giving in immediately to all her requests and demands. One set of parents in the NYLS sample appeased their difficult infant for a different reason. They had an older child with a serious physiologic disturbance of growth, which required a great deal of their time and attention. When this next child began to cry loudly and frequently they felt overwhelmed and unable to cope with this additional problem. They felt they had to give in to stop the child's crying, no matter what the cost. In another of the NYLS families, the father was highly successful in a very demanding professional field. To achieve this success he had had to defy the threats and roadblocks of several powerful hostile government bureaucrats. This he did not only without anxiety but with aplomb. He did, however, feel guilty over his neglect of his older child by a previous marriage and resolved to make up for this by being attentive to his new baby. This boy turned out to be a difficult child and the father felt he had to appease him to stop his crying, otherwise he would again be a failure as a father. The contrast between his objectivity and refusal to be intimidated by powerful threatening opponents in his work life, and his subjectivity and intimidation by his baby son was quite remarkable.

Whatever the reason for parental appeasement of a difficult child, the end result is the creation of a child tyrant. The only thing that the child can learn in such an interaction is that if she cries loudly and long enough her parents will always give in. The parents may succeed momentarily in gaining peace by appeasing the youngster, but only at the cost of acceding to the child's demands, no matter how unreasonable. For such youngsters, these victories are indeed pyrrhic ones, when they discover to their bewilderment and shock that such tactics do not work in the outside world, but instead boomerang against them.

Not uncommonly, parents feel victimized by a difficult child, whether they are blaming themselves or the child. In such cases, whether the parents feel helpless and unable to change the youngster's behavior or whether they engage in an antagonistic battle with the child to force change to occur, in either instance the sense of victimization is bound to engender resentment and anger against the child. Here again, if one is looking only to the parents' attitudes and behavior for the origin of difficulties in the child's functioning, it is easy to be misled into labeling the parents' hostility as the primary cause.

Where the parents blame the child, this means that they attribute the cause of the stress and demands on their time and energies in raising the child to some abnormality in the youngster, rather than the consequence of her normal temperament. Either she has some mysterious innate defect, or else, again for some unknown reason, she is being willful, stubborn, or trying to control the family. If the parents enter into a power struggle with the child and demand swift compliance and quick adaptation to new situations and new activities, the child may develop the very defiance and negativism that she was incorrectly assumed to show in earlier childhood.

Even when parents are appeasing or battling with their temperamentally difficult child, this behavior is often selective rather than all-encompassing for all the issues of daily living. A rigidly demanding parent will generally concentrate on those activities that are deemed important and symbolic of the question "Who's in control," and may be patient and even benign in his or her approach to other situations. For example, one parent turned a child's hesitation to attend social functions into a power struggle but, on the other hand, was quite patient and accepting of the youngster's reluctance to try a new food. As a result, the child gradually learned the rule that she must taste, but need not finish the foods, and could eat as much or as little as she wished. This allowed for pleasant mealtimes. By contrast, the antagonistic parental handling of social experiences led to a period of intense parental rage and wild weeping by the child before every outing. Another parent, who was intimidated by her daughter's outbursts of screaming, was quite clear that this toddler had to learn the rules of safety inside and outside the house. In all other areas she vacillated and appeased the youngster, but when it came to safety rules she was quietly firm and consistent. As a result, the girl had difficulties in functioning in almost all other areas, which led to a severe adjustment disorder, except with regard to safety issues, where she adapted reasonably and appropriately.

When parent or parents are locked into a battle with the child, with each trying loudly to impose his or her will on the other, and the clinical evaluation indicates that the youngster has difficult temperament, a crucial diagnostic question arises. Are the parents mishandling the child because of a lack of understanding of how they could do better? Or, is one or both of them trying to impose some rigid set of demands on the child, no matter how inappropriate to her temperament, because of some unhealthy need for control, domination, or perfectionism? The answer to this question will determine the optimal preventative and treatment approaches. (This issue of strategies of prevention and treatment is discussed in detail in the last section of this volume.)

In making this differential diagnosis, it is often possible to gather enough information from the interview with the parents to come to a decision. It may be clear that the parents only appease this one temperamentally difficult child or make rigid, inflexible demands on her, and with their other children of different temperament act with patience, flexibility, and consistency, though at the same time they are firm in their demand for compliance in important areas of behavior. This will indicate that the parental attitudes and behaviors toward the difficult child are probably reactive to their confusion, frustration, and lack of understanding of what is normal behavior for this child. If, in the interview, one parent is peremptory with the other, tries to take over the interview from the clinician, and in others ways indicates controlling attitudes to people in general, then it is likely that similar attitudes and practices with the child reflects this unhealthy parental psychologic pattern, rather than being primarily a reaction to the child's functioning.

If there is still doubt as to the dynamics of the parents' behavior, the question is usually easily resolved by their response to the initial parent guidance discussions. The basic formulation is spelled out that their child is fundamentally healthy, that her intense negative reactions to new situations and slow adaptability, as well as irregular sleep and feeding patterns, are expressions of the child's normal personality, as difficult as this makes it for the child and the parents. However, it is stressed that with proper handling, the actual behavior problem symptoms which have resulted from an unhealthy interaction between them and their youngster can be eliminated and she can go on to function as successfully and happily as any other child. However, her basic temperament may not change. If the parents greet this discussion with relief, or even with skepticism but with a willingness to try a new approach, and then do their best to carry out the new plan of management, then it is likely that their mishandling has been the result of their ignorance. If however, one parent or both respond to the discussion with a variation on the theme that "I still know it's all my fault," or that

"You're asking me to do something I can't," or that "No matter what you say, she's still a rotten kid" (the label actually applied to his 5-year old daughter by one of our NYLS fathers, himself a mental health professional), then it is likely that the parental mismanagement reflects some fixed unhealthy psychologic pattern. The prognosis for parental guidance then becomes unfavorable.

As outlined here, this strategy for differential diagnosis is applicable to the analysis of unfavorable parent–child interactional patterns with children with other temperamental characteristics and not only to the difficult child. The issue of identifying the dynamics of pathogenic parental attitudes and practices may be more obvious with the difficult child because undesirable and self-defeating parental functioning is so often intensely expressed and even stormy with such a youngster. But even if more subtle and quiet in its manifestations, inappropriate parental management with children with other temperamental characteristics requires the same analysis of its origin and dynamics if prevention and treatment is to be effective.

THE SLOW-TO-WARM-UP CHILD

As with the difficult child, the parents (and the teachers) of a slow-to-warm-up child may easily misinterpret the significance of such a youngster's typical behavior pattern. The initial quiet withdrawal response and slow adaptability, especially with social situations, may be seen as anxiety, some innate defect in social competence, or apathy and indifference. Parents who set high store by the social graces, or parents who feel that the child's behavior is a reflection on themselves, will all too often pressure the youngster to adapt to new situations at a speed entirely beyond her capacity. Other parents, who themselves move quickly into anything new, may not understand their child's hesitancies, become impatient, and also expect the child to change. Such pressures can only result in an exacerbation of the socially withdrawn behavior, which can then become a pathologic adjustment disorder.

Other overprotective parents, worried that new social situations are too difficult or painful for their youngsters, may try to insulate the child from them. This deprives the child of the opportunities to experience new activities and to discover that if she allows enough time she will finally adapt to and enjoy the activity, no matter how uncomfortable she was to begin with. Such positive sequences will give the child a basis for a positive self-image, for a judgment that she is capable of coping successfully with new challenges that are disturbing to begin with. The child will also have the experiences that will provide increasing skills in task mastery and social functioning. By contrast, the slow-to-warm-up child whose parents shield her from disturbing new situations will be deprived of these positive experiences of mastery, and is all too likely to end up feeling socially inept and unable to cope with new tasks. And in fact this self-evaluation may eventually be accurate.

The parent–child interaction in which the parents make unrealistic demands for quick adaptation on a slow-to-warm-up child does not lead to the stormy confrontations and battles, as is likely to occur with the difficult child. But the quiet withdrawal reactions of the slow-to-warm-up child in such a case can lead to a passive negativism which may be just as detrimental to healthy psychologic development as are the tantrums and violent resistances of the badly handled difficult child.

Many parents can accept the behavioral pattern of a slow-to-warm-up child without feeling threatened or challenged. They will readily agree that their youngster is "shy," an accurate description, but that the child gets over this once she gets acquainted with the new people or places. They may even remark that they, or one or another of their relatives or friends, were the same way when they were young, but that it did not do them any harm in the long run. Sometimes, a parent has to be very clear on this positive judgment to maintain it in the face of social pressures. For example, one of the slow-to-warm-up children in the NYLS was enrolled in nursery school at 4 years of age. After a slow and hesitant start, the girl made a positive adaptation and functioned well in all aspects of the school setting. At the end of the school year there was an evening entertainment by the children to which the parents were invited. When this girl entered the strange room with her mother and saw the crowd of strange adults all around her, she climbed onto her mother's lap and would not budge for the entire evening. As the mother reported the incident to us with amusement, "All evening the other parents kept looking at Kate and myself. I was sure they were thinking what was wrong with her and what was wrong with me as a mother." The mother was undoubtedly correct in her inference regarding the other parents. She was secure enough in her competency as a mother and in the normalcy of her daughter's behavior to be amused by the incident. Many another parent, however, would be less self-confident and would be shaken and pressured by such an adverse judgment.

HIGH PERSISTENCE AND LOW DISTRACTIBILITY

These two characteristics usually go together, though an occasional highly persistent individual will also be highly distractible.

The parents' reactions to the behavior of a highly persistent and nondistractible child will depend very much on the content and the situation, more so than with other temperamental attributes. If the youngster is absorbed in an activity that is convenient for the parents, and of which they approve, their response will be positive. If, on the other hand, the child is busy doing something of which they disapprove and they want to pull her away, the child's persistence and low distractibility may make this difficult without creating a big fuss or violent tantrum. Thus, for example, it is convenient for the mother or other caretaker if the toddler is busy playing peacefully with her toys and games for long periods at a time. And parents who give a high priority to education will be delighted to see their school-age youngster concentrating on her homework without taking a break, and ignoring extraneous distractions. However, when this same toddler persistently takes the telephone off the hook or tries her best to get at the knives or breakable dishes in the kitchen, cannot be distracted, and reacts with a violent and prolonged protest when pulled away, the same patient will be annoyed and all too likely to scold her child as being "stubborn" and "inconsiderate." And when the same older schoolgirl who does her homework so well insists on going on some outing the parents consider unsafe or too extravagant, she becomes an annoying and "selfish nag." Yet both the toddler and the schoolgirl are only consistently displaying the same temperamental characteristic of persistence. It is the context in which they show their persistence that gains them parental approval or disapproval.

As with the difficult child, reactions of parents to an intensely persistent youngster can take many forms, depending on the parents' own personality characteristics and their insight into the meaning of the child's behavior. The parent who understands and even welcomes this quality of persistence will learn to anticipate circumstances, such as the approach of dinnertime, that will require the child to terminate an activity. The parent will then caution the child ahead of time not to get started on an activity, or, if the child has already started, will warn her of the time limit. Such a parent will also be prepared to deal with persistent behavior of which he or she disapproves by quietly and consistently making the demand for its cessation, and, if necessary, firmly removing the child from the scene, disregarding her protests. At the same time the parent will encourage and support those persistent activities that are constructive and do not interfere with other obligations of the child or with necessary family schedules. With this kind of selective reactions by the parents, persistent children can learn as they grow older to judge by themselves when they can give free rein to which persistent activities and when, and on which occasions they should limit the intensity and time of their involvement in a specific task.

As with the difficult child, though less frequently, some parents are threatened, overwhelmed, or challenged by the behavior of the persistent child which they cannot fathom. They may become helpless, inconsistent, explosive, or engage in a power struggle with the youngster. Whatever the maladaptive response of the parent, it is all too likely to lead to a pathogenic parent–child interaction which eventually mushrooms into a behavior disorder in the child.

LOW PERSISTENCE AND HIGH DISTRACTIBILITY

During infancy and the preschool age period, the child with low persistence and high distractibility is not likely to present management problems that may evoke negative parental reactions. It is quite easy for them to minimize interruptions when the infant is being fed. In a number of ways, the ease with which such a child's attention can be deflected may even be an asset during the early childhood years. Whether the child is resisting being dressed, or poking at electrical outlets, or engaged in other potentially dangerous activities, the ease with which she can be distracted makes the parent's task easier.

As the child grows older, however, parental reactions may change drastically. The child typically fails to carry through tasks with her undivided attention for any length of time, such as homework or various household chores. If the parents (and the teachers) appreciate that the diversion of the youngster's attention and activity is not motivated by a desire to avoid completion of a task, all can go well.

Such parents will know they should make a progress check after short intervals when the child has started on a task such as setting the table or undressing at bedtime, and get her back on the track without anger or punishment. With homework, similar friendly reminders are usually effective. Such parents will often also appreciate that their child's distractibility has its positive side. The child's responsiveness to a wide range of ongoing environmental stimuli may facilitate a high level of general alertness and an awareness of the nuances of other people's behavior and feelings that may be difficult for the nondistractible child to achieve. With such an understanding parental approach, the youngster's difficulties with task completion can be minimized, and a healthy course of psychological development is likely.

Where this parental understanding is lacking, however, unfavorable judgments on the child's functioning may be quite damaging. The youngster's failure to meet the parents' standards for task completion is likely to result in severe scoldings and criticisms. Most often the parent will decide that the child is "lacking in character, will-power and a sense of responsibility" or that she is deliberately out to disobey and to defy her parents. We have seen these judgments in two NYLS subjects with low persistence and high distractibility, and in each case the parental reproach became a self-fulfilling prophecy. One boy whose mother interpreted his incomplete tasks as deliberate defiance and kept attacking him for this sin eventually did manage to transform their relationship into a back-and-forth battle with each other. Another boy who was continually denigrated by his father as having "no character or will power," eventually believed his father was right and gave up trying to succeed at school or in work.

The greatest danger of adverse parental reactions to a child who is distractible comes when she also shows low persistence. If the distractible youngster is highly persistent, this latter trait will enable her to return spontaneously and without reminder to an incomplete task from which she has been distracted. Thus, when present in the same child, persistence and distractibility will cancel each other out mostly but not always, as far as the eventual extent of task completion is concerned. Sometimes, when the child turns her attention back, she finds that the task that was begun has been completed by the person the child was supposed to be helping, that the bath water she was running has flooded the floor, or that the cake she was baking has burned. However, most parents can accept such occasional mishaps with equanimity, if in most instances the youngster's persistence serves as a check on the unfavorable potential of her distractibility.

HIGH AND LOW ACTIVITY LEVEL

The highly active child who moves quickly is more likely to break things, to get burned or bruised, to collide with others, and to present problems of restlessness in situations such as bus or automobile rides in which sitting quietly for long periods is necessary. Parental reactions to these consequences of the child's behavior can easily become one of annoyance and irritation, in which case the child will experience situations in which her normal style of behavior is considered undesirable.

Though clinically we have seen this kind of negative parent–child interaction lead to a behavior problem in a highly active child, this did not happen with this type of youngster in the NYLS sample.

These middle- and upper-middle-class families had relatively spacious apartments or private homes in neighborhoods with safe streets and backyards or easily available playgrounds. As a result, their high-activity-level children had adequate opportunity for the safe and constructive utilization of their motor energy, and at most their occasional mishaps caused minor irritation to their parents. The situation was quite different with our Puerto Rican working-class sample (Thomas, Chess, Sillen, & Mendez, 1974). These families lived in small apartments in the East Harlem area of New York City, with unsafe streets and few available playgrounds. The highly active children had inadequate space at home, and their parents legitimately restricted their access to the unsafe streets. As a result these children developed extreme restlessness, motor tension, and impulsive behavior, and a significant number did develop behavior disorders.

By contrast to the high-activity children in the NYLS, several of the low-activity children did develop adjustment disorders. These slow-moving children were mislabled by parents and teachers as being dull or inept, a judgment that became a self-fulfilling prophecy. Actually, such children are penalized in IQ testing, in which certain items only allow a specified time limit for their completion. In one girl's case, the problem was accentuated by the presence of a younger, quickly moving sister who jumped to carry out requests made by the parents, while her older, slowly moving sister was just beginning to get going. The younger sister gained the parents' approval, and by contrast her older sister was the butt of their impatience and annoyance at her "reluctance to cooperate."

Other parents, however, did recognize that their slowly moving child was trying her best, and that this slowness was no reflection on her intelligence or on her willingness to cooperate. In such instances, the parents were usually able to curb their impatience, and reward the youngster's achievements with appropriate praise, even when the tasks were done slowly and deliberately. In such instances, low activity level did not become a significant negative factor in the child's developmental course.

OTHER TEMPERAMENTAL PATTERNS

The biologically irregular infant makes more demands on the time and energy of her parents than does the regular infant in the establishment of regular sleep and feeding patterns and in toilet training. However, this consequence of biological irregularity by itself, unless accompanied by other attributes of the temperamentally difficult child, is likely to cause only minor annoyance in the parents. Furthermore, once regular sleep and mealtime schedules are achieved and toilet training is accomplished, even such minor reactions of parental annoyance disappear.

Low sensory threshold, like biological irregularity, may sometimes be productive of parental irritability in the early childhood years. A child with low threshold may complain over wearing rough or tight clothing, and the child's parents may not understand why she should be so "fussy," as compared to other children. Carey (1974) has reported a correlation between low sensory threshold and night waking in infancy, which can become a source of annoyance to parents. However, these issues arising from low sensory threshold do not tend to become sources of major disturbance between parent and child.

In this chapter, we have considered the parental reactions to the child's attributes of withdrawal, negative mood, slow adaptability, and high intensity level within the easy, difficult, and slow-to-warm-up temperamental constellations. A mixed pattern, when it occurs, may mitigate potential adverse parental reactions. Thus, a child who has initial negative reactions of high intensity to new situations and new people, but who adapts quickly, is less likely to stimulate one or another of the unfavorable parental responses as will the difficult child who is also slow to adapt. On the other hand, other combinations may exacerbate adverse parental judgments. Thus, a slow-to-warm-up child who is also of low activity level, is more likely to be appraised as dull and inept than if he or she were of moderate or high activity level.

SUMMARY

We have given a run-through of the more frequent types of parental reactions to the different patterns of temperamental individuality in their children. But we have by no means exhausted all the possibilities. Individual personality differences among parents, the many permutations of temperamental clusters that can occur in children and the various special influences that may operate within and from without the family, all these make for many possible idiosyncratic patterns of parental reactions to the child's temperament, as well as of the child's reactions to the parents. It is here that the goodness of fit model (see Chapter 2) is of special value in teasing out the dynamics of the parent–child interaction in a clinical case that may not follow the usual pattern seen in other cases.

It is also true that the parents' reactions to the child's temperament does not occur in the abstract, in isolation from their responses to all the other aspects of the child as a human being. One case from the NYLS sample illustrates this issue strikingly. This girl developed severe symptoms of an adjustment disorder starting in her preschool years. Temperamentally a difficult child, her father responded with rigid demands for quick positive adaptation, and hostile criticisms and punishment when the girl could not meet his expectations. Our discussions with him were of no avail. In his eyes she was a "rotten kid," and needed strict unyielding discipline. The mother was intimidated by both husband and daughter, and became anxious and vascillating in her handling of her daughter. A course of psychotherapy with the girl was initiated after she began school. Improvement, however, was only modest, which was to be expected, given the continued adverse and conflicting approach of both parents. But when she was 9–10 years of age, the girl blossomed forth with dramatic and musical talent. This brought favorable attention and praise, which teachers and other parents communicated not only to her, but also to her parents. Fortunately, these talents ranked high in her parents' hierarchy of desirable attributes. Her father then began to see his daughter's intense and explosive personality not as signs of "a rotten kid," but as evidence of a budding artist. He began to make allowances for her "artistic temperament," and his criticisms and punitive approach changed to praise and tolerance. With this, the mother was able to relax and also relate positively to her daughter. The girl was allowed to adapt positively at her own pace, and by adolescence all evidence of her neurotic symptomatology and functioning had disappeared. Her early adult follow-up showed a continuation of her positive functioning.

The opposite sequence can also occur, namely an adverse parental reaction to a child's easy temperament because of some other attribute of the youngster. One set of parents consulted us because of their concern over their teenage son's school behavior. He did poorly academically, tried to avoid his homework assignments, and resisted any tutoring or help from his parents. They saw him as a lackadaisical, all-too-easy-going youngster without initiative or ambition. This was in sharp contrast to their positive judgments on their two older children, who were doing superior work in school without any urging or help. A review of the boy's overall behavior with the parents revealed that his difficulties were confined to school. Otherwise, he was an actively functioning youngster at home, socially and athletically, and without any behavioral symptoms. What the parents criticized as his easy-going manner appeared clearly to be the expression of easy temperament. An interview with the boy himself confirmed the impressions gained from the parents. An IQ test was done, and gave him a score of 102, in the average range. When this finding was communicated to the parents they were shocked. They said openly that they could not accept the idea that the boy might not be able intellectually to make it to college. For them, with their middle-class expectations of higher education and academic success for their children, a less than superior IQ score was the equivalent of a diagnosis of mental deficiency. It became clear that the parents had made demands for school achievement that the boy could not meet, and that he had reacted defensively with passive resistance and avoidance of anything academic. It also seemed likely that the parents, because of their critical reaction to their son's poor school performance, had categorized his mild expressiveness and quick adaptability as undesirable attributes. It is not unreasonable to speculate that if the boy had had a superior IQ and was doing well in school, the parents would have been pleased rather than critical of his easy temperament. The parents were advised that their son was a normal youngster with many positive attributes, but that he would undoubtedly be only a mediocre student through high school, and would not get to college. Therefore, they should stop pressuring him for greater academic achievement, and be pleased at his many other good qualities as a person. The parents reluctantly accepted the logic of this counseling, but follow-up was not possible, and we do not know how well they followed our advice.

In this chapter we have detailed the many ways in which adverse and even hostile parental reactions to children's temperament can be created and expressed, as well as the unfavorable consequences of such judgments for the child's development. However, rarely do such negative parental attitudes and destructive behavior reflect any basic a priori rejection of the child. The vast majority of parents, including most of those caught up in antogonistic interactions with their youngsters, do want their children to prosper physically and psychologically. They may be confused and bewildered as to how to handle their child, they may misinterpret the meaning of their child's behavior, they may be entangled in their own unhealthy motivations and goals, but even so, with few exceptions, they search for answers which will be helpful to their child. Sometimes they may not be able to accept the advice which will ameliorate or cure their child's disturbed functioning because of their own psychologic problems, but these cases are in a minority. And it is the parents' commitment to their child's welfare which is the greatest asset to be utilized to the fullest by the mental health professional, pediatrician, nurse, or educator in helping the troubled child.

CHAPTER 4

Temperament in Infancy

Infancy, covering the first 2 years of life, is a period of immense expansion in developmental capacities. Therefore, the influence of temperament in the interactions that take place in the course of nurturing activities during this age-stage must be considered within the growing complexity of the infant's social initiations and responses. During this time, the infant is being introduced to a segment of the world; a segment delimited by the child's capacities, by the cultural caretaking habits, and by the physical properties of the environment. Thus, when we consider such areas as feeding in terms of the infant's temperamental individuality, we must include awareness of the stage of the infant's digestive abilities, the cultural habits of the milieu in which milk is presented, the steps through which there is widening of the dietary intake, and the particular foods that are available. For the sake of this discussion we will assume that initially the baby will be fed only milk, either by breast or bottle, and by the end of infancy will be eating a variety of solid foods and be capable of handling a cup or glass. Similarly it is assumed that the infant sleeps in a cradle or crib, that baths are given regularly, that diapers and clothing are part of the infant's life, and that toilet training may have been initiated.

When one describes an infant, ordinarily there is a statement as to whether the baby is a boy or a girl (usually in this order), followed by the infant's birth weight or current weight—with some comment as to how much more this is than the average for the infant's age. Generally there follows some recital of developmental accomplishments: "he can already sit if you prop him a bit," "she grabs the spoon and tries to feed herself," or "the twins are both trying to put rings onto poles—of course they have no idea yet of size order." Some comment on the presence of smiling, or of how much the babbling already has some wordlike quality, is frequent.

But parents also make comments on the temperamental qualities that they have noticed. These are the behavioral characteristics of an infant that are observable, that parents can describe, and that have a direct and continuous impact upon the modes of caretaking that will bring satisfaction to both infant and caretaker. It is noted that the baby is beginning to move his eyes in the direction of a noise and gaze at the caretaker's face; a composite of low threshold toward stimuli and maturing perceptual and perceptual–motor abilities. Comments are made of the infant's general state of contentment, or of the opposite, that there is a great deal of crying without anything specific seemingly the matter; thus predominance of positive versus negative mood has been recorded. The amount of wiggling, of high, moderate, or low activity, during the diapering process, the disturbing shrillness of the infant's cries, the ease with which a new person is accepted as a caretaker—these are of great importance to the establishing of the infant's individuality, just because they are such an important part of the everyday caretaking interactions and make for ease or difficulty of their accomplishment. Value judgments abound. Bigger is usually thought to be better. To be a bit earlier in accomplishment than the recorded dates, for sitting, feats of motor accomplishment with hand to mouth, and the like, these are welcomed as harbingers of other superiorities to come. It is forgotten, or perhaps may not have been known, that the expected weights and dates are averages compiled of normal measurements that reach past both sides of the single number used as a standard measure. Not that baby watching is to be deplored. Parents and friends should be fascinated by the unfolding of infant capabilities; but hopefully not so mesmerized as to believe that future abilities, character structure or emotional sensitivity are to be foretold by the infant's versions of these actions.

THE BABY'S IMPACT ON THE FAMILY

The arrival of the first baby results in considerable restructuring of the lives of the parents. Not only do new types of furniture become part of the decor as crib, changing table, and small bathtub have to find a place in the home, but also time assumes an entirely different meaning. As one new father commented, "Isn't it interesting how you begin to plan your day around his majesty's eating and sleeping habits?" The initial period when the mother is recovering physically from labor and regaining some degree of prepregnancy physiological identity—this has been anticipated. It may be a small surprise how quickly she tires, but basically planning has generally included provision of help for these first weeks. The extent of time reorganization has, however, generally been underestimated. Although it is true that the young infant sleeps during a majority of the 24 hours of the day, since his schedule is vastly different from the previous adult schedule that ruled the home, someone must adapt. While over the years, it is the child who learns to adapt to adult living habits, for the immediate period and for some time to come it is the adults who must do the adapting. Infant physiologic needs take priority. No matter how much one might mistakenly try to make a 3-week-old baby sleep through the night to give parents a full 7 or 8 hours of uninterrupted sleep, it will not be that way. It is during this early period that the importance of rhythmicity of function is discovered. The infant who is predictable and regular in hunger and sleep brings a measure of alertness to his parents' days; the infant who is unpredictable and irregular may have parents who move around in a haze of sleepiness until they have worked out a way of alternating nights on call, of taking catnaps when the baby is sleeping, of calling on help for periodic respite so that lost sleep can be made up and so that the parents can rediscover that they can spend time together, just themselves—that while they have become parents they still are people. Isn't this loss of sleep and drain on energy with a new baby obvious? Theoretically yes, but when it happens it is amazing how many new parents are surprised.

As caretaking continues over the days, weeks, and eventually months, the importance of temperament is discovered and rediscovered as caretakers and infant are busy figuring each other out. It comes into awareness in tandem with recognition of growing abilities. It is found that, if Laura fusses when being diapered, she is easily distracted by moving the blue powder can. Thus, simultaneously, the caretaker becomes aware that Laura can focus her eyes on a brightly colored moving object, that she wishes to do so, and that she can quickly be distracted by this. When Laura's motor skills begin to include turning over, holding a colorful object against the wall can prevent her from squirming herself over the edge of the changing table. Such parental awareness is usually communicated to helpers in terms of homely advice, "Hold the powder can near the wall, she will turn in that direction and won't fall off the table." A hungry, distractible baby can often be diverted long enough by an object or sound or playful action that has been discovered to have intriguing qualities for this child, so that the breast or bottle or solid food can be gotten ready without the accompaniment of frenzied cries. When no particular reason seems to lie behind the crying, since food has recently been taken and Billy is both dry and clean, play often works. Billy is moderately distractible, but perhaps Billy has also matured in his 3-month-old mixture of conditioned reflex, accommodation to sequential events, and cognitive advance, to what is already, or is in the process of becoming, a desire to play. And soon it may become evident that for Billy, the best distraction is social; that above all else he is interested by people; their sounds and their movements, and their interacting presence. In parental terms, and in fact, Billy and Laura are making clear that, from the beginning, they have been social beings. It just took the adults some time to figure out how they showed this quality and precisely what their preferences are in terms of sociability. By 6 months, the differences in social style, at least for this period, are clearer. Coming home from an excursion, Billy's infant seat is put down in the hall while impediments are being put away—just for a few moments. A bellow from Billy brings his parents attention. "Oh," they explain, "he never likes being left out—he has to be able to see you, and he really wants to be picked up and talked to." While at times necessity dictates that Billy be left to scream briefly while something is attended to that cannot be done with one hand, mostly Billy is not left out. Things are arranged, for the most part, so that Billy can be an active part of the social scene. Laura, on the other hand, while she coos in enjoyment when played with, can also play and look around happily for 15 minutes or so while her parents are doing other things. The routine of arrival home for Laura is to put her in her room while things are put to rights at leisure, and then Laura once again is brought into the family scene while a meal is prepared. Both Billy and Laura have each given their individual imprint to the handling they receive. Each has to a small extent determined the environment, influenced the type of stimuli that will come their way, and started a process of fit—be it goodness of fit or poorness of fit—between temperamental style of baby and caretaking style of parents.

How does the parental style fit in? Let us imagine that Billy's parents decide that he is spoiled, rather than sociable, and must learn to accommodate. He must learn some self-sufficiency, and accept being left alone. He may learn this, but perhaps he will not, perhaps he may become more fussy, more demanding of attention. His parents may then jump to attention whenever he cries, which only reinforces Billy's demands under all circumstances and strengthens their own habits of unselective response to his fussing by always picking him up. Both Billy and his parents are losing the power to discriminate the importance of different circumstances. They, the parents, should know better, having lived longer. Billy cannot know, except from the responses of caretakers, what the rhyme and rhythm are of this world into which he has been born.

On the other hand, the parents may respond differently. Perhaps, having determined that they must be in charge, they carry on each time as they have planned, without regard for Billy's fussing, making little or no distinction between different circumstances. Billy does indeed become a continuously demanding child, with the precise flavor depending upon his degree of persistence and also upon his intensity of expressiveness. He perhaps learns that, if he keeps at it long and loudly enough, eventually he will be picked up and soothed. Or, if he is less persistent and of low intensity so that his crying is softer and shorter, he gives up; social interaction with his parents then does not come his way except capriciously. In either case, temperamental styles, in the one case those of high persistence and high intensity, in the other case of low persistence and low intensity, have, together with parental attitudes and handling, created a poorness of fit. Billy has by his own temperamental style, helped to influence his environment and experiences. But of course this has occurred only in relation to his parents' particular attitudes and caretaking style. Each reacts to the events that are shaped by the behavior of the other; neither can be said to have come to a behavioral style in isolation.

Let us project an interaction of goodness of fit as an alternative. If Billy has high intensity, the parents may appreciate this, but nevertheless decide whether his immediate demand is appropriate at that time and place. Or they realize his particular low-intensity mode of indicating desire and decide on its propriety. Whether Billy is highly persistent or not, they present a decision determined by social necessities as well as by desire to provide him with positive quality of life.

NOTHING IS FOREVER

In the scripts that have been outlined, does the goodness of fit mean positive outcome for all time?; does poorness of fit mean that all is forever ordained to keep the unfavorable course that has been set? Neither is inevitable. Both parents and baby are resilient, unless an element of pathology is present. Should a parent have pathologic rages, should the infant be significantly mentally retarded or autistic, then these pathologic elements have a power beyond the interactive process just presented. But under normal circumstances, which are after all the most usual, very little is forever. Parents can decide to have another look at Billy's frequent screaming and realize that he does have a right to priority at times, that it would be better and more pleasant were they to modify their all-or-nothing stance. They may conclude that each has rights; Billy as a social individual, provided that some reasonable pattern be established; they as individuals, provided some appropriate pattern is introduced. Since babies are adaptable, even though speed of adaptation varies greatly, soon, or perhaps only after a seemingly long interval, Billy will adapt if given a consistent set of cause and effect sequences. He may not adapt totally. And when he has matured further and reaches further cognitive, perceptive, and motorically capable stages, the balance will alter and a new equilibrium will need to be set. New demandingness may become prominent, or less demandingness as Billy becomes intrigued by the properties and possibilities of toys as well as of people. Parents who have made a decision to give more of their time and their attention to Billy suddenly find that he is the one who wanders away.

On the other hand, it may be that different kinds of attention are demanded. Billy, now a biped whose standing and walking have put him in reach of cupboards that were above his crawling height, has discovered the knife drawer and that delving into this particular place brings guaranteed attention. Once again, the parents' own styles come into play. Safety usually comes first and they make other, more distant, arrangements for the housing of the sharp kitchen and shaving apparatus. But decisions must be made as to handling of pots and pans. Are guards to be put onto all doors and drawers? Or can some discrimination as to what is in or out of bounds be taught? Or is it a fact that pots and pans and differently colored measuring cups are just as capable of stimulating awareness of size, shape, and color discrimination as are the carefully subscribed baby toys labeled as to age-specific educational value? Imitating parental use of the telephone also becomes a game. Pretending to cook, to tidy up, to shave, to play tennis—to do all the actions that are going around about her become Laura's greatest interests. She is an adaptable, still highly distractible infant. Now her adaptation is directed toward replaying the actions of the world around her. It is cute when she wants to brush her teeth at age 14 months. It is not so cute when the telephone is found to have been off the hook since morning. An attempt is made to teach her to replace it, but the very distractibility that made for easier management early on, now interferes with remembering this task. It matters little that she also is easily taken from other tasks. Easy distraction from poking a spoon into an electric outlet is a boon, moving from plaything to plaything does no harm—unless the parents have determined that task accomplishment now is the key to future success. Then the attempt to keep Laura at her self-assigned task of stacking the blocks for a time period that is well beyond her spontaneous attention span, and is also cut short by her distraction by some other occupaton or event, goes against Laura's temperament. With persistence on her parents' part, Laura does not lose her high distractibility. Rather she becomes fretful and unhappy as she becomes aware of her parents' disapproval. She tries, perhaps, but does not really know what she must do. Somehow, from pleasant playtimes, these periods have become sources of mutual discontent. And Laura's parents may now be in a quandary. On the one hand, the value of stick-to-it-of-ness has been made clear in their own lives and they are convinced that it is their parental duty to help their daughter learn this habit as early as possible. If they simply allow her to go on her own spontaneous way, will she not fail to live up to her full potential? It would help if Laura's parents realized that there are many different worthy modes of accomplishment, and one can surely be found that is consonant with Laura's high distractibility. If the task were arranged so as to be accomplished in stages, if the blocks are put away, some now and some later, both distractibility and task accomplishment can be honored. And this can help Laura feel that she is pleasing her caretakers while enjoying her tasks. It may not be her parents' style of task accomplishment, but it is her own. It can become a model that the parents can reinforce with Laura over the years, and with differing kinds of tasks; a model that, if incorporated in her activities sequentially, can be exploited by her consciously with tasks at later dates. It is not the infancy management that will have a magical influence upon Laura's future habits. What will be effective will be the repetition of the message and its utility in her own endeavors; the repeated sense of being able to fulfill her goals and of being respected by others as she does so. The consonance and goodness of fit includes actual acceptance of Laura's qualities by her parents, and their ingenuity in helping her to use them in adapting to the world in which they are all striving for mastery.

PLANNING AHEAD

There have been many references to goodness of fit, and to its opposite, poorness of fit, in the previous discussion in this chapter. Goodness of fit involves respect for the infant's temperamental individuality in the course of everyday handling and caretaking, but it also involves some planning ahead for developmental stages to come and for the environmental expectations to come. In early infancy it is the here and now that is dominant, but within weeks the efforts to attain such creature comforts as a full night's sleep become part of planning ahead, and consequently of current practices. Although few people in an urban setting would wish to do so, it is possible to maintain a 4-hour feeding schedule around the clock. By contrast, it is the habit of being a bit less attentive to the night fussing, waiting a bit to see if the baby does fall back to sleep, that gradually stretches the night intervals of sleep and hunger, while the wakeful time and the nourishment is made up during the day. It is the patterned offering of food that begins to define breakfast, lunch, and dinner with snacks in between—or daytime awake alertness with naps in between. But the speed with which these adaptations to adult living rhythms are attained will be determined in important part by the temperamental quality of high, moderate, or low rhythmicity. The attempt to impose early regularity with adult time scheduling upon a highly irregular child will not work. Here it is important for parents to recognize the realities, and turn to other ways of attaining adequate rest while waiting for the belated effect of their program to show itself.

This example is easy and clear. It may be worthwhile to use the hardest one; the case of the temperamentally difficult child. Although low in representation, involving about 10% of babies, this temperamental cluster gives more than its fair share of problem to caretakers who hope to have their modes of daily management result in a contented, playful baby who brings pleasure to the nurturing interactions. Yet these infants cry more often than they appear content, their cries are piercing and disturbing, and the rhythms of physiologic functioning are irregular and quite different from day to day. This is a baby for whom anything new and different seems to be an affront, whose ability to incorporate new happenings takes days or weeks to be demonstrated. The first important fact for the caretaker is to be secure in the awareness that she or he isn't to blame, that some babies come that way, that this infant's behavior is not properly a personal indictment of attitudes toward being a parent, a negative comment about one's ability to meet an infant's needs. The issue is rather a learning task, the need to learn how to handle a difficult baby without losing one's cool, to learn how to bring about adaptations simultaneously following the infant's behavioral style while holding to the goals that are consistent with the realities of the culture and also with the personalities of the caretakers. It helps parents of a difficult child to know that this is not an unknown state of affairs, and that difficult children, if handled with a goodness of fit, do not need to become behavior problems. In fact, with appropriate handling, although careful thought may be needed, negative mood can become less prominent as higher proportions of happenings become routine events. With positive mood, high intensity of expressiveness is renamed and reexperienced as zest—a quality that adds sparkle to interactions. Irregularity can be managed—at first by caretakers and later by such children themselves so as not to interfere with the comfort of others. Negative mood, which is so extensively shown when things are new and uncomfortably unfamiliar, can be exchanged for positive mood as familiarity brings relaxation. The initial withdrawal to new experiences gradually attenuates as the new, whether foods, people, places or schedules of events, becomes the old and the expected. Finally, the lengthy period needed for adaptation to occur inevitably comes to an end and the child now fits into the new grooves as if they had always been present. True, all this must be done over and over and this may be discouraging. It can be a nuisance, but it need not be a deterrent. The demonstration of the growing competence of the child to deal with the world and the positive contingencies that it brings should be reward enough to make up for the lack of smoothness of developmental and adaptive advances.

Does this mean that the easy child, the youngster who is regular, loves to meet new events, has a positive attitude for the most part, is gentle in mood expressiveness, and adapts speedily to new schedules and situations—that this easy child bears an immunity to behavior disorder from birth? Certainly, the easy infant is more likely to give the caretaker a feeling of competence than his difficult counterpart. The easy infant coos most of the day, cries only for a definite need, and is quickly restored to contentment. A new bathtub, a change from cradle to crib, a new food; all are accepted quickly. Vacations are a pleasure— the necessary alterations of schedule are accommodated to at once. Babysitters wish to be called again as they have had a delightful time. One hopes, indeed, for first-time parents that they will have an easy child, so that their pleasure in parenthood is guaranteed. But there are circumstances, even with an easy baby, that require attention to achieve a goodness of fit. The easy baby with his moderate or mild intensity can be sick, yet not be fussing much. One must learn alternate signposts of physical discomfort—perhaps the baby lacks just a bit of the customary ebullience when ill. As the easy baby moves into the second year of life, disappointments can evoke only a mild outward sign of unhappiness—a turning down of the mouth, a silent retreat. Yet, if this had been a difficult child whose protests were loud, the parents might have rethought the issue and decided rightfully that the child's desire should be met. Similarly, were they aware of the degree of importance this denial held for their easy child, they would have also altered their decision. A goodness of fit for an easy child and his parents involves learning how this child does in fact signal feelings, and appreciating that the outward strength of expression of feelings is not necessarily a true measure of the depth of feeling.

Differences in activity level also necessitate differences in parental handling to achieve goodness of fit. This is easily recognized where a high activity level is present. The squirmy infant requires constant alertness when being changed, dressed, or bathed. As a crawling baby, doors must be closed to keep the high-activity baby within view or to prevent him from tumbling downstairs. When walking has become a fact, the probability that objects will be broken by the impact of a small running body is great; alternatives are to rearrange rooms, place a gate across certain doors, or scold. By maintaining a totally child-proofed environment, one can avoid all need to admonish, but one also unfortunately avoids giving the first introduction to the child that one does not touch certain things. And this can be begun by the decision to leave selected objects within reach but with rules as to when and how they are to be touched. Perhaps a bookcase shelf for Roger's books and toys can be set aside, along with the rule that no other books are to be touched without express permission and supervision. This injunction will not magically be honored at all times, but the repetition, without rancor but also without inconsistency, will begin the task of helping this child channel his high activity level. When circumstances require long, quiet waiting, opportunities can be found for going out to walk periodically; if this is impossible, the fussing must be endured along with a resolution to keep such situations to the unavoidable minimum. In general, one tries to honor the reality of our culture in a manner that is consonant with the reality of Roger's temperament with regard to activity level. And by achieving a goodness of fit, Roger imbibes the need to modify the expression of his high activity without feeling that he is bad or unworthy of parental liking. In fact, in some cases, to have a high-activity child may be a cause for parental pride in terms of its fit with their own temperamental qualities or value systems.

It is not so often recognized that a child with low activity level may also require careful thought as to consonant handling and parental attitudes that will provide a goodness of fit. The very slowness of movement, the lengthy quiet lying, and later sitting in one spot may connote slowness of intellect to some parents, who might find a moderately active child more to their liking. This can be especially prominent should there be a sib with quicker responses, who shoots to comply with a request while the low-active child is still gathering himself for action. Such slowness and infrequency of motor activity may be mistaken for reluctance to be helpful—even in a 1-year- or 18-month-old infant. Jenny's belated responses can bring admonitions that are quite unwarranted, giving her a feeling that she is disapproved of, not liked, and somehow she never can please her parents. A goodness of fit here requires identifying a low activity level as such, making sure that these measured actions are accepted without impatience, and also making sure that a habit is not established of bypassing this child by failing to seek her out for mutual activities. And during these joint ventures, it is more important that the parent adjust his or her pace to Jenny's, so that she can be herself in relaxation. It may be that Jenny has other temperamental qualities that fit spontaneously with parental values; perhaps she is amazingly persistent so that, despite a tardy start, she can always be counted on to complete what she has started, while her speedier sister habitually leaves her tasks half done. If Jenny's temperamental individuality contains both qualities, it will be easier for her parents to appreciate her low activity level as normal. Not that the low-active child with low persistence should be considered as abnormal either.

Or it may be that Jenny's parents themselves are deliberate and slow to arrive at decisions. In such a case, the goodness of fit comes spontaneously as far as low activity level is concerned. It might be that, for these parents, a child of moderate activity level would be seen as if at high speed. To attain a goodness of fit with such a parent–child match, readjustment of the parents' spontaneous judgments are called for. In addition, while for some parents, high persistence is seen as a plus, others may find it a nuisance as they appear to be continually waiting for the infant to finish some task.

It is most unlikely that any baby will be born with just those temperamental characteristics esteemed by both parents. Goodness of fit requires some thinking, some accommodation, and some planning ahead.

RELATIONSHIPS

The important issue of the need to form psychologic bonds between baby and parents has achieved prominence in the last several decades. Unfortunately, a number of professional discussions have created anxieties for working mothers, mothers separated from their newborn infants due to illness of either mother or baby, or to prematurity of the baby who may be kept in a premature unit geographically far from home (Chess & Thomas, 1982). Such factors often create considerable worry and soul-searching in parents who have heard that only if there is immediate and continuing interaction from the time of birth onward will the mother form a true bond with her infant. And how and when, they wonder, does the baby learn which of several caretakers is his mother or father. Since the Industrial Revolution, it has been taken for granted that fathers will not be everpresent in the childrens' lives, but there has been little doubt that children loved their fathers. Mothers have gone out to work for generations under circumstances of privation, and upper-class mothers have a time-honored practice of giving their babies into the virtual full-time care of nurses and nannies.

The present-day perspective on baby's relationships has its own flavor. Middle- and working-class mothers whose economic circumstances do not require their financial input into the family income and who have no particular desire to work outside of the home, see child and household care as their full-time occupation. Many other mothers work full- or part-time outside the home, either because of the family's financial needs, or because their interests and aspirations can only be fulfilled in this way. Such working mothers all too often are burdened with guilt feelings imposed by those "experts" who make sweeping pronouncements on the dire consequences to their young children who are left with substitute caretakers or in day-care centers while their mothers are working. But facts have been accumulating to show that, for the very young infant of a working mother, aside from the greater probability that colds will be passed around more often if the infant is in a group care center, day-care babies and young children with good substitute caretaker arrangements can flourish physically and psychologically (Scarr, 1984). At the same time, these babies have no doubt that the person who collects them and spends the remainder of the day and night with them, is indeed in a special class.

A relationship grows out of mutual activity. And there is ample opportunity for mutual activity in the period after day care has concluded. Whatever the pattern of that particular household—whether the infant is in the kitchen in an infant seat watching food preparation go on, is fed separately or at the table with parents, is bathed by mother or father or by each in turn, is part of special ways in which the family does things together, or plays certain games as part of ordinary household events—all these activities become the basis of close relationships.

Babies are resilient; they are capable of making several simultaneous close relationships, and no one relationship diminishes any other. The infant who is comfortable and reaches with pleasure to the baby-sitter is not losing his relationship with his parents; it is not necessary that there be a crying scene at parting to prove that mother is important. Grandparents, and numerous brothers and sisters have, for generations, been part of an infant's daily interactions without the special relationship between child and parent becoming diluted—unless there is something about this relationship itself that is out of joint. In that case it will not have been the fact of a working mother, of a busy father, that has caused the distance or antagonistic quality of the infant–parent relationship, but rather the nature of the interactions between infant and parent that require examination. Relationship arises from mutual activity and the joys that derive from these. Quality is quite as important as quantity, sometimes more so. And let us remember that a busy mother at home may in fact spend less time with her new infant, given her other household duties and the demands of her other children, than does the working mother who comes home fresh from work and ready for a change of pace.

ATTACHMENT AND DETACHMENT

The concept of analyzing one's child's behavior in terms of temperament and of guiding management techniques so that they are a good fit conjures up pictures of detachment, of coldness and artificality of relatedness. The authors have been asked whether such detached handling may not cause the infant to sense a distance between self and caretakers. Detachment, it is true, has several connotations; one can in fact assess a situation in a detached fashion because one doesn't care, or because it is exceedingly important and some distance of viewpoint is necessary in order that one can ensure that closeness is maintained or regained. When one stands at a distance for a period of assessment of the parent–infant interaction, if it is for the purpose of selecting a type of caretaker activity that will bring better-planned approaches, it is no more detached than standing at a distance long enough to assess whether a new toy is developmentally appropriate. From this scrutiny of toy and baby will come a decision either that there is a good match and play should go full speed ahead, or that there is a poor match and the toy should either be retired for a period or presented with the expectation that the infant will either ignore it or adapt it to his proper developmental capacities. It is then possible to go ahead with mutual play, knowing how to bring about mutual joy in the playing. In the same way, standing at a distance long enough to figure out what is inappropriate to the infant's temperamental individuality leads to an alteration of approach that can change an unhappy interaction and transform it into a positive series of close interactions.

CHAPTER 5

Temperament in the Toddler Stage

Each culture has different expectations for the successive stages of childhood. In some cultures, small children are expected to partake usefully in meaningful household and work chores of the family, while in others the same age-period is assumed to be properly one of innocent play in which, at best, there are miniature playful imitations of adult activities. In western urban culture, for the most part, there is a script in which toddlers are encouraged to use toy cars, typewriters, and household implements that will introduce them to the demands that will be made of them in adult life.

We should not expect that, when toddlers imitate adults, they do so with the same motivations, the same cognitive awareness of cause and effect, or the same empathic and sympathetic abilities as would be found in the adult. Many adults often overlook this truth, so that at times there is much misjudgment and adultomorphic bias. Not too surprisingly, the child is then judged to be sadly lacking in the eyes of such a demanding beholder. However, the concept of goodness of fit reminds us that we should match our expectations of a toddler to her abilities: cognitive, perceptual, motoric, and social. And throughout the myriad interactions of child demand upon adult and adult demand upon child, the mediating influence of temperamental individuality plays a part. At times, this part is minimal. But often it plays an essential role in shaping the goodness of fit that will aid a child who is being competent at being a young toddler to organize and reorganize her functioning as body, abilities, and environmental realities move through sequential developmental stages. Toddlers welcome new demands. They frequently make demands upon themselves that are beyond their own abilities, and then deal with the consequences in various ways. In a game of jumping from first one step, then two, then more steps higher up, one 3-year-old girl said confidently, "I can jump from here," as she moved five steps up. Not too surprisingly she fell instead of landing on her feet. A temperamentally easy child, she said with the best of humor, "I bet you can't do that trick!," thus converting defeat into an accomplishment. A difficult child might have had a tantrum, or blamed the fall on a companion.

DEMANDS AT THE TODDLER STAGE

A brief and incomplete summary of our society's common demands upon toddlers can first be given. These are, of course, not invariable; they differ in close-packed versus isolated life; they differ in cultures with varying traditions brought from foreign lands, they differ in myriad socioeconomic settings. But for the sake of continuity of discussion that does not demand the constant statement of exceptions, let us state certain generalizations. It is assumed that, if the child has not already been toilet trained during infancy, this sphincteric mastery is a task the parents expect will be accomplished in the toddler stage. We can expect that the toddler will be introduced, if this has not already been done, to playing with peers in protected situations, such as in a sand box at home or recreational center, or at nursery school. Mastering the fact that, in other settings than at home, acceptable rules of behavior have new additions and restrictions is a part of this 2- to 6-year old child's growing social competence. Knowing how to assess the expectations and opportunities of a new situation, learning a group of safety precautions, sharing toys in both hostess and guest position, are all part of toddler stage growing sophistication, as is learning to play alone at times. And in our society, knowing when to give in gracefully and when to make a valiant effort to retain a possession or a position or to gain a new and better one—the complicated rules for these social accomplishments are part of a toddler's education. True, these rules may become different at an older developmental stage, but what remains constant is that there is rhyme and reason behind the decision when the triumphant cry, "It's mine!" brings proud possession, or instead brings admonition and disapproval. To learn that one speaks and acts differently to a peer as opposed to an adult also becomes part of the toddler's social education. So, too, is the awareness that adults and children differ; that strategies that will work with one are misplaced with another. When stated all at once, these accomplishments expected of the toddler appear manifold and bewildering, but to the toddler this does not need to be so. If imparted with a temperamental goodness of fit, at a pace and in a style that are consonant with temperamental qualities, these learning experiences are a bit like the jumping off the stairs. Give the child the direction, and usually she is away and trying before you have gotten started yourself.

LAURA AND BILLY

Let us take up the tale of the infants mentioned in the last chapter. We will start with Laura, with her high distractibility. In early routine care, this quality was a boon, but during later infant stages, with dissonant parental values, Laura's high distractibility obtained mixed reviews. Now, during the toddler period, high distractibility once again is to be measured against current expectations, as highly valuable or a disadvantage. Or, in more balanced judgments, it is an attribute that has both valuable and problematic aspects, depending upon the specific activity and the attitudes of those responsible for her nurturing and learning experiences. Mornings in Laura's household are timed. Mother and father must go to their jobs, Laura must go either to the babysitter or to nursey school. Or mother is at home much of the day, but organizes her household tasks so that Laura's dressing and breakfast are best completed by the time daddy leaves the house. Laura is a "I want to do it myself" sort of child. But in the middle of putting on her panties, she sees a toy and starts to play with it. Or, having been given a set of rules designed to get her panties on back to back rather than back to front, Laura forgets again and again that she is supposed to place them on the bed back down and elastic toward her, for the task to come out right. But distractible Laura forgets, and even at times becomes hopelessly entangled with both feet in one panty leg. Funny? Perhaps the first few times. But with time so dear, and with Laura both determined to do it herself and guaranteed to become distracted from recalling the correct procedure, dressing can easily become a daily battleground. Clearly, in this case a poorness of fit needs to be prevented. Perhaps, after all, Laura's motor and cognitive skill are not yet up to her motivation. A firm rule is made that either mother or father do part of the task, allowing Laura to complete it and begin to master the lesson in stages. It may involve some protest, but it also can be made into a game of taking turns. Praise for an accomplishment consonant with cognitive, motor, perceptual, and temperamental qualities is then possible. In this way, a positive experience can take the place of the turmoil and hassle that had previously started Laura's day.

Laura has begun to do a jigsaw puzzle when it is time to leave for a visit. The trip is long and time is precious. It is a boon that distractible Laura is ready and willing to put aside her puzzle gracefully, turning her attention to asking questions about whether her favorite cousins will also be there and what kind of ice cream will be served. But it is a birthday party, and Laura has taken the present from the spot where her mother had placed it to avoid a last-minute delay, and Laura has no recollection where she may have left it. Distractibility here is no boon. It requires some restraint on the part of both mother and father to gain perspective. The "why must you always make us be late?" is a question that 4-year-old Laura has no power to answer. Indeed, after reflection, one hopes, the parents will conclude that , if Laura is involved, it is their timing, not Laura's, that is off the mark. They must simply account for the extra time needed to get ready with Laura, in addition to that which strict efficiency would demand. Would they, after all, not make such allowances for an unfeeling car which required an extra 10 minutes to warm up lest it stall? If everything goes smoothly, to be early does not harm, while if things go their worst, serenity can still rule the day and make the excursion the pleasant event that had been planned.

Billy, in infancy, seemed to be an insatiable child because of his intensity and persistence. But when it became clear that it was social contact that he wanted, the parents' delightful knowledge of how important they were to Billy made his frequent demands for interaction with them acceptable—even though it required some extra planning ahead. When Billy discovered the interesting complexity behind toys, his parents were less relieved by his diminished demandingness than they would have anticipated; in fact they feel a bit rejected. Now in toddlerhood, with his augmented cognition, perception, and motoric skills, Billy is avid for new and intriguing occupations. After some solitary explorations for a period, once again he demands company as he plays, asking constant questions, many of which go to the heart of reality, but well beyond the reach of his ability to understand. Often he leaves his parents behind while they are still focused on the old, previously treasured game. Mother realizes one day that she has put down her preparations for dinner just to be available to Billy, but finds herself building alone with the blocks while he has gone off to use the toy village. This has happened before. With sudden insight she reverses roles and realizes that she had indeed selected the blocks repeatedly in the past when they were in fact his favorite toys. But Billy had now altered his interests and she had not kept up. Billy, in his 2½-year-old way, still maintained his high sociability, he was taking care of her, giving her those toys that were, in his experience, her favorites, before moving on to his preferred occupation. Funny to mother? One hopes so. And when Billy's toy village goes wrong and he bellows for assistance in his usual highly intense manner, the decision as to whether to come to his aid immediately or to ask him to wait, will be made, one hopes, in keeping with whatever program of socialization has been the rule, rather than out of pique.

ENTRY TO NURSERY SCHOOL

Many toddlers attend nursery school, some start school attendance only at age 5 with kindergarten, and others only begin formal schooling at 6, the next developmental period. School includes many new demands: cooperative peer group interactions, being away from home for several hours at a time with another adult besides parents in charge, a set of rules that differs in many respects from those of the home; these now come all at once and continue. For the easy child, the school experience may bring only fun and positive excitement. For toddlers with the difficult child temperamental cluster, every new aspect of school may bring stress. If handled well, such stress is not harmful, but rather brings mastery and competences that are a prototype of demands that will recur throughout life. Many nursery schools have a regular procedure that takes such needs into account. The school may be visited several times before actual regular attendance. Mothers or fathers may remain for the first few days. The child's peer group may be built up gradually. Nevertheless, for the child this is a very different experience than life has heretofor brought. Time begins to be a focus of living, whether there is a school bus or the child is brought by a parent. "School today?" brings the awareness of days of the week having different qualities. The meeting of the other youngsters at school, learning to hang or fold clothing in cubbies, differentiating between one's own possessions brought for comfort and security, and the school possessions to be shared, brings a concept of "mine" and "me" as well as "yours" and "you." Happenings are scheduled for all. While they are planned to be in tune with the average attention span, interest level, and speed of adaptation of the child's particular age, be it 2, 3, or 4, no one arrangement can be best for the wide diversity of children's temperamental styles, cognitive competences, perceptual capacities, and motor skills. The low-active child may often be left out, while the high-active child finds rest periods a trial and is often admonished because of accidental pushes and grabs. The regular child finds that the rhythm of awakening, toileting in school, snack time, and nap or rest time gives little difficulty. The irregular child may have trouble accommodating to some or all of these. The toddler with definite likes and dislikes in food and with low sensory threshold is exquisitely aware of the unwelcome differences in taste, texture, and temperature of the school food. Yet all of these demands and others are the template of things to come. Learning quickly or gradually, with smiles or howls, to become familiar with and to enjoy the elements (all or perhaps only some) of this first brush with formal schooling will not be an inoculation for life. Other nurseries, kindergarten, and later grade school, all have their differences of tempo and demand which will also have to be mastered in sequence.

As they move on through the toddler years, both Laura and Billy will find that their behaviors bring reactions from peers with whom they play. Laura's sunny nature and the ease with which she can be distracted from a toy that her visitor has taken from her makes her a favorite for visiting and also as a guest. When, at age 3, she begins nursery school, her start is fine. She is intrigued by the changing events and is ready for changes. But soon this same quality of high distractibility brings her into some disfavor. In her nursery school she leaves toys strewn about and constantly forgets to clean up. She loses her mittens in winter, misplaces her exhibit for Show and Tell, pays little heed to the rules of games so that she fails to sit down when put out in musical chairs, or forgets that she is supposed to be a bunny or a butterfly at dance and mime time. In general, Laura requires special watching and she repeatedly makes her group lose games through her forgetfulness. Here it is the teacher who may find herself scolding constantly without effect, creating a confused and unhappy child.

Laura wishes to please, but as has happened before during the infancy period, she does not know what to do. Now, at a more advanced cognitive developmental stage, she has an uneasy awareness that others find her very essence wanting. True, she obtains approval when she, long before her classmates, notes the silent withdrawal of another child and moves to comfort her and find out what has happened to make her unhappy. This sensitivity is a composite of low threshold and high distractibility. She notes stimuli too faint for the others, and her high distractibility makes her constantly aware of and responsive to events that are peripheral to the main occupation. Teacher does not realize, it seems, that both the annoying "forgetfulness" and the prized compassion have the same basis. Laura could not be the compassionate one without also being the forgetful one; they are composed of the same temperamental qualities. Yet the compassion is to be nurtured while the forgetfulness will be a hindrance if left unchecked. Awareness of temperament as the unifying cause of both behaviors is a start to finding the solution. The ability to be compassionate, to be alert to the feelings of others, can be encouraged, although Laura will have to learn that this concern for others will not always be reciprocated. When some friend whose sorrow she has shared now turns upon her and excludes her from a "secret society," Laura will need to learn that loyalty is not forever, that people have many sides, and that her own behavior was still good, even though now apparently forgotten.

But Larua's forgetfulness does need attention. There is a world of difference between the individual who, knowing of her high distractibility, works out practical maneuvers for reminding herself, puts the Show and Tell material always in the same place so as not to forget, folds up the sweater immediately because she knows from experience that otherwise some other distraction will cause her to forget—versus the one who says in essence, "Well, that's the way I am." Others may, in response to the latter attitude, take up the slack for a time, but after a while people tire of doing someone else's remembering for them. So Laura, with parents', teachers', and friends' help, has to learn that she is a highly distractible person, that sometimes this is a help, but often it is a hindrance. She is not a bad person for this, but it is her responsibility to do something about it. The something must be consonant with her temperament, as well as with her motivation to be a positive part of the group, and also with her cognitive awareness that she may lose important opportunities if she fails to take remedial measures. But of overriding importance is the fact that, by virtue of the messages she gets from others, she is liked and respected, that her high distractibility is a normal quality, not a demon, and that with constant awareness she can, with some exceptions, remain on top of her life plans. She will forget again and again, she will aggravate herself and others, but with constant repetition over the years of the positive message from others as to her basic worth, the positives and negatives of high distractibility will fall into place. It is not the way she was treated as a toddler that will create a magical protection for Laura's life-span. It will be the repetition over the years of this fundamental message that will reinforce the self-esteem and the self-confidence that permits Laura to take responsibility for her own behavior and its effect on others and on her own level of performance. And even were there to be a bad start, a poorness of fit, later relationships and events can go far toward reversing the process and creating a goodness of fit once again.

For Billy, as well as for Laura, a whole world of new events, schedules, restrictions, and opportunities appears with entrance to nursery school. For one, it is now decreed in preparation for this great new event, that toilet training must be accomplished. For Laura, a regular child, motorically quiet, and capable of being easily distracted by being read to, the sitting on a brand new potty was a delight. By habit, she absentmindedly deposited her regular evacuation in it after lunch and just before her nap. It then became a small step for her to announce that a B.M. was coming, and to run to pull down her panties in time for the deposit to be made in the proper receptacle. When, at school, the children were toileted daily, for Laura this was an accepted procedure. Not so for Billy. Irregular in biologic rhythm, there had been no set time for Billy to evacuate his bowels. One attempt to sit him arbitrarily on his potty at what seemed to be a propitious moment revealed that, with his high activity level, a moment's sitting still was an eternity. No relationship between the potty and his own B.M. had been learned, even though by watching he had made a relationship between his parents' toilet-sitting and their production of bowel movements. Indeed, he had announced grandly that, when he was a big boy and went to nursery school, he would make his B.M. in the toilet and not wear diapers like a baby any more. He had sat for a moment pushing his belly in and out and looking hopefully for the results. Billy indicated by a myriad of means that his motivation to be toilet trained was there. What was missing were the temperamental qualities that would make this motivation operative; the regularity of biologic functioning that could be harnessed to voluntary control, the ability to sit comfortably long enough, the approach rather than withdrawal to the coldness and height of the seat. Was Billy destined to start school in diapers, a sad disappointment to himself and a possible focus of teasing by classmates? Billy was able to announce a B.M. immediately after its occurence. Thus, before it became a messy business, it was possible to put him in big boy pants, secure that he would not soil the furniture. Exuberantly pleased by this success, in line with his high intensity, after a while Billy began to announce, "I think it's coming," and so it was. Sometimes it was caught, sometimes not, but the next step toward actual mastery of his sphincter was gained. Little by little, Billy learned to understand his inner messages, and by the beginning of nursery school he was toilet trained—that is, accidents were less frequent than successes. Thus, Billy's milestones of toilet training was accomplished in a manner consonant with several of his temperamental qualities; not, to be sure, in the easiest manner, but with a goodness of fit for him.

Billy entered nursery school with his usual sociability, so that he looked forward with pleasure to making new friends. His persistence with puzzles and games evoked much praise from his teachers. However, his persistence was not always a plus. Having started a mammoth architectural project of building a three-story house with blocks, Billy shrieked with disappointment when the almost completed structure overbalanced and crashed. Persistently, he started again, and once more his desires outstripped his execution and again it toppled. Howling, Billy started a third time—but now outdoor playtime had arrived. To distract Billy from his impossible task was itself impossible. Yet he could not be left unattended, and both teachers were needed to monitor the outdoor play. A scene was inevitable as Billy was picked up, dressed, struggling, in his snowsuit, and conducted outdoors. Within a few minutes, sociable Billy had become engaged in a game with his friends, happy and persistent. But the teachers felt torn and bleeding and were very aware that another day might bring another such battle. Somehow the positive side of persistence must continue to be rewarded. But also, where Billy was concerned, they would be well advised to estimate the time and deflect Billy from initiating a task too lengthy for the time at hand.

In marked contrast was Billy's cousin George, who was in the same class. George entered nursery school with more than slight trepidation. New events had always been hard for him. Although he had visited the school building, and although school attendance was started with the company of only 2 other children at first and mother present for the first days, nevertheless it was a new building, the use of cubbyholes for possessions had not been part of George's previous habit, the daily presence of 20, not 2 other children, the fact that Jane and Mildred, the teachers, are in charge instead of mommy—all these areas of newness must now be incorporated in the daily rhythms of living. True, George has had the experience of visiting away from home, of having the rules determined by the parent of the child he was visiting. He has developed some awareness of sharing, though he is not yet accomplished at its nuances. Without these bridges from the old to the new, George would be in even greater distress than he is now. But everything is indeed somewhat new, and George, when overcome by this realization, gives voice to his distress in loud tones, as is his usual habit. The teachers, who are pushed to the limit by this frequently unhappy child, are all too often likely to label him "immature" and to say to the mother, "I'm afraid he isn't yet ready for nursery school." But if one went by George's outward reaction, he has rarely been ready for anything. He was not ready for his first bath, if one went by the screaming and struggle; but after several weeks he was ready, if one went by his smiles and anticipatory gurgling. He was so ready that removing him from the bath brought on screams of protest at terminating this now delightful experience. He had not been ready for any new food, if one went by the fuss each new food evoked. But it had become clear that, if each new food was presented again and again, giving intervals of several days between presentations while old and accepted foods were offered, eventually the new became the familiar and in fact George now had a wide repertoire of favorite foods. That George was considered to be "not ready" was old stuff, and fortunately George's parents had a formula ready. They suggested to the teachers, who were so prepared to believe that George was being sacrificed to his parents' work ambitions, that they hold out until Thanksgiving. By then, it was clear that George was indeed ready, and by the Christmas recess he was enjoying the now-familiar routine of nursery school with his typical high intensity—now called "zest" in view of its association with positive mood.

To make more clear the complexity of dynamics of behavior disorder during the toddler stage, when temperamental qualities must be considered together with cognitive abilities, the meaning to the toddler of events that have befallen her, and the demands and needs of the environment, the case of Arthur seems appropriate to recount. Arthur, at age 4½, was presenting multiple problems. A sleep problem which had been overcome during infancy had now recurred in much magnified and complicated form. In infancy Arthur had awakened irregularly at night and had been easily soothed back to sleep. Alert to concepts of temperament by their own reading, his parents had noted that Arthur was irregular in biologic rhythms and they had willingly accommodated to this fact. He had finally been sleeping mostly through the night, and when he did awaken it was understood that he had his parents' permission to turn on the light and play quietly—provided his baby sister did not awaken. Irregularly the light was found on in the morning while Arthur was now peacefully slumbering, and sister was now awake after a seemingly good night's rest.

However, in the previous 6 months Arthur's sleep began once again to be broken. At first this seemed merely a recurrence of the old sleep irregularity, but soon it began to be accompanied by nightmares and fears about going to bed. Being put to bed, previously a pleasant routine which had included being read to and tucked into bed in a special way, now begun to be contaminated by demands for new and time-consuming additional rituals, so that in the end confrontations and angry feelings on both sides had become dishearteningly typical.

A further complication was the frequency with which Arthur came to his parents' bedroom during the night, crying because of some nightmare—at times too vague to be described clearly. Patient at first, they began to feel that sometimes there was less fright and more manipulation, especially as Arthur had begun to make threats. "If you don't let me stay in your bed, I will make pee-pee in mine," and so he did one night when his presumed bluff was called. Daytime requests had also turned often into demands with threats attached, even though the request itself might be quite reasonable and one which he would not have been denied. "If you don't let me have bread and peanut butter I will cut up the rug"—and one day he did cut into the living room rug after a confrontation. Ordinary events were now often turned into struggles—events that had previously been accepted easily or even looked forward to. Even a car ride to visit relatives whom Arthur liked might become a struggle over selection of clothing.

With all this troublesome behavior, at times Arthur seemed himself to be striving to find some way out of this situation. He asked his parents on several occasions to lock their bedroom door so he couldn't get in at night. This they had not done, since they then might not hear one of the children if sick or in distress. Arthur had also, several times, suggested punishments for himself for misbehavior. But his proposed punishments were extreme, such as tying him to a chair so he would not be able to carry out a threatened retribution.

Other qualities remained unchanged. Always a bright and inquiring child, Arthur continued to pursue knowledge and enjoyed asking insightful questions, and there was mutual pleasure still in the discussions that followed with either parent. The child was fond of his sister, 2 years his junior, and his geniune tenderness for her and appropriate play with her continued as before. He went to nursery school with the same old pleasure—except for the sudden and seemingly unprovoked fights over some aspect of the morning routine. Always sensitive to sights and sounds, this low sensory threshold continued in evidence.

Sometimes its presence was a plus, as when he noted some bird's song or showed delight in music. Sometimes it was a distinct disadvantage, as when he complained about a garment because of the slight roughness of its texture.

More than anything, Arthur's parents were disturbed at their own growing negative feelings. More and more, they found themselves expecting an outing to be spoiled by the child's behavior; they worried that they were in fact beginning to dislike their son. They had come to the end of their reasoning powers. They sought help for Arthur because he was patently unhappy and everything they did to help seemed only to make things worse. They also sought help for themselves because they were growing increasingly unhappy at the growing gulf between them and their child.

The basic history showed Arthur to have been the product of a wanted pregnancy and a normal delivery. In infancy, other than a tendency to be biologically irregular, to be moderately withdrawing from new stimuli, to need a moderately long time to make adaptations, and with high intensity of expressiveness, he had been reasonably easy to care for. There had been no major illnesses. Developmental milestones had all been not only within normal limits, but mostly early. He had shown awareness of colors, differences in temperature, and sensitivity to tastes and sound early—a combination of low sensory threshold and developmental precocity. Observation during a play session showed an alert, intelligent, and expressive child.

Probing into the events that had preceded the toddler sleep problem, there had been a family visit to his father's father in another state. This grandfather had been ill at the time and had subsequently died. Arthur's parents had thought that, because of distance and few prior visits, little meaningful relationship had been present between child and grandfather, so that the death would be experienced as no actual loss for Arthur. As we talked about this further, however, it appeared that Arthur had noted his father's grief and had asked a great many questions about death. Did only old people die? Did children's fathers die or did that only happen after the children were grown up people themselves? These had been penetrating questions and had been answered honestly and apparently to Arthur's satisfaction. But in retrospect, the night fears had been initiated not long after this event.

This very intelligent child, whose cognition outran his 4-year-old emotional developmental status, was struggling to learn the facts about permanence of relationship, control of relationships, and abandonment. This struggle to understand and be reassured had taken place within the temperamental context of low threshold, hence high sensitivity to nuances of parental feeling; in the context of his irregularity of biologic functioning, so that Arthur's state of concern had brought back the sleep irregularity. And nighttime, when one is all alone in the dark, is the best time to awaken fears and panic. Yet, this toddler knew what he shouldn't awaken his parents so frequently, that their desire to respond to genuine emergencies was not a desire to be disturbed nightly. Striking out blindly, he struck at those closest—not at school where people didn't matter quite so much, but at home where parents are supposed to make everything come out right. So Arthur suffered, and expressed his suffering with his characteristic high intensity. His threats were those of a toddler, and consisted of toileting regression and simple destruction of objects. But, partly because he was so intelligent, Arthur's parents expected him to behave in tune with his cognition rather than with his 4-year-old emotional state. They saw his behavior as a vengeful campaign to make their daily functioning difficult. What Arthur was saying with his suggestions for parental control—to lock the bedroom door so he could not wear out his welcome, to tie him to a chair so he could not carry out his destructive threats—was a plea for them to take control again. Arthur had a bear by the tail and he couldn't let go. He was pleading with his parents to stop this progression of negative moves leading to reprisal, and going on and on in a vicious circle.

In fact, once the parents were able to take their distance and see that the very temperamental qualities with which they had coped so well during infancy were now showing up in terms of a cognitively higher conflict on their son's part, that he was responding to his own feelings and needs, and not merely making an onslaught on their needs, things fell into place. They no longer felt victimized by their son. They were able to let Arthur know that they were indeed in control. No, they would not lock their door because they loved both their children and must be able to hear if one of them were ill. If he awakened during the night, he could come into their room and lie down on the blanket they placed for him—but he was not to awaken them unless he was feeling sick. If he broke the rule, they would not like it, but no, they would not punish. When he asked for something with threats, he was to ask again, but politely. They knew he didn't really wish to do the things he threatened. Yes, grandfather had died, and sometimes children's parents did die, but they felt quite healthy and were not about to die—but he could ask about this as often as he wished. And indeed a new equilibrium was established. It took several weeks for the most obnoxious behavior to disappear, and several months before Arthur was entirely back to his normal self, and his parent to theirs. Without his high intelligence, perhaps Arthur's particular temperamental qualities might not have erupted in this series of problems. Perhaps with his high intelligence and other temperamental qualities, his worries might have shown a different form. But the effect of a child's temperament in the toddler stage, as at other times, can only be understood in the light of cognition, perception, motor abilities, and environmental events and responses.

CHAPTER 6

Temperament in Middle Childhood

A colleague of ours, a general psychiatrist who had moved to an area where there were no child psychiatrists, was called upon to help Arlene, a 7-year-old girl who was having considerable difficulty in keeping friends and was showing growing apprehension about going to school. Feeling obligated to assist, but knowing his inexperience, he asked one of us (S.C.) to be available to review the diagnostic data and treatment approaches—a task that was accepted. The diagnostic evaluation made clear that there was no thought disorder, and the developmental history had been normal. Since this child had been living in a semi-isolated place, she had had few opportunities prior to kindergarten for group play, but with sibs and family no difficulties had previously arisen. As a result, Arlene had become a clinging child who worried about where she was going, who would be there, and whether "they" would like her.

The initial treatment phases went well. Arlene made friendly responses to the psychiatrist's expressed interest in her troubles. Indeed, she had always gotten along well with adults and enjoyed talking to them. She chatted about her teacher, the mean things the boys did during recess, the way her "best friend" Jackie made friends with another girl, Beth, and began to tease Arlene, how Susan wanted to copy Arlene's homework and she didn't let her, and how Susan is now telling everyone to hate her. The therapist, Dr. Z., was disheartened. He had waited for Arlene to talk about important issues, but here she was chatting on about these trivialities; how could he be of help unless he could get her onto important topics. I asked what he would be doing and thinking had an adult patient with relationship problems spent the treatment time discussing events in the office with fellow workers. That, said Dr. Z., would be different. It would be possible to pick out of these interactions the patterns of attitudes and the actions that gave insight into the problem areas. Once these were clear to him, he could raise them at a rate consonant with his patient's ability to explore them, and give interpretations that could be mutually discussed.

Knowing that this was indeed the way in which he functioned with adults, I pointed out that, for a 7-year-old, the events that Arlene had been bringing up were quite the equivalent. These were the effective material of her existence at her developmental level. She was telling him that social relationships were very important to her. But she was also informing him that she was attempting to find social security in binding one friend to her, and interpreting a desire on the part of such child to have additional friendships as disloyalty. If Dr. Z. explored the precise actions that Arlene had taken, he might learn what she had done in her pique at Jackie's assumed disloyalty that had evoked the teasing. He must reorganize his own mental set to realize that in fact Arlene was bringing to him the details of her interactions out of which her pattern of functioning could be analyzed. Dr. Z. must prove his respect for Arlene's concerns by remembering the names of the children about whom she spoke, the nature of her interactions with them, and the patterns of pleasure and pain that occurred in these daily events. These data were not only the prelude toward making a therapeutic relationship, but were also important in themselves. They were the meaningful content of Arlene's 7-year-old life, and provided the clues for identifying the attitudes that needed examination. Her improvement would come in the same terms, by means of his reinterpreting within her 7-year-old cognitive and affective ability, the significance of these daily coalitions and ruptures of Arlene's relationships with other children, of the manner in which she considered friendships to be cemented, and what she thought to be a hostile action denoting enmity. Once this reorientation had been solidified, Dr. Z. was able to proceed, although his ability to think and talk in terms of the world of middle childhood needed restructuring from time to time.

How did Arlene's problem arise, and what part did temperament play in its development? Her early behavioral history indicated clearly that temperamentally she had always been a slow-to-warm-up child. She had always needed several exposures to new stimuli before feeling comfortable with them. Adaptations had always been slow, although they eventually occurred. But her parents had always been patient with her and did not pressure her to accommodate quickly to the new. Neither did they try to shelter her from a new experience because of her initial discomfort. The one exception had been Arlene's first experience with school, when she was enrolled in kindergarten. Here, her distress was so evident that her mother withdrew her after a week's trial, saying "after all, kindergarten isn't important and she can wait for first grade."

Handled with such a basically positive goodness of fit, Arlene's development had proceeded normally through the preschool years. Given her initial discomfort with most new situations, however, Arlene tended to stick strongly to what had become familiar and was no longer new, whether this was a favorite toy, her next-door neighbor playmate, or "helping" mother clean the house. At the same time she resisted any innovations that might change a familiar routine.

Starting first grade could not be avoided. Arlene was indeed very uncomfortable to begin with, but this began to lessen as the first weeks went by. Also, she made one friend in the class, Jackie, but then, in her established way of functioning, Arlene stuck to Jackie, expected that Jackie would reciprocate, and could not cope adequately when Jackie also became friendly with another girl.

The same lack of flexibility was evident in her classmate Susan's request to copy Arlene's homework. When Arlene had asked her own mother to do some of her work, her mother had said quite firmly that the purpose of homework was for Arlene to learn and not to turn in a perfect paper that was done by someone else. Arlene, having accepted this quite accurate statement of her mother, had applied it in the same manner in which she stuck to any accommodation she had learned. She imitated her mother, and had given Susan her mother's lecture. Susan's teasing had then been in reaction to what appeared to be a superior moralistic preaching approach. Arlene did not realize that she was setting herself up as the conscience of the class, nor had she intended to do so. She was merely holding inflexibly to a lesson she herself had learned from her mother. But behavior has repercussions, and Susan had indeed told everyone she could that Arlene thought she was better than everybody. That the coalition set up by Susan included only a few children—the rest didn't care—and that it lasted but a day, these facts had gotten lost in Arlene's reaction to this new atmosphere. Arlene was afraid to go to school the next day; a school phobia was in the making. Her mother consulted Dr. Z., who, after consulting me, suggested that Arlene be taken firmly, but with reassurances, up to and through the school door, but that her mother not speak to the teacher or in any way blow up the matter. And in fact, Arlene found out at once that her classmates were absorbed in the new day's activities, had no recollection of this very minor episode, and that she was in no way an outsider. Had there been parental intrusion, and had the teacher chided the other children, then Arlene might indeed have been labeled by the other children as an oddball outsider who made trouble for others.

Arlene was a slow-to-warm-up child, but this had not been a problem until middle childhood. In the toddler period, she had mastered the expectations of limited social interactions, had become a capable youngster who was content, knowing the routines that each day would bring, and who showed both her enjoyments and her disappointments in low key. The demands of the middle childhood period were challenging and stressful because there were so many new elements occurring simultaneously. However, with an opportunity to talk out with her therapist what was happening, the discussions themselves acted as rehearsals and preparations that helped her gain understanding and mastery, as well as familiarity with the ways of her new world. And, in addition, Arlene had parents who alerted themselves to any incipient trouble, brought the issue to the therapist's attention, and were able to act as colleagues in the therapeutic endeavor.

Little by little, Arlene built up a coterie of friends, and at least cognitively, began to realize that a change of groupings, while still distressing to her, given her temperamental attributes, was a temporary disequilibrium and that she was in fact capable of adapting to it as she had to other changes. Excessive stress had been converted to a degree and pace of stresses that allowed her time for mastery of each in turn. With each new distress, Arlene now came to talk of how to deal with it, in place of her previous complaining that people should behave in a way that she was used to. Remaining a child with a small number of friends, she nevertheless had sufficient friends so that her self-esteem as a person no longer depended upon just one child's exclusive relationship to her. Quietly content, she now looked forward to attending school, although any change, such as a substitute teacher, a new subject, or a new bus driver, required advance rehearsal or after-the-fact reconstruction. Would this adaptation take Arlene through all of school? Probably not. In junior high school, with its many alterations of place and persons, with changing class schedules and multiple teachers, it is not at all unlikely that apprehension would again occur. But the fact of her earlier mastery would help Arlene in coping anew with the many new types of settings and expectations that would come her way during later childhood and adolescence. It would be the aggregate of masteries that would feed her self-image as being someone who did cope in the end, although it was hard in the beginning.

THE "LATENCY PERIOD" CONCEPT

What, then, is the world of middle childhood? In many psychiatric discussions, the middle childhood period is frequently and casually labeled the "latency period," as if this were a descriptive term understood by everyone. Yet the term "latency" actually derives from a specific hypothetical concept in traditional psychoanalytic thinking. To Sigmund Freud, this age period was a period of psychosexual "latency" between the passing of the Oedipal stage and the beginning of adolescence, a period in which the energy of infantile sexuality is turned away either wholly or partially from sexual utilization and directed toward other aims (Freud, 1924). While, the more recent psychoanalytic literature has tended to emphasize that middle childhood is a period of active developmental change (Erikson, 1968; A. Freud, 1965), there remains a widespread concept that "latency" implies an absence of any significant change during this period. Thus, as one writer has put it, latency is "an unfortunate term since it suggests that nothing really important is happening and that the child is simply waiting for puberty to begin" (Shaw, 1966).

Even with regard to sex, in the NYLS and in other studies in which middle childhood has been studied, sexual curiosity and sexual experimentation have been very much in evidence. Thus, Jersild, a leading student of child development, has pointed out that: "When viewed in the light of empirical studies of children's interests and actions during this period, 'latency' cannot be taken literally. For many children, interest in sex during this period is not latent or inactive or held in abeyance, but is distinctly manifest and active. In normal development, sex never takes a holiday" (Jersild, 1968).

SEX IN CHILDHOOD

In infancy, awareness of all body parts occurs. During diapering it is a common question of mothers whether to do anything when a baby boy grabs at his penis. Although they would be quite capable of dealing with the fact of grabbing at a foot or any body part that interfered with putting the diaper in place, they hesitate to take action here, having often been told that playing with the penis has a special significance. They may wonder if they should take special measures to discourage this interest, such as giving a toy to play with as a distraction, or showing signs of disapproval so as to teach the infant that this part is not to be handled. Alternatively, parents have read that it is extremely bad to interfere with body exploration, especially of sex organs. They themselves may be made uneasy by the baby's action, but feel that they may do grave damage to adult normal sexual expression were they to interfere with such spontaneous exploration on the part of the infant. Little girls, in infancy, having no protruding sex organ to grab, are not so evident in their awareness of their sex organs. Such parents need to be reassured that the infant boy or girl's sexual exploration has no special meaning and should be handled by the parent in the same way as any other body exploration.

Girl and boy infants alike do masturbate, either by touch or by rubbing or rocking their bodies in such a way as to obtain stimulation of sex organs and gain pleasure thereby. In the NYLS parental histories of the infancy period, parents did not bring up masturbation as a problem, but when direct questions were asked as part of the protocol about this, most parents had noted its occurrence. It was not clear whether the failure to speak of masturbation as a problem was due to actual lack of parental concern about this issue, or whether they had read that they ought not to have such concern, and hence suppressed any outward expression of it. In no children in our sample did masturbation in infancy reach such a frequency of occurrence as to interfere with interest in other activities or to be the expression of a compulsive action. Some infants were reported to have urinated while standing up in the bath, and to have shown great interest and pleasure in this phenomenon. In fact, some little boys were described as watching their penis in subsequent baths, even drawing in their belly muscles and pushing them out, apparently in an effort to repeat this intriguing scene. Or they reached with their hands, girls and boys, to touch the place—but not knowing what button to push, usually they were unable to bring about this interesting act of water on demand.

During the toddler period, children's interest in all body parts continues. While parents play games with older infants and with toddlers that involve the naming of body parts or pointing to them when named, usually the penis and vulva are omitted. During toileting at home or at school, or in watching parents bathing or using the toilet, the awareness of similarities and differences in anatomic structure becomes more definite. Sexual identity through observation of peers and parents leads to children making special announcements of identity with the same-sex parent. In present-day society, neither haircut nor clothing are the marks of being a girl or a boy as once was the case. Nevertheless, despite our society's official attempts to root out sex typing with its value judgments, it is still not unusual for parents and other adults to admonish a toddler by saying "little girls shouldn't be rough" or "Of course you must expect him to be so active, he's a boy." Girls and boys alike are usually in pants, but when dressed up the appearance of a pretty dress or jazzy dress-up pants make the child's sexual identity clear to the children and to the watching world.

Playing doctor during the toddler period seems to be part of many children's experience. This is an opportunity to strip and examine visually how each other is made, to note the similarities and the differences. Often it includes repeating the actions that have occurred during illness, so that parents are concerned when they find "thermometers" thrust up small anuses by inventive children. While this imitation is in its essence not different from the imitation of any other adult activity, akin to the attempts at self-washing or trying to peel vegetables, because of adult sensitivities playing doctor is often seen as incipiently evil and as meriting punishment. And indeed, one should be cautious as to any object introduced within a body orifice, but this is the issue, not that sexual curiosity is in itself bad and likely to lead to depravity.

When children enter the developmental period of middle childhood their sexual interests take on the cognitive advances of that period. Whereas naughty words during the earlier periods tended to be toilet talk, now "dirty" language tends to add on the currently popular obscene words with explicit sexual meaning. This too is part sexual curiosity and part imitation of the adolescent and adult language that connotes being grown up. And along with the imitative part of sexual curiosity, there is also a cognitive desire to understand how babies are made, how they grow, and how they get out of the mother's belly. In all these aspects of sexual interest, temperament plays a modest part. The persistent child pursues the exploration of sex organs and sexuality by continued evoking of the special sensations or by questions; low or high threshold to stimuli will influence the child's degree of interest.

More important is the growth of ability. This brings questions as to both current and adult sexuality—here the degree of openness on the part of adults will add some idea that this is an area of privacy, or of secrecy or of shame. And indeed here is the opportunity to teach the child the difference between privacy and shamefulness. Parents who find little trouble identifying for themselves and for the child that, while a degree of undress is not proper in public places, but is acceptable at home, often find that they have trouble with sexual questions as far as making this same distinction is concerned. In fact some parents are stumped by the request that the child watch them having sexual intercourse. The child, having been given a willing and open answer to his queries, does not have any idea that this demonstration has different connotations than other demonstrations that have been offered. Once this is seen by the parents as a learning experience for the child—that the child is permitted to learn that parents' sexual activity is private to them—these parents who are so conscientiously striving to ensure their child's later sexual fulfillment are given the privilege to be private without having to feel that they are somehow being hypocritical in saying that sexual activity is simultaneously private and also a wholesome and important part of life. They now must describe, just as they no doubt did during the infancy and toddler period in appropriate nonverbal as well as in verbal ways, in what ways society approves of openness of the expression of sexual interest.

Children must also learn that there are many family concepts and standards that may not be the same as those held by others, and that the feelings and beliefs of others must at times be respected. Such social differentiation applies not only to sex, but also to virtually every area of living. The rules of the society in which the child is to live are important to know. Whether and when to accept them, and whether and when to defy them, are value judgments that also must be learned. And such decisions will be different ones at different developmental stages. To teach the child at the middle childhood stage that the family's ideas are always superior to any from outside that differ, is sometimes done—this is prejudice and closed-mindedness. Awareness that one's own beliefs should be reached only after experiencing and thinking about a variety of mores and beliefs, can be initiated by explanation and by precept in the middle childhood years.

SOCIAL COMPETENCE AND TASK MASTERY

Far from being a period of "latency," middle childhood is a rich developmental period. New levels of social expectations are experienced, and the youngster's opportunities for achieving social competence are progressively expanded. In addition, the first formal years of academic learning, with their sequential schedules for increasingly complex tasks which the child is required to master, introduce him to the world of work, and the demands this makes on his own capacities and behavioral characteristics.

Friendships become very important, both in the formation of close and "best" friends, as well as in the experimentation with the category of good friends who are not one to whom one tells "everything," as well as the larger group who are friendly acquaintances. All these differentiations are learned through trial and error. For the temperamentally easy child, this is most often a comfortable period of social exploration. A best friend may give away a confidence, but the lesson of making judgments more carefully is rehearsed in company with another best friend who brings consolation. True, such a lesson may need to be learned again and again, with different friends who have differing personalities, and in differing kinds of circumstances. And even though it may be mastered firmly for the type of events that occur in middle childhood, the lesson must be reviewed again during adolescence. But all learning requires repetition and application to varied circumstances before the child can separate the essentials from the accompanying accidental factors.

In contrast to the temperamentally easy child, the slow-to-warm-up or difficult child may find the increased complexities and variations in the patterns of social relationships in middle childhood stressful and bewildering. As a result, behavior problems may arise, or may become intensified in their severity and range of symptomatology if they had already begun to crystallize in the toddler period. Coping mechanisms that were adequate at earlier ages may no longer prove adequate in this new and more demanding age-period. The history of Arlene, cited at the beginning of this chapter, is a case in point. On the other hand, social difficulties in middle childhood for such youngsters are by no means inevitable. Carl, one of the most extreme temperamentally difficult infants and toddlers in the NYLS sample, was handled well by his parents throughout. Not only did no behavior problems develop, but Carl learned from his repeated experiences with the new that any initial discomfort with the new was temporary and disappeared once he stuck to the situation patiently and consistently. In middle childhood and adolescence, he lived in the same neighborhood and went through successive school years with the same friends. New academic subjects were introduced gradually so that he had no difficulty mastering each one. For Carl, middle childhood and adolesence, were periods of smooth, successful mastery of the new complexities of social relationships and academic demands. Actually, excessive stress and a period of malfunction developed only when he went off to college, when he was faced with the need to make a number of new adaptations simultaneously entirely on his own—a strange environment, very different living arrangements, a curriculum structured and scheduled differently from his previous school experiences, and a complex relationship with a young woman which presented problems he had never encountered before. However, his previous positive school experiences gave him clues as to the way out, and, together with several brief counseling sessions with one of us, he reorganized his schedule and way of working so that he quickly began to cope adequately with all the new demands that had been pressuring him.

The highly active youngster usually has little difficulty with his social relationships in middle childhood. His liveliness is an asset, except at times when the group is engaged in some rather sedentary activity. Low-activity children may find themselves chosen last when teams are arranged for athletic or other lively games. But if they are not threatened by this, and prove themselves reliable and dependable team members, little harm is done. The highly intense child may get a reputation for being impulsive and "blowing off steam" too easily, but again, if he otherwise is a social asset to the peer group, little harm is done. The persistent, nondistractible child may clash with the peer group at those times when his persistence interferes with their sudden decisions to change plans. Otherwise, the knowledge that this child will stick to any activity until completed, come what may, usually makes him an asset to the group. The highly distractible youngster may be a nuisance to peers when he forgets an appointment or fails to complete a task, but his sensitivity to the nuances of feelings and attitudes of others (this is the positive side of distraction by extraneous stimuli) usually weighs the balance on the plus side.

DEVELOPMENT OF VALUE SYSTEMS

During middle childhood the youngster begins actively to build habits of conformity, and simultaneously also individual values that may go against the crowd. Values are not developed in the abstract. They can only be built out of specific actions and their consequences. Group pressures are powerful, and just as toddlers can best learn how to fall and pull themselves up to stand again when they are small and close enough to the ground that no bones will be broken, so youngsters in middle childhood can learn without catastrophe which of their own attitudes and actions they themselves should learn to disrespect and refuse to repeat no matter how persuasive their companions may be. The following example may be of interest. A mother, looking out of

the window saw a boy of 9 going past the house, fleeing from small
stones that were being thrown at him—and her own son was among
the stone throwers. Recognizing the running child as her son's classmate, she recalled that comments had been made that indicated this
youngster to be a clumsy child who was largely left out of the peer
group. She felt that this situation of persecution necessitated sharp and
immediate action. Running out, she called back the victim and all the
other children involved—these being neighborhood friends of her son
whom she knew well from their frequent visits to her home as well as
their own street play. "Why," she asked her son, "did you throw
stones?" "They told me to" he replied. The mother then gave a brief
and pithy lecture. First, she informed the victimized child that never
again would he need to worry that he would be attacked when passing
this block, since it would never happen again—and she sent him on
his way. Then she informed her son that, as his hands had thrown the
stones, it was he who was responsible for doing so. No matter what
anyone told him to do, it was his business to decide whether it was
right or wrong. This was wrong and was never to happen again. She
then told the other children that this was wrong—to make the point
stronger, she said that, if such a thing ever happened again, she would
talk to their parents about it. Since she had never before reported the
children's mischief, taking whatever action was called for entirely on
her own when it occurred in her home, such a threat indeed gave this
event a gravity different from simple ganging up or minor destruction
that had been dealt with privately in the past. What lesson the neigh-
boring children learned was never clear, except that the youngster who
had been victimized often passed that way and was never again mol-
ested. But this was the first of a series of opportunities this mother had
to teach her own son that there were values that transcended being part
of a group and that he must take personal responsibility for the kind of
person he was. This one event alone would not have been enough to
form this moral value, but the succession of events by means of which
the moral point was made forcefully did have a cumulative effect and
became the basis of this boy's personal moral standard.

TASK MASTERY

Work takes on a new dimension in middle childhood with the successive and increasingly demanding expectations of academic learning.
In many, if not most families, the child is also expected to take

responsibility for specific household chores, simple at first, but more demanding as he or she grows older. Recreation also becomes not only fun and games, but learning to play by the rules and how to work with a team. Toddlers have usually done an apprenticeship when they have imitated parents and older children carrying out tasks and playing games. In middle childhood it is not only expected that the child will be assigned some tasks, but he is also expected to carry these out in keeping with the standards set for their accomplishment. For the most part, children like to be included as part of ongoing work, although getting out of certain jobs (such as taking out the garbage) is also part of the scene. Children begin to think of the future in terms of what they may do or become. Such dreams are to some extent shaped by what they see adults working at, and the degree of prestige given to specific recreational undertakings.

Children experiment with future occupations, at times by playing at them or dressing up to fit heroic roles, or by statement and pursuit of knowledge in the area. A very few do find an abiding interest that comes to the fore early and remains as a major goal. Certain arts, such as music and dance, or graphic arts, may become early interests at which the child persists and even makes this a final occupation. But for the most part, early interests are try-outs, valuable in that they give the child an opportunity to explore and find out what really is involved in becoming a doctor like a television hero, a baseball star, or a farmer or mechanic. Persistence comes to the fore here, when the activity requires much difficult preparation and practice. But temperamental attributes of other kinds play a part also; low threshold for those fields requiring high sensitivity to sensory events; attention span when an endeavor necessitates a long uninterrupted pursuit; high distractibility for activities requiring that peripheral events be not only noted but also given full attention immediately.

At other times ambition and temperament may interfere with each other. One high-school-age boy, with ambition to enter a profession, who also had moderate persistence, might seem to be an excellent candidate for success, inasmuch as his intellectual ability was in keeping with his ambition. But his cognitive ability was enough to bear fruit only if he studied assiduously, for he did not have an extraordinarily high intelligence nor total recall. This he was willing to do. But since he also was a highly active boy and a natural athlete, in after school hours he all too often made the decision to join a neighborhood or school team and forego his homework, promising himself that he would make it up later. Sometimes he did, but all too often insufficiently to maintain the high academic ratings of which he was capable. At this point in his high school career, the ultimate issue is in the balance—will his athletic skills prove an asset, or will they divert him sufficiently from his professional ambitions so as to limit seriously his career success. Multiple abilities, however, do not have to be counterproductive. Another boy, with high persistence and intelligence, applied himself thoroughly to both academic interests and athletics, and became both a scholar and an outstanding high school and college athlete. What made the differences between the two boys? Perhaps the difference in degree of persistence was a factor, perhaps the different value systems of their families and communities made a difference, and perhaps we really don't know the full answer.

SCHOOL FUNCTIONING

School attendance and all its ramifications are a central part of middle childhood, which covers the grade school period. Even for those youngsters who attended kindergarten and perhaps nursery school as well, there are new and qualitatively different expectations during this time of formal scholastic participation. The seriousness of school is clear to children; witness the old first-grader's jingle, "kindergarten baby, stick your head in gravy." Being a first grader is a triumph, a passage to grown-up status. Getting to school without absence and on time, wearing the precise type of clothing acceptable to that time and school tradition—these outward evidences of the seriousness of being a school child are demonstrated by the fierceness with which most children will insist upon this conformity. Notes from the teacher to be brought home, homework assignments, bringing requested supplies for posters or other special projects, are treated by and large as solemn obligations.

But the very importance given to this first formal learning experience brings new or heightened demands to be met. These expectations include new ways of social functioning, as well as actual learning. Temperament plays a most important role in this beginning. So important is the role of temperament that we devote a special chapter in this volume to it—Chapter 13, "Temperament and School Functioning." The goodness or poorness of fit that develops between the child's temperament and other characteristics and the school's expectations and demands in this initial phase of formal school can have profound psychological consequences. It can provide the child with a sturdy foundation on which to build a positive self-image. Or it can set the stage for self-doubts, lack of self-confidence, and fear of exposure of presumed inadequacies.

But nothing is forever. There is always the possibility that during the next developmental period of adolescence, new and unexpected skills may emerge, or that unanticipated new environmental influences may emerge to reverse a negative self-image. But it is in the highly active and rich new social and school experiences of middle childhood that a positive or negative self-image begins to crystallize. Even in those youngsters in whom nothing remarkable appears to be happening, a quiet self-satisfaction may be growing that provides a positive basis for later endeavors. Even if there are later poorer periods of functioning, such youngsters can tell themselves, "this isn't me," and mobilize themselves, with or without help, to recoup the unsatisfactory situation. For the middle childhood youngster whose efforts have been replete with near or actual failure of performance, a self-image of ineptitude may be in the making. With the expectation that "everything goes wrong for me," or "You know me, I always leave things until it's too late," the stage is set for repeated poor performance, excused because it's habitual—"It's me." Even if later experiences can change the middle childhood positive or negative self-image and its consequences, a good start in the preadolescent period can make it substantially easier or harder for the youngster in his later years.

The middle childhood years are full of promise and opportunity, of challenges and demands, and of opportunities for youngsters really to begin to know themselves. To call these years a "latency period" appears highly inappropriate.

CHAPTER 7

Temperament in Adolescence

We have become accustomed to think of adolescence as a period of high turmoil, as a time when rapid bodily and psychologic changes occur that alter both physical appearance and behavior patterns, sometimes beyond recognition. Children on the threshold of the teenage years jokingly say, "Next year my parents are going to hate me, because I will be a teenager," and parents who have survived earlier developmental periods often anticipate with dread the expected conflicts in adolescence over authority, morals, manners, and general respect. The issue of the controlling parent versus the child in control, or the manipulative parent versus the child tyrant may come sharply to the fore. However, more adolescents pass through this developmental period smoothly than in turmoil, and the data of recent studies indicate that intergenerational communication does not appear to diminish (Coleman, 1978; Offer & Offer, 1975; Rutter, 1979). The bodily metamorphoses between the newborn state to that of the toddler are certainly as great although different from those of adolescence. And throughout all the previous developmental stages, the child has gradually been making forays into independent thought and action, has expanded progressively her mastery of cognitive understanding, motor self-sufficiency, and task competence, has learned the delicacies of social skills, and has practiced accommodation or defiance of rules that are dictated by the adult world.

Adolescence itself is a by product of modern times. Prior to the Industrial Revolution, children were apprenticed at age 7, and were expected to be self-sufficient as adults at ages that we now consider part of preadult life. In affluent families in which self-support was not a part of life, boys sowed their wild oats as young adults while daughters at puberty were considered of marriageable age, as was Shakespeare's 13-year-old Juliet. In present-day industrialized society, by contrast, economic possibilities depend not only upon the family's socioeconomic status but also strongly upon educational preparation for the work arena. There is variability from country to country among economically advanced nations as to school-leaving age, but generally the youngster's education and resulting economic dependency is prolonged, thus creating the period that we call adolescence. The high school years are those of adolescence, and schooling continues into early adulthood for the economically advantaged who select careers that require years of preparation and training beyond high school. Thus, for much of the population, the teenage years do, in our historical period, have a special character in which demands and expectations asssume that complete adult self-sufficiency will be postponed to the next life-stage. Adolescents, then, must come to terms with a changing body, expanding academic or training demands, new levels of work expectation, widening choices as to the management of daily life, and sexual activity or the decision to defer sexual experience. All this occurs in a world in which adults also have to alter their relationship to their offspring. They must give up their authority in many areas. They have to adjust to the concept that their dependent child is on the way to being an adult and is no longer a youngster to whom they have the obligation and the right to give directions and rules, but is becoming an equal who may or may not wish to have parents' opinions in making decisions, and is prepared to take decisive actions on his or her own. In contrast to the developmental stages of previous periods, when adults were encouraging their children to advance in competence and independence, during adolescence there is frequently ambivalence for both parent and youngster over the quality and speed of change.

Parents wish their adolescent children to begin to take their lives and decisions into their own hands, but they also realize that certain areas are a one-way street, in which a reversal of direction may be difficult if not impossible. The children, pushing for the outward evidence of independence, may not realize that with their demand to be completely independent also comes the ending of the parents' obligation to provide bed, board, and financial support. It is in this context that the contribution of temperament to the mastery of the demands and expectations of the adolescent period is to be considered.

SCHOOL

In the United States, it is generally expected that education will continue through completion of high school. For those intending to become trained for skilled occupations, this training may have commenced and may perhaps be completed during the high school years, while for other adolescents specialization begins only after high school graduation. For the academically and professionally inclined who have the good fortune also to have parental encouragement and financial support for this inclination, college and possibly postgraduate academic studies will be assumed. For other middle-class youngsters, it is assumed that college will follow high school, even though the adolescent may not have any particular purpose in mind for which higher education is needed. In all of these ways, the adolescent's high school academic record becomes linked in the youth's mind to the future, whether this is to be an assumption that learning and school grades do matter for what she wishes to do, or whether these grades become suddenly of importance, in that they will determine whether college will be reached and, if so, which college. In turn, the type of college will influence the next possible level of academic training and consequently the job market that will be open. Motivation, at this age, becomes a powerful companion to temperament. Motivated to learn, the easy child at adolescence becomes quickly tuned to the style and content of work and may now, possibly for the first time, acquire effective study techniques. The difficult child, finding the stepped-up expectations unfamiliar, will tend to be uncomfortable—but with sufficiently high motivation will continue to pursue goals until they have become familiar and can be mastered. On the other hand, other adolescents with this temperamental cluster may give up, deciding that it is too late and they are too far behind. Sex stereotypes may play a part. Boys may be urged to persevere in achieving academic credentials so that their job goals in the future can be achieved. For girls with academic reluctance, adults may acquiesce all too early, on the basis that marriage and children eliminate the usefulness of training for specialized work or for higher academic activities. The hard facts that interest in being a working person is not biologically sex linked, that certain occupations or professions not previously thought "feminine" may be found desirable by girls, that more than half of the mothers with children under 6 are part of the work force—all of these seem not to have penetrated sufficiently to many of those who guide high school youngsters to plan for their own future.

The influence of temperament on school functioning, because of its special importance, will be considered in Chapter 13. The comments made here are not, therefore, a complete discussion of the issue. In general, most high school youngsters treasure the concept that grades achieved prior to the junior year "don't count," and will be disregarded by colleges or special training facilities. For those with ambitions toward post-high school schooling, the junior year brings resolution for greater work effort and for good marks. How effectively this project can be carried through depends greatly in many youngsters upon temperamental factors. Work habits may need to be learned for the first time, even by the highly persistent youth. The difference between turning homework in and learning the material asssumes a new reality. Adaptable children who have serious intent are likely to address themselves to this task competently, asking for adult aid as needed to make sure that they have truly understood the assigned material. Gone are the days when doing homework consisted in finding in the text the wording that answered the question, without much desire to understand what the words meant.

The slowly adapting adolescent is likely to find the changing of old attitudes and their conversion into altered modes of functioning more difficult. Old habits are cherished. The fact that, when put to the test, genuine understanding has not been acquired is often blamed on the teacher who "asked the wrong questions," the excuse that "I studied the wrong pages," or any number of variations on the theme that second-guessing the teacher is equivalent to adequate studying. The adolescent with short attention span now finds this quality to be a drawback whose reality must be faced so that compensations can be devised. The highly distractible youth who is sidetracked from assignments and comes into class to face a test whose prior announcement had been forgotten, must now deal with this propensity by devising mechanical reminders. The student with low persistence gives up, intending to return later to complete the study task, but other interests may intervene and drive away the memory that she still has an incomplete task to be finished. The highly persistent but slowly working child carries on with no awareness of the passage of time, only to find out that the test papers are being called in while she is still only at the halfway mark.

Whether it be those temperamental qualities just mentioned or others, for the adolescent now motivated toward further education and training goals, who wishes to meet these new demands and expectations of the adolescent developmental period, temperamental self-awareness is necessary. With self-awareness also comes the need to take personal responsibility. The distractible youngster makes many resolutions, but finds that resolutions do not alter the fact of high distractibility. She must make resolutions so that they fit her needs. Methods must be found to guarantee remembering—methods that assume that forgetting will be the spontaneous end result in the absence of use of special efficacious devices. Strategies used in previous periods by parents can often assume new perspectives now, when personal motivation has come into its own. Lists taped to mirrors, timers whose ringing announces that the recess for relaxation is over, the placement of obstacles in front of the bedroom door to act as alerting devices for tasks not yet completed—these tactics and others like them now become welcome tricks to defeat temperamental obstacles, instead of "silly" ideas thought up by the parents. The adolescent for whom every new subject is strange, confusing, and distasteful can now realize that those subjects that are now familiar, clear, and absorbing did not start as such. A personal campaign to create the sequence through which familiarity and mastery will emerge is now the child's own desire and no longer an unwelcome parental edict to be outwitted by any strategem.

Even biological irregularity now can be harnessed in favor of academic mastery, as the youth in whom sleepiness does not overcome concentration at fixed hours can, by harnessing full power of concentration, stay up all night to complete a term paper or study for an important examination. Alertness to nuances of teacher emphasis, the other side of the coin of high distractibility, can cue a student to the issues that the instructor considers important. The highly active girl or boy may now practice for adulthood, so that the advantages of a high degree of energy can come into the foreground, as long as disorganized movement for its own sake is eliminated. Utilizing acceptable reasons for movement is the key strategy—volunteering to retrieve the projector needed for this class lesson, accepting extra assignments that permit moving about, even the old trick of sharpening pencils at frequent intervals—these devices will allow muscular movements that are useful and do not interfere with the actions of others. On the athletic field, high motoric activity ceases to be a problem, but in the classroom this kind of planning ahead is important. A low activity level can be either harnessed to academic needs, or may be a potential hazard. A slow and careful approach is ideal for certain tasks, especially those in which only the final product is of importance. Where timed tasks are of the essence, low activity level requires genuine self-knowledge from the adolescent. All too often, the adult world equates slowness of output with slowness of cognition, so that the slow-moving youth may be unfairly penalized. Certainly she will suffer on timed intelligence or achievement tests. However, with determination and self-awareness, effective explanations can be mounted, and evidence of high-quality work presented by the adolescent as indication of her capability and motivation for satisfactory and even superior performance.

Nonacademic learning follows a similar course. Depending on their temperament, as well as ability and motivation, youngsters fascinated by machinery will be adaptable, turned off, distracted from, or persistent in the basic technique of their trade and the mastery of the intricacies that make for expertness. Many an adolescent who learns thoroughly becomes the neighborhood bicycle, motorcycle, computer, or automobile fix-it person, and gains invaluable experience for her chosen craft. And a determined and competent girl, although she may still meet opposition if she has a technical work inclination, can persist, pursuade and prove her way into fields that had heretofore been considered strictly male domains.

SOCIAL SKILLS

In the adolescent period, social relationships have even greater importance than during the middle childhood years. Boy–girl relationships move into prominence. While the progression from group mixed-sex activities, to boyfriend–girlfriend links, to serious dating, to sexual activities, with or without deep affectionate ties, is a general trend, this is by no means universal. Despite the sexual revolution, some young women prefer to remain virgins until marriage. Despite the ploy, so effectively used by boys when the new sex attitudes had just arrived on the scene, that sexual activity was virtually necessary as a badge of freedom, many adolescent girls have now learned that freedom includes both the privilege of saying "no" as well as that of saying "yes." Some boys, too, despite the former and current stereotype that sexual activity is a signal of true masculinity, defer active sexuality until a deep and abiding emotional tie has been reached. As we discovered in private interviews with adolescents in our NYLS study, not everything claimed by these youngsters in boasting to their peers about their supposed sexual exploits, was in fact true. We found also that when premarital sexual activity was a part of life, there was less guilt and more taking this as an accepted style by both girls and boys than would have been the case in previous generations. Such a statement is a generalization, and clearly there are some exceptions. Many adolescents work toward a self-determined standard that sex should be part of an emotional meaningful bond, although often such a standard is only reached after a period of active and perhaps promiscuous adolescent experimentation with sex.

Unfortunately, when it comes to pregnancy, adolescents are prone to the myth that "this won't happen to me," so that the possibility of pregnancy and its consequences are not anticipated. Also, there is sometimes a period of adolescent sterility, so that the appearance of menses does not always coincide with fertility. Some adolescent girls who are sexually active fail to realize that if they don't become pregnant, this is merely accidental. They fail to take contraceptive measures and adolescent pregnancies have recently become more frequent and constitute a significant psychosocial problem. Whereas unwed middle-class girls in the past usually gave their infants up for adoption if abortion had not ended the pregnancy, an increasing number of single women of all socioeconomic classes now keep their babies. The phenomenon of the unmarried single mother is now more tolerated by society, so that such a status has now become accepted in many communities. Also, in poor families, adolescent girls hold the illusory view that motherhood and the ability to collect welfare benefits it brings will enable them to enjoy greater freedom, not realizing that caring for a young baby will effectively cut into their lives, leaving them equally but differently manacled. It is of interest that many adolescent unmarried mothers typically are afraid to give their babies unstinted affection, and virtually obsessed with the concept that "spoiling" the baby is undesirable. This finding is consistent in different studies, for reasons that are still obscure. The result is a degree of emotional neglect that these young mothers do not recognize. Another consequence of adolescent motherhood is the end of schooling. While this may be a relief to an unmotivated youngster, it effectively cuts off the opportunity to learn a trade that, now or later, will bring upward mobility or at least the opportunity to enjoy a modest but decent standard of living. And for a temperamentally withdrawing adolescent girl, moving to her own apartment with a baby may result in almost total social isolation.

For the most part, sexual interest in early adolescence occurs without explicit sex. Dating is negotiated both with the opposite-sex friend and with the family in regard to curfew. The curfew issue is often a stressful area of disagreement between child and parents.

The mores of the teenager's peer group are most intrusive, and parents often find themselves evoking a standard that was held during their own adolescence but has long been out of date. The manner and degree of this parent–child disagreement will be greatly influenced by the temperamental qualities of each. When there are intense reactions on both sides, the anticipated turmoil of adolescence may indeed come to pass, with escalating parental warnings, groundings and lectures on the one hand, and growing feelings of alienation, testing of limits, and sheer rebellion on the part of the adolescent. At times, the battle grows so fierce that youngster's no longer even know what they wish to do, so determined are they to act counter to parental ultimatums. It is not unknown for an adolescent to act in a manner contrary to his or her own desire simply to defy parents. The low-intensity youngster will do this in a quiet and unobtrusive manner, while the high-intensity adolescent can create a constant degree of turmoil. This may not only discomfit parents, but may also interfere with the needs of sibs to have the home available so they may entertain friends there, and who also wish their share of parental attention.

Withdrawing adolescents, whether this is quietly carried out as in the slow-to-warm-up youngster, or becomes a stormy process as in the case of the "difficult child," will find it difficult to bring themselves forward in group or individual social encounters. Such a child may be viewed by peers as snobbish, because they keep their distance socially. When the withdrawing adolescent has a close friend from a prior developmental period, by hanging onto her friend's shirttails, such a shy or difficult youngster may succeed in becoming part of a group. At first she may be on the periphery, but later when familiarity has been achieved, the youngster succeeds in becoming an active part of the group. Unfortunately, should there not be such a bridge available for the withdrawing adolescent, and she does acquire a reputation as an oddball or a snob, the actions of the adolescent's peer group are likely to perpetuate such behavior with increasing fixity, leading the youngster to experience depression, to develop a self-image that he or she is unlikeable, and to suffer from general unhappiness.

Adolescence is a period most marked by conformity, to the peer group's mores, language, even gestures. A shy or otherwise withdrawing youngster is influenced by this aspect of this developmental period. The strong wish to become incorporated in a group may give the withdrawing youngster the impetus to do something about the isolation that he or she had previously either denied or tolerated as inevitable. With such strong motivation to be part of the group, with or without outside help, the shy adolescent may find methods to enter adolescent society in a manner consonant with her temperamental individuality. Here, any previous insights into one's self are invaluable. Even without such insight, prior patterns used by parents to arrange gradual familarization with new people and endeavors may now be copied with profit. This is in fact the developmental period when temperamental self-knowledge can be gained to a significant degree. This will then provide a model for later behavior that will promote the intentions and desires of the person without engendering the wish to deny personal qualities and to become someone else. The case of Martha provides an apt illustration.

Martha had first been referred for evaluation at age 10. In contrast to her older sister, whose social life had always been active, Martha had never brought a friend home nor had she been invited by anyone to visit—except for parties to which the entire class had been invited. School gatherings, like interclass athletics and after-school contests, had been avoided by her with varying reasons for non-attendance. While Martha kept herself busy with personal projects, and was a good student, her parents felt that the girl did feel left out and was lonely.

Her temperamental history showed that, from babyhood on, Martha had shown negative mood to new stimuli expressed with moderate to mild intensity and had always been slow to adapt. She had gradually moved into home routines and was pleasant to live with. Martha filled the criteria of a slow-to-warm-up child.

While mental status had shown no pathology, Martha first denied being friendless, then when details of friendships were enquired into, she agreed that she had none, but declared that her way of functioning was her own choice and she preferred her personal intersts to those of her peers. Clearly no psychotherapy was possible since Martha was not motivated to change.

At the time of junior high school selection a year later another consultation was held. The choice lay between the town junior high school fed by three grade schools or a small private school. Martha was in a panic and did this time have strong motivation to explore possible solutions. In the local school there was a policy of scattering the members of incoming schools so as to give an opportunity for new acquaintanceships to develop—and Martha saw herself as a stray among a mass of total strangers. The private school, being small, seemed at first consideration to provide serenity. And, as this school started with the seventh grade, no previous friendships would have been formed among students. On the other hand, with only girls in the class, Martha had a panicky vision of finding no one with whom she could have even a detached but accepting acquaintanceship. Torn equally between these choices, I (S.C.) finally made the judgment that she go to her local school, but that we must simultaneously start psychotherapy. In this preteen period, Martha accepted my interpretation that her temperamental style was to be our focus. She did in fact cooperate with suggestions to use events such as school evening basketball games as opportunities for her to be present and noticed by others. Fortuitously, in private tennis lessons, which her parents forced upon her, she was paired with another shy girl who attended the same school. Once she obtained this minimum social comfort at school, Martha's motivation and cooperation vanished. She declared herself satisfied with one friend plus token attendance at school affairs, and psychotherapy had to be suspended.

At age 14, high school in a new building altered Martha's comfortable but restricted social life. Again she came for discussion with anticipatory panic. It was possible this time to use not only the evidence of former events, but her secret crush on a boy classmate as combined organizing principles of discussion. I now insisted that she, desiring to be in charge of her life and relationships, must understand the part her temperamental style had played in her previous decisions. I would restart psychotherapy, but our joint strategy would be for Martha to take responsiblity for plans while I would act in an advisory capacity. Martha was now able to recall how her parents had virtually forced her initially into activites, like the tennis lessons, which later had become pleasurable and faithful standbys. She was able to realize that now she was no longer willing to retire into a social void, and as it was beneath her adolescent dignity to accept parental maneuvering, she must understand her own temperamental contribution to her social habits. Her junior high school friends, acquired with such difficulty, were now her solid backup and Martha could envision a widening horizon—needing courage initially but bringing comfortable and interesting rewards.

These insights and positive changes on Martha's part made it possible first of all to develop an expanding and satisfying social life. Furthermore, these positive experiences became the basis for a thoughtful self-examination of her temperamental characteristics, and the formulation on her own of a set of effective strategies by which she could adapt successfully to new situations and new people in the future.

ADOLESCENCE AND WORK

The work ethic is a strong part of our society. In fact, one longitudinal study found that the strongest predictor of whether a member of a cohort of inner-city low-income boys would achieve positive mental health, career success, and capacity for interpersonal relationships by age 47 was capacity to work in childhood, by age 14 (Vaillant & Vaillant, 1981). While many children begin to earn money by odd jobs such as snow shoveling or carrying groceries, it is in adolescence that serious job searching begins. Work is sought to provide pocket money for items that the family would not find important or that might be financially impossible to provide even if approved in principle. Some adolescents begin seriously to think ahead and save for large purchases; some of these desires are derived from the items that provide conspicuous consumption in the teen-age world, other savings are actually motivated by thinking ahead to academic goals that are beyond family income. Some youths also feel the need to prove that they can, in fact, be self-supporting in whole or in part, as part of the self-image they wish to acquire. And some look for experience in a field for which they may wish to train, trying it out before making the plunge.

In job hunting, temperament plays a strong role. The high-approaching youth enjoys the very act of job hunting, and finds the act of returning day after day to enquire whether a possible opening has in fact materialized to be socially rewarding effort. The very persistence of an adolescent job hunter may give a most positive impression, making the youngster the top person on the list when the opening does come through. In contrast, the shy adolescent can bring defeat in his or her very manner of asking for a job. The negative wording, the seeming indifference, the inability to converse, gives both the impression of a lackadaisical manner that would bode ill for job efficiency, and also gives the impression that the desire for a job is wanting. Offering oneself for a work position again and again, and experiencing rejection repeatedly, is also deeply painful to such a youngster. Often it is only on the job that the shy adolescent can prove that she is indeed competent, reliable, and work-oriented.

The match of job and temperament is important, and at times crucial. One high-active adolescent boy, who would have found sedentary work disastrously uncomfortable, obtained a job as a stock clerk in a store. The constant physical activity, so necessary for this youngster's comfort, was seen by the employer as willingness to oblige above and beyond the call of duty and this, plus the boy's demonstrated intelligence, led to quick promotion. The high persistence of a girl who was assigned to filing papers, brought constant compliments that she would never stop when she had started at *A* until she arrived at *Z*. Had she been given an assignment requiring many shifts of activity, it is probable that her strong tendency to continue on and on until an end point had been reached might have been so out of line with what was needed as to make her a poor worker. In the work arena, as has been mentioned above, the adolescent has the opportunity, and at times the necessity, to become acquainted with her temperamental identity. This will help in selecting areas of training toward future work, insofar as it is possible to match temperamental qualities with work demands. When this is not possible, or when deep interests are at variance with the temperamental qualities called for, techniques for bringing personal temperamental qualities into consonance with the essentials of the work are necessary. In most cases, these can be learned. Committing facts to memory can be done equally efficiently while sitting still or walking about. A delicate mechanical task can be brought to completion either in a single uninterrupted period, or in several separate sessions, provided provision has been made to meet the deadline. A slow pace of work, if due to a low activity level, can be used to shape a personal work strategy that covers both personal temperamental qualities and ensures that the necessities of the task will be accomplished.

PARENT–CHILD RELATIONSHIPS

There is a wide spectrum of adolescent–parent relationships. In some situations there is complete harmony. Harmony does not mean total agreement. As in music, harmony means many notes that form a pleasant and meaningful relationship. An example of a most positive relatedness between an adolescent son and his parents was summed up by a 14-year-old youth who said in amusement, "My friends don't understand me. I don't fight with my parents, they don't fight with me, and most of what I do seems to be all right with them. And if it isn't, my parents say so, and either I do it their way or my way—but that's where it ends. My friends think I should be fighting with my parents and that there must be something wrong with me because I don't." In this situation, the harmony included mutual respect, a basic consensus of values, and agreement that there would be times to agree to disagree. This adolescent was temperamentally "easy." He was mostly in a good mood, and had moderate intensity of mood expressiveness, quick interest in new situations and people, and easy adaptability, but nevertheless was also persistent. Having formed concepts of functioning that were to his liking and conformed to his own values, he had no overriding need to conform to the group mores and act out an artificial adolescent turmoil. And with his pleasant temperament, he still retained the friendship of his peers.

A different type of harmony occurred with one of our NYLS subjects. Hank's parents asked for a consultation to find out whether there was any problem. Hank, at age 16, had made a decision to leave his town's high school and attend one requiring an hour's ride each way, that was organized on the plan of an open curriculum. Prior to this announced but not discussed decision, there had been several years of dissatisfaction on Hank's part with his school, which had been openly discussed with his parents. They considered Hank to be fundamentally in the right, and when the boy had formed a student committee to meet with the principal, the parents had helped him to plan his strategy. Changes had been promised by the school prinicpal but none had occurred. Hank was, and had always been highly persistent, and despite the failure of the school to arrange for the teaching of subjects close to his interests, and despite the continuance in the school of computer-based rather than student interest-based individual curricula, he had pursued his particular interests on his own. Thus, while Hank's dissatisfaction with the town school was not a surprise, his decision to change schools had not been arrived at by preliminary discussions with his parents who, in fact, had not previously been aware of the existence of this alternative school. When they had made inquiries about the new school, they had only been able to learn generalities—all positive but none from individuals who had in fact had any contact with the school or any of its graduates. Hank's parents' worries were twofold: one, would the new school really prepare Hank for his chosen career, or would it on the contrary leave him ineligible for college?, and, second, was there some factor needing redress that had alienated Hank, so that he no longer saw his parents as allies?

Inasmuch as the NYLS was just at that point preparing to initiate direct interviews with our adolescent subjects, we scheduled Hank's interview among the first. He and his parents received our form letter, in which it was stated that there would be a follow-up telephone call to arrange the interviews. When I (S.C.) phoned, Hank was out, but had told his parents that if Dr. Chess phoned, to give her the following times when he could come in to New York to see me. He had given no explanation and had they not also received the letter, they would not have known from him what this was all about. Hank arrived promptly, was friendly, and expressed his belief that it was a good plan for us to learn our subjects' views directly from them. When he came to the topic of parent–child relationships, Hank stated that he thought he and his parents got along very well. He told me about the school situation and his new plans. I asked whether he had formulated his decision to change schools with his parents. Hank said he had not, and expressed puzzlement that anyone would think this necessary. The old school was a washout, his parents had done what they could to help his campaign to make it successful, and this he appreciated. He then, in a manner that he saw as proper and responsible, had initiated enquiries about the new school of which he had heard, concluded that it answered his needs, was ready to add the hour's train ride each way daily, had made application and been accepted, and then simply announced the accomplished fact, knowing that his parents could afford the fee and presumably would be in agreement with him. He simply assumed that he was old enough and responsible enough to make such decisions, and saw them as consonant with his parents' views. It had neither occurred to him that they should be consulted in advance nor that they might be in disagreement. I received permission from him to go over this portion of his interview with his parents. He gave it easily as if it were no great issue for him. And, in fact, Hank's parents were quite satisfied when they learned that his silence on the matter during the decision-making period had not amounted to a deliberate, calculated exclusion of them from his life. The basic trust of parents by son, and of son by parents, was firm.

Disharmony in parent–child relations also occurs frequently. Perhaps the most extreme example in the NYLS is Bernice. A well-functioning youngster through middle childhood, during adolescence she became the embodiment of extreme adolescent turmoil. Quick to act, intense, previously positive in mood, highly adaptable, and having throughout childhood usually received positive feedback, Bernice in adolescence applied her temperamental qualities destructively. She deteriorated in home and school functioning, failed to carry out chores and assignments, lied her way out of showdowns, and went into violent tantrums as a last resort. Adapting to a delinquent peer group, she lost her old friends because of her unreliability, and was asked to leave one school, then a second because of unacceptable work and behavior. The death of her father left the full responsibility for the family upon her overburdened mother. Bernice's sisters felt harassed by the scenes Bernice created, and every attempt by her mother to institute rules and restrictions ended in Bernice's hysterical accusations of being picked on. Because of the distress Bernice was causing to her sibs, and because Bernice herself would not be helped (she had gone through the empty motions of psychotherapy several times), the family's disharmony was judged sufficient to warrant asking the girl to leave the home when she reached her 18th birthday—after having somehow managed to achieve a high school diploma. To bring the story to a happy ending, the need to fend for herself finally led Bernice to a fairly adequate level of adult functioning.

Between such extremes, there have been all shades of adolescent child–parent relationships. In some there was harmony on some issues but not others. In a few there was distancing by the adolescent due to parental overintrusiveness—sometimes a continuation from earlier developmental periods and sometimes a newly acquired maneuver during adolescence. However, in the majority of child–parent relationships there was mutual tolerance and liking, expressed in the characteristics temperamental styles of both adolescents and parents, the latter being informed and sympathetic regarding the expanded and changing needs, capacities, and goals of their sons or daughters.

CHAPTER 8

Temperament in Adult Life

The task of identifying and rating temperament in the adult is complex as compared with the childhood period. Behavioral repertoires are elaborate; cognitive and motivational patterns are highly conceptualized and symbolized. Temperament enters into complex interactional processes with these other psychologic attributes of the adult and with a host of environmental factors. This makes the identification of the stylistic component in any item or pattern of behavior in adults more difficult than in children. But this does not in any way mean that temperamental characteristics are unimportant in shaping the developmental course in adult life. Quite the contrary. In fact, it was our impressionistic identification of temperamental patterns in both adults and children that we knew personally and professionally, and our judgment that these patterns had functional significance in the adult as well as the child, that stimulated our original interest in studying this psychologic attribute.

TEMPERAMENT AND DAILY ROUTINES

As in the child or adolescent, temperament in the adult is a significant factor in shaping the person's style of coping with the daily routines of living. The high-activity person may become an enthusiastic jogger and tennis player; his or her low-activity counterpart may have little interest in vigorous sports. The highly intense adult may express his pleasure, excitement, or displeasure openly and vehemently, and even wish he could "keep his cool" more easily. The low-intensity person may be quiet and calm when everyone around him is in turmoil—an asset at some times, but not in other situations. Adults with easy temperament may adapt easily and quickly to all kinds of new situations and problems, but worry over their tendency to be "a pushover" when pressured by others for their own benefit. Individuals with difficult temperament, by contrast, are not likely to change their behavior easily to suit a new demand made upon them, which may be an asset at some times, but not in other situations. The slow-to-warm-up adult may be cautious in attempting anything new and may feel uncomfortable in any new social setting, but once the adaption has been made, will then proceed as easily and effectively as his quickly adaptable counterpart.

The highly persistent, nondistractible person is likely to get deeply absorbed in any task or project that catches his attention, a most valuable attribute for the sustained mastery of difficult and demanding tasks. On the other hand, there is the possibility of the "absent-minded professor" syndrome, in which this selective mental absorption is accompanied by the oblivious inattention to the details of daily living which can be so exasperating to family, friends, and coworkers. By contrast, highly distractible adults are in tune with their social environment and are alert to the nuances of attitudes and messages of those around them. But they suffer from the danger of leaving tasks half-completed, unless they discipline themselves to turn their attention back after being distracted so that they can fulfill their responsibilities. The low-threshold adult may suffer from exposure to heat and cold, loud noises, and rough fabrics, and may limit certain activities and expeditions to avoid these uncomfortable extremes. At the same time, this low-threshold may give this type of person an appreciation and enjoyment of subtle shades of colors, music, and texture. The high-threshold person may lack this kind of sensitivity, but he will be able to adapt more easily to variations in temperature, noise, and roughness of fabrics.

In contrast to earlier life, especially early childhood, the temperamental attribute of rhythmicity appears to have limited functional significance in adult life. Sleep and mealtime patterns are shaped primarily by the requirements of work schedules, family routines, and social commitments. Even adults with a temperamental tendency to biologic irregularity appear to be able to make the necessary sleep and mealtime arrangements without appreciable difficulty. The question of regularity of bowel movements, which influences the ease of bowel training in childhood, becomes a matter of little concern to the great majority of adults in our culture.

TEMPERAMENT AND ADULT DEVELOPMENT

Until recent years, it was generally believed that psychologic development leveled off with the transition from adolescence to early adulthood, and that little that was new was added thereafter. This view was
strongly influenced by traditional psychoanalytic and behaviorist theories, both of which pointed to early childhood as the decisive period
for shaping future psychologic development. It has become clear,
however, that development does not stop in adolescence, and that new
psychologic stages can emerge in adult life. Erikson (1963) has emphasized this point with his broad characterizations of adult life in terms
of generativity versus stagnation, and ego identity versus despair. A
number of empirical studies have also begun to spell out specifically
the view that psychologic development proceeds throughout adult life
(Baltes *et al.*, 1978; Gould, 1972; Levinson, 1978; Neugarten, 1979;
Stein, Holzman, Karasu, & Charles, 1978).

For the adult, as for the child or adolescent, temperament by itself
does not determine personality structure, or act as the exclusive cause
of a behavior disorder development. As in the earlier age-periods, it is
always an issue of goodness or poorness of fit, that is, the consonance
or dissonance between the person's characteristics, abilities, and motivations and the expectations and demands of the environment, that is
decisive. The elements making for goodness of fit in an adult may be
more complex and difficult to identify than in a child, but the dynamic
issue is the same. A distractible person may find that he is frequently
late for work and social appointments, which annoys both his employer and friends, and interferes with career and social life. If the
distractible individual has insight into the cause of this problem, and
monitors his own behavior, all may be well. However, all too often,
such a person is confused and bewildered as to the reason for the
unfavorable sequence of events, and reproaches himself for being
irresponsible or lazy, and lectures himself that he must do better
without knowing what is required to do better. This confusion and
self-derogation can only lead to anxiety and defensive maneuvers,
which make the situation worse. And, unfortunately, if such a person
seeks professional help for his distress and undesirable behavior, if the
therapist does not identify the role of the temperamental pattern,
interpretations of an "unconscious wish to fail," or neurotic conflicts
over work commitment or social activity, are likely to be offered. Such
interpretations can only intensify the persons's self-derogation and

leave him in a blind alley as far as effective action goes. Instead of getting better, such an individual will be unimproved or the difficulties may only grow worse.

In the adult, perhaps even more frequently than in the child or adolescent, poorness of fit can sometimes involve issues in which temperament plays a minor or negligible role, in contrast to its major importance in other cases. Motivational patterns, defense mechanisms, moral and ethical standards, and enduring personality characteristics become more complex and influential in the adult as compared to the child or adolescent. Environmental demands and expectations, whether in work, social life, or intimate personal relationships, also become more challenging, and require levels of mastery and adaptation beyond these that are relevant at earlier age-periods. But the clinical judgment in any individual case that temperamental characteristics are of negligible importance and can be ignored should not be made in any a priori fashion. No matter what the presenting clinical problem may be, the evaluation of the role of temperament requires an assessment of all the factors that appear influential, and a determination of the dynamic interaction among these factors. This approach is in line with the clinician's diagnostic procedure in physical medicine, in which the functioning of all major organ systems is reviewed before deciding which play a significant role in the genesis and evolution of the symptoms manifested in any specific case. Even where the etiology of a psychiatric disorder does not have a significant temperamental component, such as in schizophrenia, manic-depressive illness, or organic brain syndromes, temperament may be substantially influential in certain individual cases in shaping the specific pattern of symptoms, or in affecting the patient's ability to cope with the consequences of the illness.

TEMPERAMENT AND SELF-IMAGE

The process of developing a self-image and sense of identity starts in childhood, expands rapidly in adolescence, and matures in adult life (Thomas & Chess, 1980). This self-image has profound consequences for the individual's level of self-confidence and for the patterns he develops to cope with the demands of the environment. The self-assured adult will face even difficult challenges directly and with the conviction of success. The adult with an inadequate self-concept will respond to environmental demands with self-doubt and even anxiety, and is likely to utilize neurotic defense mechanisms which only serve to guarantee failure rather than success. In this way, self-doubts are reinforced by self-fulfilling prophecies.

Though the self-concept typically shows consistency with the passage of the years, major changes in the sense of identity can occur at any time in adult life, as well as in childhood or adolescence. A qualitative alteration in role functioning, a radical change in the social environment, an important success or failure in life, a crisis that is surmounted or not—all these can have important and even profound consequences for self-concept.

Temperamental characteristics often play a significant role in shaping the adult's self-concept. If the person possesses those traits that are highly regarded by his society, this will tend to stimulate or reinforce a positive self-image. If, on the other hand, the person's temperamental characteristics are devalued and even considered abnormal by the society, this will have a negative effect on his sense of self-worth. Thus, for example, the work ethic gives approval to the qualities of high persistence and long attention span. Correspondingly, low persistence and short attention span will typically meet with critical reactions, including interpretation of such behavior as reflecting "laziness," "lack of interest," or "lack of will-power and self-discipline." And in middle-class American society, the person with easy adaptability to new people and to change meets the "hail fellow well met" standard of easy and quick sociability. By contrast, the adult who warms up slowly, who is hesitant and uncomfortable with strangers, is likely to meet with various kinds of derogatory judgments on his personality characteristics. Two case vignettes will illustrate this issue of temperament and self-image.

A young woman, Frances, one of the subjects in the NYLS, came to consult one of us (S.C.) because of problems experienced in job hunting. Now age 22, she had recently graduated from college with a major in graphic arts, and was seeking a position in this field with an advertising agency. She discovered that, as she approached an interview, she felt hesitant and uncomfortable, and was tempted to find one excuse or another to delay or avoid what she felt was an impending ordeal. She was highly self-critical of these reactions and was convinced there was something wrong with herself as a person. She kept repeating, "Why can't I be like my sister. She just plunges right in; she doesn't have any trouble with interviews." It became clear that Frances's whole family had this same derogatory, judgmental evaluation of her hesitations as she had of herself. Frances was so firmly fixed in her own mind that she suffered from terrible inadequacies as a person, that, after describing her problem to me, she stopped and exclaimed, "You're not batting an eyelash over what I'm telling you. Doesn't it shock you?." Of course it didn't, since she was describing the initial withdrawal responses of a slow-to-warm-up person. And, having reviewed her childhood records, I also knew that she had displayed this same temperamental constellation in her childhood years. Also, in her college years, she had made friends slowly. This had not bothered her, because she did end up with several good friends. Furthermore, there had never been any evidence of psychopathology in her functioning, either in childhood or adolescence, or now in early adulthood. Finally, I was impressed by the effective coping mechanism she had developed to deal with her distressing reactions. When a job interview was scheduled for her, Frances had worked out on her own the strategy of rehearsing the interview to herself in detail ahead of time—what she would say, what questions the interviewer was likely to ask, how she would answer, and so on. Ironically, she saw this coping mechanism as further evidence of her deficiency as a person, rather than as an affirmation of her positive resources. "Other people don't have to rehearse this way, why do I have to?"

I pointed out emphatically to Frances that there was no evidence that she was suffering from any psychiatric disorder. Neither was there anything wrong with her as a person. Rather, she had a particular temperamental characteristic, perfectly normal in itself, but which did create hesitation and discomfort when facing a demanding new situation. Many young adults just out of school found job interviews stressful and even intimidating. Her sister apparently was an exception. On top of this stress, her temperamental reactions magnified the tension of a job interview which meant so much to her. And, rather than scolding herself for her rehearsal strategy, she should feel proud of herself that, completely on her own, she had worked out such an effective method of dealing with her problem. Finally, I told her that when she did obtain a job in her field, she should expect to find the initial work-period stressful, again because of her slow-to-warm-up temperament. But, she should also expect that she would adapt gradually and successfully, as she had always done in other new situations throughout her life. Frances left the interview, her self-esteem still shaky, but holding on to the assurances that she was indeed a normal person psychologically. This single discussion, while clearly of great value to her, by itself could not accomplish miracles. If Frances succeeds in obtaining a satisfactory job, and adjusts successfully, then we can expect that a progressively positive self-image will crystallize. If, on the other hand, she meets with successive disappointments in her job interviews—a not remote possibility, given the present-day job market for young inexperienced adults—then her shaky self-esteem will undoubtedly require professional reinforcement to prevent a downhill development.

Kevin, a successful professional man in his mid-30s, came for psychotherapy because of several psychological problems. Prominent in his concerns was a stormy and stressful marital relationship. His wife was a person with intense emotional expressiveness, while Kevin was quiet and low-keyed in his emotional responses. The wife, who actually had much more severe psychiatric disturbance than did her husband, had intimidated him into believing that she was the normal one, that he suffered from "shallow feelings," and that he was seriously "emotionally inhibited" and barely alive as a human being. He accepted this judgment, especially since he had always been uneasy as to his inability to display strong emotional reactions in the way many other people could and did.

In the therapeutic sessions with Kevin, this issue was explored in detail because of its effect on his self-image and its consequences for his marital relationship. It became clear that Kevin was in no way a shallow person emotionally. He experienced strong feelings appropriately, and this had always been the case. But temperamentally he was a person of mild intensity of expressiveness, which was normal for him. He was not "emotionally inhibited," but was intimidated and inhibited in expressing his feelings and thoughts when these challenged and opposed his wife's attitudes and behavior. As this issue was clarified, it became evident to Kevin that his wife's intense emotional outbursts were all too often excessive and pathologic, and quite the opposite of her claims to heightened sensitivity and depth of feeling. The truth was that he was the basically healthy person psychologically, while she was the one who suffered from psychiatric problems. This became more and more evident as the years went by and her mental disorder became more severe, in spite of active psychiatric treatment. This insight into himself and his wife did not make Kevin's marriage easier, but this was because of her problems, not his. But the insight did free him of the self-doubts that had plagued him all his adult years, and permitted him to accept his own temperamental pattern as normal. This enhancement of his self-image then enabled him to deal forcefully and effectively with people and issues in his professional life, but in his own quiet low-keyed manner.

It is of course, true that the hesitation and discomfort in new situations that Frances experienced, or the mildness of emotional expressiveness that characterized Kevin, might in some cases reflect a psychologic disorder, rather than a normal temperamental attribute. The differential diagnosis cannot be made on the basis of any a priori judgment, but requires in each case the kind of data-gathering and data-assessment procedures to be outlined in Chapter 9.

TEMPERAMENT AND INTIMATE PERSONAL RELATIONSHIPS

In the goodness of fit model, psychologic outcome is determined by the interplay between the individual's characteristics and capacities and the environmental demands and expectations. In a close personal relationship in which two people live together, whether in a formalized marriage or not, each person in effect provides an important part of the environment for the other. With a goodness of fit, in which each one's demands and expectations are consonant with the other's characteristics, a favorable course for the relationship is likely. With a poorness of fit, on the contrary, difficulties and excessive stresses between the two people are predictable.

Many factors enter into the interplay between the two partners in a marriage or other long-term intimate relationship—temperament, goals, and ambitions, personal standards and moral values, sexual compatibility, and special interests. As in the parent–child interaction, goodness of fit for an adult couple does not demand identity of temperament, interests, goals and life-styles. On the contrary, differences between the two partners may serve as a positive stimulating factor that may widen the horizons of the relationship and enhance the activities and functioning of each partner. And, in fact, in many marriages where husband and wife appear to have identical interests and life-styles, this is achieved only by the suppression of differences, often at great psychological cost to one or the other or both partners.

This issue of goodness of fit as reflecting consonance rather than identity is evident when the functional significance of temperamental individuality is considered. What is of central importance is that husband and wife *respect* each other's temperamental characteristics, and that the husband not demand that the wife change her individual style to suit him, or vice versa. Actually, similarity in temperament does not guarantee a goodness of fit. One or the other partner may come to the relationship with a deficient self-image, and without real respect for his or her own temperamental style. In such a case, similarity of temperament in the partner may bring disrespect, and not acceptance.

Respect for a partner's temperament does not mean toleration of any and all behavioral expressions of temperament. This would only make the partner into a tyrant, just as it makes the child into a tyrant when the parent sets no limits to the permissive acceptance of all the child's impulses. The wife of a husband who is slow-to-warm-up should expect him to participate in new social situations, and at the same time understand that his involvement will be quiet and even peripheral to begin with. The husband of a wife with intense expressiveness should expect her to control any tendency to explosive emotional reactions, when these would be embarrassing or even harmful, and at the same time understand that she cannot and should not try to imitate his calm, mild responses.

The importance of the reciprocal recognition and acceptance of temperament in creating a goodness of fit in a marriage has been emphasized in a pioneering clinical study by Burks and Rubenstein (1979) on temperamental styles in adult interaction and their implications for psychotherapy. We ourselves have also been impressed by the significant role of temperament in many of the instances of marital discord that have come to our clinical attention over the years. The case of Kevin, as outlined above in this chapter, is one example. A marital problem can develop and escalate if one or both partners disrespect and derogate the normal temperamental characteristics of the other, and assume that such a behavioral pattern is somehow a matter of choice and represents a willful refusal to make a change "for the better." If the husband or wife who is attacked in such a fashion accepts the partner's judgment, as Kevin did, then at best a precarious peace is achieved at the cost of intimidation and damaged self-esteem. But this does not provide any basis for a healthy relationship, and all too often the tenuous marital balance is disrupted by periodic conflicts and hostile outbursts of one kind or another. In some instances, the husband or wife whose psychological integrity is being assaulted has the self-understanding and self-esteem to assert the right to his or her own individuality and to challenge directly the partner's derogatory judgments. Or this understanding and assertiveness may be achieved through psychotherapy, as was the case with Kevin. In these instances where the one partner refuses to be intimidated, a confrontation and even a marital crisis is likely to ensue. How such a crisis is resolved can depend, on the one hand, on whether the one partner's demand for respect and understanding is made constructively and patiently or takes the form of a hostile counterattack, "It's you who is all wrong, not me." On the other hand, the outcome will also depend on whether the partner who is being challenged is capable psychologically of understanding and accepting the validity of the other's demand for respect for his or her own normal temperamental traits, as Kevin's wife was unable to do.

Where husband and wife are entangled in destructive conflicts for other reasons, temperamental differences between them often become the source of additional stress and disruption. Typically, in such cases, the inconvenience or frustration that the one partner's temperament creates for the other is interpreted as another evidence of willful intent to annoy and harass. A simple example, but one we have seen more than once, occurs in a couple with marital friction, where the wife or husband has a low sensory threshold and is sensitive to cold, and the partner has a high sensory threshold with a greater tolerance for low temperatures. The wife will complain, "My husband insists on opening the windows, even when it is freezing cold outside, and he does it just to make me suffer," while the husband will charge, "My wife insists on keeping the windows shut even when it is hot and stuffy in the house, and she does it to annoy me." More complex manifestations of this type of interchange over temperamental differences are not uncommon; the quiet, reserved husband who is embarrassed by his wife's emotional openness and vigor in social gatherings, and resents what he interprets as her willful refusal to copy his behavioral style; the wife who judges her highly distractible husband's failure to carry through to completion many routine household errands and chores quickly and promptly as evidence of deliberate sabotage on his part; the husband who blows up when his highly persistent and nondistractible wife is so absorbed in a task that she fails to respond to a question or request he raises, because he considers her behavior as evidence of lack of interest in him and his needs.

Such destructive interactions over temperamental differences, even when they are not the primary cause of a marital problem, nevertheless merit serious attention in marital therapy. It may be easier to bring the battling partners to understand their misinterpretations and distortions of each other's behavior with regard to the issue of temperament, than it may be with regard to other disturbances which are plaguing their relationship. When such a change can be effected, it may affirm effectively the therapist's thesis of the need and the possibility of mutual respect and understanding as a basic goal of the treatment.

There are, of course, many marital problems in which discord over temperamental differences is not a significant issue. But this should be determined by a careful clinical evaluation of the data in each case, and not by any fixed allegiance to some theoretical framework that does not give temperament a potentially significant role.

INSIGHT INTO ONE'S OWN TEMPERAMENT

Self-knowledge is potentially a profoundly important psychologic asset. To know one's own capacities, temperament, and motivations, to be able to assess one's own strengths and weaknesses accurately, and to know what the impact of one's own behavior on others is likely to be, all these are of enormous value to an individual in mastering the demands and expectations of social, educational, and work life. This kind of self-knowledge is not possible in early childhood; it begins to emerge in middle childhood and to crystalize in adolescence. It is in adult life that a comprehensive self image and self knowledge can mature, not overnight, but gradually over time. How fully developed an accurate self-image is in any adult is certainly one basic measure of healthy psychologic maturity.

Self-knowledge as to one's temperament can be an important asset, but only if it is free of distorted derogatory judgments. Both Frances and Kevin, as detailed above in this chapter, were all too aware of certain of their temperamental characteristics. However, this self-awareness had brought them only distress and self-devaluation, as they compared their behavior to that of others, and accepted the derogatory judgments of others. At the same time, acceptance of one's own temperament as normal is only the first step. What is also necessary is the determination by any person when the expression of temperament can be free and spontaneous, when it should be curbed, and when it may be necessary to behave in an opposite direction. Thus, for example, the intensely expressive person first has to know that he has this quality and that it is normal for him. Such people then have to learn through their life-experiences when it is desirable to give full expression to this trait, when it is preferable to modify it somewhat, and when it is necessary for a specific time and purpose to act in a low-keyed manner, no matter how strong their urge to explode. Such a person's mildly expressive counterpart, by contrast, will have to learn that there are occasions where it is desirable and possible to give forceful expression to feelings and needs. The same issues are pertinent for all other temperamental traits and constellations.

The clinician is often faced with the responsibility of helping the patient to master this multiple need in the self-knowledge of temperament: to know his or her temperament, to know that it is normal for himself or herself, to know when and how to express it fully, or within limits, and to know when it is necessary and possible to go counter to one's temperamental urges.

PART TWO

Clinical Applications

CHAPTER 9

Obtaining Data on Temperament in Clinical Practice

When a child or adolescent is brought for clinical evaluation, the history obtained from the parents or other primary caretakers represents a prime source of data on temperament for the clinician. With a younger child this is supplemented by the information gained through a playroom session. With the older child or adolescent a direct interview with the youngster is indicated. In the case of an adult who seeks help because of a psychological problem, the clinican usually has to rely exclusively on information obtained through direct interview, including observations of the individual's behavior during such interviews.

The clinician uses these data-gathering procedures in the overall diagnostic evaluation of the child or adult's problem. (In some cases, of course, additional data may be required through psychological testing, neurologic evaluation, or other techniques.) In this regard, gathering temperament data does not require separate interviews or playroom sessions, but can be accomplished in the course of the clinician's overall diagnostic procedures.

GENERAL PRINCIPLES

The clinician has the task of identifying the significant elements in a child or adult's deviant behavior—what is temperament, what is motivation (including defense mechanisms), and what is inadequate or distorted sensory functioning, perception, or cognition. Then there is the interplay among these factors with each other and with the important aspects of the environment, both within the family and in the outside social world, to be analyzed.

As regards temperament, there are several useful guidelines that can aid the clinician in the determination of which temperamental qualities, if any, are of importance in the etiology and evolution of the child or adult's behavior disorder. First of all, the significant temperamental traits in such a case will almost always be at the extreme: high or low intensity rather than a moderate level, high or low persistence rather than an intermediate rating, a definitely difficult or easy temperamental pattern, rather than a borderline classification, high or low activity level rather than moderate activity, and so on.

Then, temperament can be identified by its nonmotivational character. A specific behavioral pattern in a specific environmental setting may reflect temperamental characteristics or motivations or a combination of both. The child who stands at the periphery of a new nursery school group may do so because she is temperamentally slow-to-warm-up, or because she is afraid of mingling with strange children and avoids this perceived threat by remaining on the outskirts of the group, or because she is both slow-to-warm-up and afraid. Adults who resist major changes in their work schedule similarly may do so because of a temperamental withdrawal response to new situations, or because their self-esteem is low and they are afraid they will fail any new challenge, or because they are withdrawers temperamentally and are afraid of failure. The child or adult who is low-keyed and reserved in her emotional expressiveness may be of low intensity in temperament, or may be emotionally inhibited and fearful of the consequences of exposing her feelings, or both.

It usually requires information on the person's behavior in a wide range of situations and circumstances to identify a particular behavioral pattern as either nonmotivational and temperamental, or as motivational and goal-directed. Thus, in the case of a child who stands quietly at the periphery of a new nursery school group, if she has behaved in a similar way in other new settings, such as at a playground or outing to a beach, but then has gradually become an active participant as familiarity with the places and the people has grown, then it is likely that the nursery school behavior reflects a slow-to-warm-up temperamental pattern. If, on the other hand, the child remains aloof and resists efforts to draw her into play activity even when the other children or adults are no longer strangers, then it is probable that this behavioral pattern is motivational and represents a defensive response to anxiety. The reason for such anxiety will then require further investigation. In some cases the etiology may be excessive pressure by parents and others on a slow-to-warm-up child for a speedy adaptation to new situations and people which is beyond the capacity of such a youngster. In these instances the pattern of behavioral withdrawal will be a combination of both temperamental and motivational factors.

As another example, an adult who is concerned over her low-keyed reserved emotional expressiveness can be asked whether this tendency is shown in different types of situations, even when there is no possibility of adverse reactions by others, and even when the person knows that an open full expression of his or her feelings will be welcomed and encouraged. If so, then it is probable that the person's behavior reflects the temperamental trait of low intensity. If, on the other hand, the person can and does express anger or delight easily with people that are known and trusted, but is reserved with all others, then it is more likely that the emotional reserve reflects one or another pattern of emotional inhibition, rather than temperament. Or, the data may indicate an overall temperamental pattern of low intensity, but with a marked accentuation in certain situations where, for whatever the reason, the individual is afraid to express even her normal low-keyed level of feelings.

Finally, information on temperament, whether obtained from the individual herself, parents, teachers, or other informants, is most likely to be accurate and useful if the objective details of behavior in specific situations are obtained, rather than a reliance on global judgmental statements. The latter type of data may often be useful in providing clues to an individual's self-evaluation or to parents' attitudes toward their child, but they will not provide the factual information necessary to identify temperamental characteristics. It is helpful to ask the informant to illustrate a general statement by giving several specific examples. Thus, for example, parents who report that their child is "stubborn and self-willed" and "throws tantrums to get her own way" should be asked to describe several recent incidents of this kind of behavior in detail. Such a description should include the nature of the initial stimulus that set off the child's behavior, what the parent did in response to the child's behavior, how the child then reacted to what the parent did, and so on until the incident is brought to a close. With this kind of information drawn from several examples, the clinician will be able to estimate whether the child has difficult temperament that the parents are handling badly, or whether the parents are in fact making inappropriate and rigid demands on a highly persistent child that the youngster is resisting actively, or whether some other type of undersirable parent–child interaction seems to be operating.

Similarly, if a teacher reports that one of his pupils is not learning because she is so inattentive, a description of several instances may clarify that the child is actually eager to learn but gets easily distracted, or that the child has a high activity level and gets restless and inattentive when forced to sit still for long periods, or that the problem may involve cognitive or motivational issues that require further classification. Or, if an adult is concerned that she is considered aggressive and inconsiderate by friends and coworkers, and "maybe they're right," the subject can be asked to describe several recent incidents in which she was charged with this kind of behavior. The resulting data may then indicate that the problem is one of very high intensity of expressiveness that the individual has never learned to modulate when necessary to give others a chance to communicate easily with her. Or, the information may be sufficient to rule out a tempermental basis for the problem, and to suggest alternative possibilities as to etiology.

THE PARENT INTERVIEW

As the clinician takes the overall history from the parents on the presenting problem, pertinent temperamental issues may become evident. A few questions may then serve to confirm this impression. For example, one set of parents came for consultation because their 5-year-old son, whom they had enrolled in kindergarten 1 month before, cried loudly for an hour or more each morning after being deposited at school. The teacher also reported some temper tantrum outbursts, not daily, but frequent enough to make for a difficult adjustment. Both parents and teacher were concerned that this behavior reflected some hidden source of maladjustment and anxiety. With a few questions it was evident that the boy had shown a pattern of loud crying on exposure to most new situations from early infancy outward. The parents had not been concerned over this reaction, because they had learned that the youngster would always adjust gradually if they were patient. From this history, it seemed likely that the distressing response to school represented another example of the temperamental pattern of the difficult child, with intense negative reactions to the new with slow adaptability, rather than an expression of anxiety. This judgment was confirmed when the complete history from the parents and the playroom session with the boy failed to reveal any other etiology for the problem behavior.

As another example, the parents of a 10-year-old girl came with the complaint that their daughter was bedeviling their lives by her "refusal" to cooperate in the daily routines of the household. If asked to do something, she would start the task but then often drop it in the middle and leave it half finished. Her clothes and belongings were scattered over the apartment, in spite of stern injunctions to put them in her own room. She took an inordinate time to get to bed at night, and was often late getting off to school in the morning. The mother especially was convinced that her daughter was bent on defying her, and described many explosive interchanges between the two of them when she, the mother, tried to enforce obedience and discipline. The father was overwhelmed by this battle between his wife and daughter, and tried to stay on the sidelines. On questioning them, both parents agreed that their daughter did not seem antagonistic when asked to do something or reminded to go to bed. Quite the contrary, she usually started off cheerfully, but then something went wrong. All she would say was "I'm sorry, I forgot." Furthermore, the parents reported that their daughter's "forgetting" was not restricted to the home, but also occurred frequently with her friends. It was not unusual for one of her friends to come by or telephone and complain "Where were you? We made this date to go out together and here you are doing something else." When this occurred, their daughter was invariably upset at having missed something she herself had wanted to do, and could only say "I forgot." This latter information made it clear that the youngster's problem revolved around the temperamental quality of high distractibility, which the mother had distorted into an issue of willful disobedience.

In other cases, the nature of the presenting complaint will leave it uncertain as to whether the child's temperament is a major factor in the pathogenesis of the behavior disorder. In such a situation, an inventory of the child's temperament gained from the parents, and supplemented by information obtained either in a playroom session or direct interview with the child, will be necessary. With this identification of the youngster's temperamental characteristics, its role in the dynamics of the origin and evolution of the behavior disorder can be evaluated.

In other instances, the parental description of the presenting problem will make it clear that temperament does not play a major etiologic role, as in a child with a definite history of organic brain damage, with pathologic behavioral consequences. In some such cases, however, the youngster's temperament may be influential in either ameliorating or exacerbating the symptoms and the clinical course. Thus, for example, in our NYLS sample, there were 3 subjects with symptoms due to brain damage from early childhood onward. Two subjects had easy temperament, while the third had difficult temperament. Severity of symptomatology and difficulties in functioning were greatest in the girl with difficult temperament, and this appeared to be clearly due in part to this temperamental constellation (Chess & Thomas, 1984).

It is therefore useful to obtain an inventory of the child's temperamental characteristics in the parental interview even when the etiology of the disorder appears clear and does not involve temperament directly. It is usually desirable to assess first the child's current temperament inasmuch as this may focus the inquiry into the temperamental characteristics at earlier age-periods.

Activity level may be estimated from a child's behavior preferences. Would the child rather sit quietly for a long time engrossed in some task, or does she prefer to seek out opportunities for active physical play? How well does the child fare in routines that require sitting still for extended periods of time? For example, can she sit through an entire meal without seeking an opportunity to move about? Must a long train or automobile ride be broken up by frequent stops because of the child's restlessness?

Rhythmicity can be explored through questions about the child's habits and their regularity. For instance, does the child get sleepy at regular and predictable times? Does she have any characteristic routines relating to hunger, such as taking a snack immediately after school or during the evening? Are the bowel movements regular?

Approach/withdrawal, or the youngster's pattern to response to new events or new people, can be explored in many ways. Questions can be directed at the nature of the child's reaction to new clothing, new neighborhood children, a new school, and a new teacher. What is the child's attitude when a family excursion to a new place is being planned? Will she try new foods or new activities easily or not?

Adaptability can be identified through a consideration of the way the child reacts to changes in environment. Does the child adjust easily and fit quickly into changed family patterns? Is she willing to go along with other children's preferences, or does she always insist on pursuing only her own interests?

Threshold level is more difficult to explore in an older child than in a young one. However, it is sometimes possible to obtain information on unusual features of threshold, such as sensitivity to noise, to visual stimuli, or to rough clothing, or remarkable unresponsiveness to such stimuli.

The *intensity of reactions* can be ascertained by finding out how the child displays disappointment or pleasure. If something pleasant happens does the child tend to be mildly enthusiastic, average in the expression of joy, or ecstatic? When unhappy, does the child fuss quietly or bellow with rage or distress?

Quality of mood can usually be estimated by parental descriptions of their offspring's overall expressions of mood. Is the child predominantly happy or contented, or is she a frequent complainer and more often unhappy than not?

Distractibility, even when not a presenting problem, will declare itself in the parents' descriptions of ordinary routines. Does the child start off to do something and then often get sidetracked by something her brother is doing, by a coin collection, or by any number of several circumstances that catch the eye or ear? Or, on the contrary, once the child is engaged in an activity, is she impervious to what is going on around her?

Data on *persistence* and *attention span* are usually easier to obtain for the older child than for the infant. The degree of persistence in the face of difficulty can be ascertained with regard to games, puzzles, athletic activities such as learning to ride a bicycle, and schoolwork. Similarly, after the initial difficulty in mastering these activities has been overcome, the length of the child's attention span for and concentration on these same kinds of activities can be ascertained.

It is also frequently important to obtain as accurate a picture as possible of the child's temperamental attributes in infancy. A poorness of fit between the child's characteristics and the parents' attitudes and child-care practices may have started at that early age-period and initiated the youngster's unfavorable developmental course. Such an inquiry has the possibility of distortion of parental recall, due to faulty memory or special biases influencing the recollection of the past. This problem of retrospective recall, of course, applies not only to temperament, but to all other kinds of information, such as the attainment of developmental landmarks, the medical history, patterns of parental functioning, and special environmental events. Greater accuracy of parental recall is likely if the questions focus on the infant's behavior and the parents' handling in discrete specific situations that were meaningful in the child's life at the that time. General questions, such as "was the child easy or hard to take care of as a baby" are least likely to evoke accurate recall, as they are often translated by parents into judgments on whether their infant was normal or not.

The following protocol for identifying temperament in the infancy period is offered as a guide to the clinician. All the items do not necessarily have to be covered in detail. In any individual case, the data obtained from the history of the behavior problem and the assessment of current temperament may suggest an emphasis on certain questions and a quick survey of the other items in the protocol. It is also desirable to pick a specific age-period between 4 and 9 months of age, and ask the parents to respond in terms of their child's behavior at that time. Some parents may choose a specific age, because special circumstances may have fixed their memory of that age-period more exactly. If the parents have no preference, an arbitrary time, such as 6 months of age, can be chosen.

Activity level. When you were changing the infant's diaper, did she lie rather still, or did the infant's constant movement make it a difficult job? In dressing or undressing the infant, was it a struggle to get her kicking legs and moving arms into garments, or was it quite easy because the infant's movements were quiet? Did she tend to remain in the same position in the crib when asleep, or move around all over the crib?

Rhythmicity. Did the infant awaken about the same time each morning? Were naps regular or not? Was hunger predictable, so that you could start to do a task that would take an hour or 2, or was it so uncertain as to timing that you might or might not be interrupted to feed the infant? If you were planning to take her somewhere, could you time it for just after a bowel movement?

Approach/withdrawal. How did the baby behave with new events, such as when the first tub bath, offered new foods, or taken care of by a new person for the first time? Did the child fuss, do nothing, or did she seem to like it? Were there any changes during the child's infancy that you remember, such as a shift to a new bed, a visit to a new place, or a permanent move? Describe the child's initial behavior at these times.

Adaptability. How would you describe the way the baby responded to changed circumstances. For example, when she was shifted from a bathinette to a bathtub, if the child didn't take to the change immediately, could you count on her getting used to it quickly or did it a take long time? (Parents should be asked to define what they mean by "quickly" and what they mean by "a long time" in terms of days or weeks.) If the child's first reaction to a new person was negative, how long did it take the child to become familiar with the person? If she didn't like a new food the first time it was offered, could you count on the child's getting to like it and most other new foods sooner or later? If so, how long would it take if the new food was offered to the child daily or several times a week?

Threshold level. Suppose the child didn't like a food, could you disguise it by putting something she liked on top, or would the child reject the food anyway? How would you estimate the child's sensitivity to sound, light, heat, and cold, and textures of clothing? For example, did you have to tiptoe about when the child was sleeping lest she be awakened? Did bright lights or bright sunshine make the child fuss or cry? Did you have to be careful about clothing you put on the child because some textures were too rough, or didn't this matter?

Intensity of reactions. When the child was hungry, did she fuss mildly, cry loudly, or was it somewhere in between? If she resisted going to bed, or was offered a food that wasn't liked; was the protest mild or loud? If the child liked something, did she usually smile and coo or rather laugh vigorously? In general, would you say that pleasure or displeasure was shown loudly or softly?

Quality of mood. If the child fussed or cried, did this happen usually only with definite discomfort, like hunger, sleepiness, or a soiled diaper? Or were there some or many times when she seemed uncomfortable or upset and yet you couldn't tell what was amiss? Would you describe the child as being mostly in a pleasant state, or was fussing predominant?

Distractibility. When the child was busy feeding and someone walked by, did she merely look while she went on feeding, or did she stop and turn her head to watch the person? If the child was hungry and fussing, could she be diverted easily in some way so that the crying stopped while you got the food ready? Or would nothing distract the child? If she was resisting being changed or dressed, could you get the child to lie still and quietly by providing a favorite toy, or would nothing stop the fussing and squirming?

Persistence and attention span. Would you say that the baby usually stuck with something she was doing for a long time or only momentarily? For example, describe the longest time the baby remained engrossed in an activity all by herself. (Examples might be playing with the cradle gym or watching a mobile.) If the baby reached for something, say a toy in the bathtub, and couldn't get it easily, would she keep after it or give up very quickly?

The survey of the child's temperamental characteristics in the current and infancy period should be coupled with inquiries as to which aspects of the child's temperament the parents found difficult or upsetting and why, and how they handled these issues. With these data, the clinician will then usually be able to identify those aspects of the child's temperament that appeared to be significant factors in the development of the behavior problem. Further information can then be obtained on these characteristics at various age-periods between infancy and the current period. For example, if the presenting complaints indicate that the child currently finds it difficult to undertake new endeavors or to join new groups of age-mates, and if the early temperamental history suggested a characteristic pattern of initial withdrawal coupled with slow adaptation, it would be important to obtain descriptions of the child's patterns of initial responses to situations and demands that arose at different points in her developmental course. And it would be equally important to determine how the parents, other family members, peers, and teachers reacted to the child's patterns of behavior with the new. For it is not temperament alone, or parental functioning alone, that determine the origin and sequential course of a behavior disorder, but always the poorness of fit in the interaction of the child with the parents and/or other significant persons in the environment.

In tracing the manifestations of any one temperamental attribute or pattern over time, care should be taken to focus on behaviors that are appropriate to each age-period, and especially those that are responsive to new situations and experiences. Otherwise, the history may appear to show a blurring or change in temperament if the inquiry concentrates on routine situations. Routine response patterns, once they shaped as an adaptation to a cultural norm, may serve to minimize individual uniqueness. For example, the first attempt at toilet training will cause one child to scream and struggle violently, another child to fuss mildly while sitting on the seat for only a few minutes, and a third child to smile and play while sitting on the seat for many minutes. A year later, when all 3 children are fully trained, their behavior on the toilet seat may be very similar or show only slight differences as compared to the marked individuality of response to the initial toileting demands. Similar blurring of initial differences in behavioral responses as progressive adaptation to the social norm develops may occur with a variety of other experiences, such as entry into nursery school, the beginning of formal learning, changes in the family group, new living quarters, and so forth. Therefore, when the behavioral history suggests an apparent change in a child's temperament over time, the data should be scrutinized to determine whether the change is evident or disappears when the responses to new situations at the different age periods are compared.

In some cases, there may actually be a significant change in a temperamental attribute over time (see Appendix B). When this appears evident from the parental history, special attention should be given to obtaining a detailed picture of the child's environment preceding and concurrent with this change in temperament. In some cases, the reasons for a shift in temperament at a particular age-period may be obscure, in other instances an important change in the child's home setting, parental functioning, or in the child's play group or school experience, may be identified as a responsible cause. Such an environmental change may then be influential not only in modifying the child's temperament, but also in shaping the subsequent course of the youngster's behavioral development.

The protocol for obtaining temperament data from the parents, as detailed above, may appear burdensome and excessively time-consuming. In our own clinical experience, however, the collection of behavioral information by parental interview, from which an evaluation of the child's temperament can be made, has presented no greater difficulties than the inquiry on other aspects of the clinical history. Much of the data pertinent to temperament will be suggested or even clearly indicated in the questioning regarding the presenting complaint, the child's attainment of developmental landmarks, or special environmental events. Thus, for example, if the parents report that their 6-year-old son had a severe upper respiratory infection several months previously, information can easily and quickly be obtained on whether the youngster fussed mildly or cried loudly, whether he tossed and turned or lay quietly, how quickly the child accepted the prescribed medication, and whether he could be distracted easily or not when in acute discomfort. Furthermore, the systematic inquiry for temperament involves the focus on new or problem situations and tracing the interactional sequence to completion. Thus, if a parent reported that the child cried when put to bed at night, the next question would be "What did you do when he cried?" followed by "How did he react to what you did?" and "What did you do then?" and so on until the sequence of interaction was completed. In such an inquiry, information is obtained not only on the child's temperament, but also on the parent's attitudes and patterns of handling. In other words, the clinician's history from the parents on other aspects of the child's behavior and life experience can elicit information upon temperament, and the specific inquiry as to temperament can add to his or her knowledge of these other significant aspects of the clinical history.

THE PLAYROOM SESSION

The playroom is a useful setting for the psychiatric examination of the child. For the clinician to observe and identify personally a slice of the child's typical behavior, it is necessary to provide a relaxed environment in which the youngster's movements are not restrained, and where toys, puzzles, and other play objects can be provided that can allow a demonstration of developmental level. And once involved in informal and spontaneous play activity, conversation with the child is more likely to reveal what the child is thinking than in a restricted formal interview.

The playroom session is analogous to a diagnostic physical examination. In both, the history very often will have provided clues as to area of malfunction, or will even have suggested the likelihood of a specific diagnosis. In such cases, the playroom session, as with the physical examination, can be focused on several features to be evaluated in detail, at the same time as an orderly inventory of the child's overall functioning is obtained. Where the history leaves the diagnosis unclear, the child's behavior in the playroom may illuminate the nature of the deviant behavior.

In the playroom session, the clinician, while engaging the child in play and talk, can determine whether the child's developmental level is appropriate to chronological age, can gather data on language and cognitive functioning, and can note whether behavior is goal-directed or aimless, organized, or chaotic. The child's affective relatedness can also be assessed, both in terms of the manner of relating to the examiner and in the association between action and emotional expression.

Temperamental attributes can also be evaluated in the playroom session, except for rhythmicity of biological functioning, which requires data over a more extended period of time. One can note whether the child is easily and quickly engaged with the new situation or requires time to warm-up; whether she uses the playroom materials quietly or is in constant motion; whether there is or is not awareness of minor degrees of visual, auditory, or other stimuli; whether there is mildness or intensity of expressiveness; whether there is largely positive or negative mood; whether suggestions and rules are accepted adaptively or not; whether the child shows high or low distractibility; whether her attention span is long or short; and whether there is persistence with a difficult activity that's started or the activity is given up easily.

The use of the playroom to evaluate a child's significant temperamental characteristics can be best illustrated by several case examples.

Case 1

Martin's mother consulted one of us (S. C.) when he was 4 years of age. This was in the late winter of his second year of nursery school, and the teacher had advised his parents that Martin was showing signs of marked anxiety, which indicated a serious adjustment problem requiring treatment. The teacher based this judgment on Martin's failure to participate actively in his classmate's group play routines. Instead, he sat or stood silently on the outer edge of the group. The mother was surprised at this report, inasmuch as Martin typically reported a pleasurable involvement in the various play activities of the day on returning home from school. Also, during this same period, when she took him and his older brother to the neighborhood playground after school and on weekends, Martin not only joined in group play, but actively sought out the other children. The history, as I took it from both parents, showed no other evidence of behavior disorder, either past or present. There had been no sleep or feeding problems, regressive behavior, difficulty with toilet training, or excessive clinging. However, a clear history was obtained that Martin needed the opportunity to become familiar with people, places, and things before he could become comfortable with them. Thus, as an infant, his parents knew that his first reaction to a new food would be a refusal. But if the food was offered every few days, he usually ended up by adding if to his growing menu. It was the same with people. A new babysitter had to be present several times before he would play with her actively. When visiting he was shy, but after several visits to the same place he relaxed and usually wanted to go again. He had shown this shyness on first starting nursery school the year before, but this had disappeared after the first month.

The history indicated that the key issue in Martin's apparently disturbed behavior in nursery school might be a slow-to-warm up child's temperamental pattern. As to why this second year of school should be so different from his first year with its positive adaptation, his health history suggested a possible answer. In his first year Martin had had only a few mild episodes of upper respiratory infections, and had been able to attend school regularly. By contrast, in his second year, he had had a number of more severe infections, starting soon after school began, so that his attendance was irregular, with a usual sequence of 1 week of attendance and 2 weeks of absence.

I asked Martin's mother to bring along at least one of his favorite toys. The playroom session began with his refusal to enter. He leaned against his mother and whispered his refusal, which she repeated to me. I then suggested that she come in to look at the room, and Martin could come with her or stay in the waiting room as he wished. Both entered and I showed the mother the various toys, then asked him if I might look at the toy he had brought. Martin hid behind his mother, but his small arm held out the paper bag holding varicolored beads that snapped together. I took them out and inspected them gravely, tried to snap one onto another but made certain that I did it incorrectly so that they failed to join. After a few moments, Martin apparently could no longer bear my ineptitude, and came over to show me. I followed his instruction, then looked to him for more guidance which he also demonstrated. Soon we each had constructed a line of joined beads with identical succession of colors, when Martin became suddenly aware that he was involved with me. He darted behind his mother again for a few moments, then rejoined me. I began to make a tower with the blocks, and reached for a block to balance another. It was too far, so I asked him to get it, which he did. From this time on, there was a rising crescendo of his involvement in play, mostly without words, but at times we exchanged requests or offers of help.

From this play activity, it was clear that Martin's concepts of size and shape, of color, and of weight were all up to, and perhaps above chronological age. His motoric skills were age-appropriate. Martin's naming of objects was accurate, as were the grammatical constructions of the few sentences he uttered. His functioning was goal-directed and organized and activity level moderate. Affective relatedness was muted but normal, as shown by his facial expressions and body movements. Thus, the playroom session elicited no evidence of psychopathology. Rather, his behavior was typical of a child with the slow-to-warm-up temperamental pattern.

It had been possible to note these aspects of Martin's behavior in one session, because the bridge from home (the familiar toy), and permitting his mother to accompany him into the room, had short-

ened the time needed to achieve a sense of familiarity and relaxation in
this new place with this new person. The judgment that the boy had
indeed warmed-up and had begun to enjoy this new play expression
with a stranger was confirmed at the end of the session. I explained to
Martin (and his listening mother) that it was now time for us to end
the visit. I thanked him for coming to see me, and said what a good
time I had had playing with him. Martin, saying nothing to me, flung
himself against his mother's chest and whispered to her, then looked at
me. He had said, his mother dutifully repeated as instructed by him,
that he wanted to stay and play some more. I extended the visit for
5 minutes, and then, to his dissatisfaction, we terminated. One can
postulate that, had there been a visit of several hours, I would then
have seen his more active interrelatedness, typical of the playground
behavior reported by his mother. One can also postulate that, were
there to be another visit after several weeks, we would have once again
started as at the beginning of the visit just described, with an initial
cautious retreat followed by an increasingly active participation. It is
also likely that this warm-up sequence would have proceeded more
rapidly than on his first visit.

My clinical evaluation, thus, which I communicated to his
mother, was that Martin was not suffering from any behavior disorder
that required treatment. Rather, his nursery school behavior was a
reflection of his slow-to-warm-up temperament. With his irregular
school attendance because of his upper respiratory infections, he had
not had the consecutive time he needed to adapt to the group and,
instead, remained a peripheral observer rather than an active participant. Now that the winter was ending, hopefully his health would
improve, he would be able to attend school continuously, and the
behavior which had so concerned the teacher would disappear. And,
indeed, this is what happened. Martin remained well physically, and
within a month's time he was an active and lively member of his
school group. When this happened, no one could have detected any
difference in his behavior from those other youngsters who had been
able temperamentally to adapt to the new quickly and easily.

Case 2

Karen's parents brought her for evaluation at age 7 years because her
second grade teacher considered her to be a pathologically hyperactive
child. She kept wiggling in her chair in the classroom, whispered to

the children around her, her pencil point seemed to need sharpening too often, and her requests to go the lavatory were too frequent. All in all, her movements and desire to get out of her seat were, in her teacher's eyes, not only excessive, but evidence of some behavior disorder.

Karen's parents themselves had not considered her to be a behavior problem. True, she had required great alertness from them early infancy onward because of her high level of motor activity. Changing her diaper or dressing her required careful watching lest she make a sudden lurch and fall from the changing table. Once she was crawling and walking, sharp objects had to be placed higher and higher much more rigorously than had been the case with her older sister. While Karen accepted in principle that certain actions were out of bounds, such as opening particular drawers and taking out the contents, in practice she looked to see if she were observed while doing the forbidden act (at 15 months), and excused her trespasses by saying "I forgot" (at 3 years). In fact, the family had a saying that Karen looked with her hands, because the request for something was simultaneous with taking it.

While the extra alertness required on their part was an extra strain on parents' energies, they had not considered Karen's behavior as actually abnormal. They were confirmed in this judgment by her otherwise healthy development and functioning. Her developmental milestones had all been within normal range, she was a sociable child who had many friends, she did well academically in school, and she had no other symptoms of behavioral malfunctioning. She did often act before she thought or asked—taking a ball from a friend simultaneously with asking for it, or pushing to get in front to go up the stairs to the slide first. Other children liked her, nevertheless, and tolerated these slight inconveniences because she was, for the most part, good natured, sharing, and ready to comfort anyone who was hurt.

On entering the playroom, Karen was immediately at home. Although I pointed out several toys, she scarcely listened, but immediately ran around looking. Very soon she discovered the punching-bag and hit at it. I pulled it into the center of the room for greater range of movement, and said, "if you watch, I will show you how to give it a big punch" and demonstrated how she must stand on the platform so that it would remain upright when she hit it. Karen immediately took a swing at it, and the punching-bag fell over. I said, "You forgot to stand on it." Karen then took a stance, placing her feet precisely as I had done in my demonstration, hit it and waited to see if it would fall—which it did not. I said, "You can hit it harder than that, it won't fall over now." She then played with it some minutes before turning her attention to other activities, but returned to it several times during the 45 minutes of the session. Her actions were well coordinated throughout. In turn, Karen played with the dollhouse furniture, built with the blocks, drew pictures at my request of the members of her family, and threw the darts with vigor. All these activities were goal directed and executed at the level of a 7-year-old. Although Karen was inclined to act quickly, before listening to full directions, when this did not work she either asked for help or used the directions she had just before failed to heed. I made a paper bird that flapped its wings; Karen ran out to show this to her parents, crumpling it in her enthusiasm. I fixed it and again showed her how to hold it and pull its tail. This time she complied and it worked.

During this playroom session it was possible to note Karen's mental status in general, and also the specifics of her activity level. Karen's affective relatedness was good, both with the examiner during the play, and as shown by her desire to share the enjoyment of the paper bird with her parents. Her gross and fine motor coordination were commensurate with her age level. Mood was positive and related to activity. During conversation that accompanied her play, Karen talked vivaciously about the things she did with her friends, what she was good at (swimming and baseball), and what she didn't do so well (homework). She was looking forward to day camp and the special treat her father had promised for Karen and her older sister soon. That was the best thing that was happening, but she could not think of any worse thing. She considered herself a good girl, except that she forgot and did things that she wasn't supposed to and sometimes her mother got angry. She liked school, and was seemingly little aware of her teacher's disapproval of her actions.

As far as Karen's activity level was concerned, it was distinctly very high, but not frenetic or disorganized. When she was unsuccessful, this was largely due to Karen's hasty approach to her task, as with the punching bag. Her first hasty drawings were also a jumble, but were repeated more slowly and at a better level on request. Play and verbalizations were age-appropriate.

In essence, the playroom observation had verified what the history had indicated; Karen's high activity level, although inconvenient, was not pathologic. Her parents' attitude was a good fit. They accommodated to Karen's need for motoric expression for the most part, yet also indicated to her that there were times and places when she must do the

accommodating. They had refrained from allowing the child's boisterous energy to be turned into confrontations and had upheld her
positive self-image. What was required was a discussion with her
teacher and principal to orient them to the normal temperamental
basis for her behavior in school. Karen's tactics for achieving the extra
motoric activity she required through such devices as sharpening her
pencil and going to the lavatory were in fact constructive. She did not
disrupt the class nor did she do anything destructive. Such a child
should be able to function well in the classroom, provided her geniune
need for more motoric expression than the average child is given
planned and constructive outlets.

Case 3

Brian's parents, like Karen's (Case 2), also came for consultation because of their child's high level of motor activity. But, by contrast to
Karen, Brian's behavior was not the reflection of a normal temperamental attribute, but constituted a psychopathologic pattern. His case
vignette is presented briefly here to illustrate the usefulness of a playroom session in defining what is and what is not temperament.

Brian had been referred by a nursery school to which his parents
had made application. Since Brian, during the school visit, had broken
a goodly number of toys and pieces of equipment, the school director
had not only stated her inability to accept him, but had also suggested
a psychiatric consultation. He was an only child, mainly because his
parents believed they could not manage another child, given the
energy required to keep this one safe. As an infant, he had been fairly
easy to manage. A wiggly young infant can, after all, be managed
when diapers are changed and during bathing. Once Brian was crawling, and especially once he was walking, child-proofing the house had
become more and more difficult. During the day, Brian's mother now
found it impossible to do anything other than follow him around, and
even then he moved so swiftly that he was in danger before she realized,
or had broken still one more object. Shopping at the supermarket had
long been impossible if Brian was there; no baby sitter would come a
second time, and the parents had not been on an outing together
without Brian since his birth. He could not be trusted to play without
supervision, and he was not welcomed in the playground or in other
backyards by other mothers—at least not after a first try, when he
pushed other children or took their toys. Despite all the mayhem he
caused, Brian's parents were certain that he did not intend to be

destructive. Nevertheless, their relationship to the boy now seemed to consist of ceaseless prohibitions and admonitions, all of them unheeded.

The history as obtained from the parents appeared objective and accurate. Nevertheless, it was possible that they were distorting the development sequence that had led to his present behavior, which was so destructive in its consequences. Perhaps Brian was essentially a youngster with a high activity level, like Karen, but whose parents, unlike Karen's, had reacted with rigid punitive rules which so restricted and constrained him that his behavior had become oppositional and disorganized. The playroom session offered the opportunity for differentiating between these two possibilities.

Brian, age 3 years 5 months, was a tall and well-built child who could have been taken for a 4- or 5-year-old. He entered the playroom, was attracted by the toys, and immediately began to use them. He picked up one of the wooden jigsaw puzzles, scattering the pieces in his hurry. He then picked up a second puzzle by edge, as before, and shook the pieces to the floor; then repeated this with a third. Reaching for still another, Brian found that the pile was finished, looked up and saw the blackboard. He ran to it, saying, "I'll draw a mommy." Grasping the chalk, he drew a circle and placed two eyes in it, when his eyes was caught by a punching bag. He ran to the corner in which the punching bag stood and scribbled with chalk on it, then looked to me mischievously. I simply watched, and over my shoulder the child noted some puppets. He ran to them, placed one over each hand, began a mock fight between them, saying "I'm gonna hit you!" and replying "No you won't." He then saw the toy furniture, began to arrange a room, and was distracted to something else. Soon the floor was strewn with toys with which he had initiated and abandoned activity after activity. All actions had been goal-directed and had begun at an age-appropriate level. With each activity it seemed likely that, had he continued any of them, it might have been brought to a higher degree of organization and complexity.

From this playroom behavior, it was possible to conclude that Brian had normal or above-normal intelligence, that he related well affectively, and that his motor dexterity was at least up to age-level. His behavior was goal-directed, and he was not oppositional or deliberately destructive. The validity of the parents' report therefore established, and the diagnosis was made of a pathologic with a secondary unhealthy parent–child interaction. The activity pattern was pathologic in nature, and was not the expression of a normal high-activity temperamental attribute.

THE DIRECT INTERVIEW WITH AN OLDER CHILD
OR ADOLESCENT

For an older child or adolescent, the direct interview serves the diagnostic and therapeutic purposes as does the playroom session for a
young child. For the middle childhood age-period, it is sometimes
desirable to schedule the interview in the playroom itself. These are the
cases in which the clinician judges that the child is still relatively
immature in direct verbal communication, and that a combination of
direct discussion with play activity will be most effective. Indeed, for a
highly active child, the insistence that the youngster sit still for the
duration of the interview may lead to discomfort and restlessness, and
interfere with a free flow of communication. One may say, "If you like,
we can talk in here. Some kids like to use the darts or other things
while they talk," thus making it clear that one is not treating the
youngster like a "baby." For an adolescent, one would not place the
interview in the playroom, unless the boy or girl wished to demonstrate some skill and use the playroom equipment to do so.

It is the parents who bring the child or adolescent to the clinician
because of their concerns over problem behavior, though older adolescents occasionally will come on their own initiative. In some cases,
youngsters are also openly worried about their behavior and are
looking for help. In these instances the establishment of a friendly cooperative atmosphere for the interview is no problem. In many cases,
however, youngsters view the situation as one of unfair parental inter-
ference in their lives, and the clinician is seen as an advocate of the
parents. Here, the discussion begins with reluctance at best, and sometimes even with open hostility. The clinician's first task is then to
convince the child or adolescent that he or she does not want to hear
only the parents' version, but does wish to take the youngster's opinions also into account, and can do so only they are put forth by the
youngster herself. The specific strategy the clinician uses to achieve
this initial goal will vary from case to case, depending on the specific
nature of the youngster's opening remarks and behavior, and the
clinician can usually expect to be at least partially successful in opening up a meaningful discussion. The hostile negative mood displayed
by a youngster who is resentful toward the parents and the clinician,
should not be interpreted as the expression of a typical temperamental
characteristic, inasmuch as it is so heavily influenced by the youngster's view of the interview situation. The manner in which the youngster expresses antagonism—quietly or loudly—may, however provide
evidence for judging temperamental intensity.

Once sufficient rapport has been established to permit a fruitful discussion, the clinician will, of course, be concerned with a comprehensive an evaluation of the youngster's psychologic status as possible. As in a playroom session with a younger child, data on temperament will not require a separate interview, but will emerge in the course of this overall assessment. Some items will require direct questions, others can be evaluated by the youngster's behavior and manner of expression, as well as by the adolescent's report concerning living routines, special activities, and patterns of adjustment at home, in school, and in various types of social situations.

As to activity level, one can ask youngsters directly how they feel when there is no opportunity for athletic or other physical activity, as during a long automobile ride. Does this make them restless and uncomfortable, or doesn't it prove bothersome? One can also estimate whether active sports play an important part in the youngster's life or not. Approach/withdrawal can be explored by asking whether it bothers the adolescent to move to a new home, go to a new school, be assigned to a new teacher, start a new academic subject, or meet a new peer group in a summer resort or summer camp. If any of these new situations did upset the youngster, did he or she then adjust quickly, or slowly, or did the subject do her best to avoid further contact? Here, the clinician will have to distinquish, from the other data available between slow adaptability as a temperamental trait or as a consequence of some cognitive or motivational problem, such as some type of learning disability. If there are a number of discussions with the youngster, the speed of adaptability can also be estimated by the tempo of the youngster's accommodation to the clinician, the office environment, and to the discussion of disturbing topics.

Mood quality can be evaluated, once rapport has been established, by noting the manner in which peers, routines, adults, and tasks are discussed. The youngster with predominantly positive mood will comment cheerfully on these activities and experiences, but will also tend to view any setback due to temporary ill luck that will soon pass. By contrast, the youngster with predominantly negative mood is likely to make comments such as "With my luck, I won't get chosen for the basketball team," or debating team, or be allowed to use the new school computer, or whatever. Intensity of expression can be noted in the play of facial expression, in the tone of voice, and in the content of ideas. Comments such as "I don't mind" and "I guess it is alright" are typical of low-intensity subjects whereas such phrases as "I always get so mad when———" and "I had a terrific time———" would be indicative of high intensity. Or these types of intensity of expressiveness can be noted during playroom occupation, as when the dart hits the bull's eye, or a craft task is completed and scrutinized.

Threshold may play a part in problems. For example, a youngster with low threshold (high sensitivity) to touch or taste, may find certain clothing uncomfortable, or may find some tastes repellant. Rather than state this, she may avoid situations such as a camping trip in which unexpected demands may arise for wearing itchy clothing or eating disliked foods. If the history or prior discussion suggests this possibility, a direct question that shows an understanding and sympathy for such sensitivities will usually result in direct accurate answers, including the various devices used to cover over or avoid embarrassment. Distractibility can usually be evaluated easily while talking to the youngster or observing the play pattern. If the subject digresses often, jumps to a new idea, and forgets to return to the original topic, it can be safely assumed that this is a stylistic component and not a measure of anxiety. Low distractibility will show itself by the firmness with which a topic or endeavor is maintained despite the intrusion of other stimuli.

Rhythmicity is unlikely to be a significant aspect of problem behavior development in older childhood or adolescence (or adult life). Biological functions are likely to have been fitted to social schedules by these ages. Whether bowel function is regular or not matters little. Only if there are strong idiosyncratic circumstances in which regularity of sleep or of appetite conflicts with rigid expectations, will this be important. Should the history suggest such a possibility, direct inquiry will usually elicit an accurate reply, such as "I get so sleepy every night at 10 o'clock that I can't stay up and talk like the others do" or "My parents make a big fuss if I don't eat everything they put on my plate, but my appetite isn't the same every day, then they accuse me of filling up with junk food."

The use of the direct interview to obtain significant temperamental data in the older child and adolescent can be illustrated by two case vignettes.

Case 4

Theodora, age 9, was brought for consultation because of a rather dramatic symptom. One morning, her upper eyelashes had all fallen out and lay on her pillow. This had occurred once previously, and the parents had scolded her for pulling them out in retaliation for a refusal she had received the day before. They were confirmed in this opinion by the regrowth of the eyelashes to their former long and attractive state. When the symptom recurred, however, the parents consulted a dermatologist, who made the diagnosis of alopecia. He suggested that she have a psychiatric consultation with special emphasis on stress, as this has been identified as a precipitating factor in such cases. An immunologic deficiency is also present in such cases, but as this is not currently amenable to reversal, the psychiatric approach was more promising.

In taking the history, although the parents' guilt level was high because of their false accusation, in general their handling of Theodora and her brother Robert was positive. Theodora was, however, a difficult child to please. Highly intelligent and competent in many areas, she was superior in a number of ways to her brother, despite the fact that he too was above average in both intelligence and all-around abilities. Nevertheless, whatever Robert showed an interest in, Theodora was guaranteed soon to declare this as her own lifelong interest. When restrictions were placed on her special endeavors, she complained loudly and to all that she was deprived of activities just because these were reserved for her brother. In general, given a finger, Theodora demanded an arm, and stated and presumably felt grossly deprived. At times, guilty at so many refusals, the parents would give into a next request only to feel manipulated, as Theodora was not fully satisfied, and Robert had once again been put unfairly into second place. Furthermore, Theodora had few friends, about which she complained loudly and often. Accounts of sneaky actions and unfair reprisals by others abounded, with sophisticated Theodora giving reasons for their "jealousy" based on her superior performance. On occasions when one or another parent had intervened, and the entire story emerged, it appeared that, while Theodora's account of the other child's actions had been accurate, she had left out the essential element of her own initial provocation. The parents had become concerned about a growing feeling that they disliked the kind of person Theodora was, and wondered in turn whether this rejection was causative of the stress and alopecia. Even had this obvious symptom been absent, Theodora was clearly suffering from a severe adjustment disorder, which deserved therapeutic intervention.

Direct interview showed a highly attractive 9-year-old child, who was not affected by the absence of her upper eyelashes. Since Theodora was poised and spoke with superior choice of words and grasp of concepts, it was also easy to overlook the fact that her emotional developmental status was only at age level. In an earnest manner, Theodora recited her litany of complaints. Without knowledge of her overpriviledged status, one might easily assume her to be a highly deprived and discriminated against child. While mood was positive toward the examiner, in her accounts of how she had retaliated against her tormentors it soon emerged that a high proportion of her interactions were of adversary nature. She was quick to go to top authorities, phoning her mother and father at the drop of a hat, and reported their intervention on her behalf with complaisant self-righteousness. She had done this the previous summer at camp, saying, "Just like always, I was stuck with a bunch of kids who were all against me." She described phoning her parents to complain, and also going to the camp director after her counselor "wouldn't do anything." Theodora was not aware that the camp had requested that she not be reenrolled, although her brother Robert was most welcome. The high intensity of this youngster was very evident in the vigor with which she gave her complaints—and even on direct questioning, she could think of little positive to report. That her activity level was varied was evident in her categorization of preferred activities: sports, gymnastics, dramatics, singing, playing chess. Clearly, she made her triumphs evident to others with boasting of high intensity.

Although, from her account, Theodora moved into new situations rapidly and hence was a high approacher, her adaptation was slow and she usually found something to her dissatisfaction, or refused to go along with the general organization of the situation. Rhythmicity seemed not to be a factor, and its determination was unclear. Her threshold was low, with high sensitivity to touch, taste, and auditory discrimination and visual changes. From both watching her in play-room activities of her own choosing and listening to her dramatic accounts of events, it was clear that Theodora's distractibility was low and her persistence and attention span high.

It was possible to conclude that Theodora's tempermental attributes had played a significant role in her life being so full of stressful situations. Of equal significance was the fact that her talented and hard-working parents had a high sense of guilt at possibly having neglected her, especially after the dramatic symptom of alopecia had appeared. In fact this guilt was not justified in terms of their arrangements for specific times totally devoted to their two children and their easy communicative availability. Nevertheless, this guilt had potentiated the parental overintervention until they realized that the events for which they had been called had, for the most part, been initiated by their own daughter. Her capacities, too, played a part in this complex interplay of features. Had Theodora been less intelligent and less talented, the arenas of discontent might have been less and her private versions of events less sophisticated.

On the other hand, Theodora was herself distressed by certain features of her life; the moments of parental disapproval, her friendlessness, the constant feelings of being discriminated against. With these motivations present, her intelligence and intensity could be harnessed to the therapeutic task. She was a colleague whose high intelligence and low threshold could be used now in the service of genuine scrutiny of her own actions and how these made others feel— imparting understanding of the reasons for their dislike of her. While initially such a therapeutic program would hardly decrease the stress and provide a quick cure for the alopecia, in the end stressful situations could become fewer. To avoid stress altogether for such a child would be to reinforce the incipient child tyrant characteristic and the consequent destructive course.

Temperamentally, Theodora's striking characteristics were her marked intensity, frequent negative mood expressions, and her slow adaptability. These are the attributes that make up the difficult temperament constellation, together with irregularity and initial withdrawal tendencies, which were not evident in Theodora's case. Her parents confirmed that she had shown these tendencies to negative mood, high intensity, and slow adaptability from infancy onward. It also became clear in reviewing this history of Theodora's development that her father had always appeased her to put an end to her loud insistent demands, and that her mother had vacillated between appeasement and the setting of rigid limits that never worked. The end result of this type of poorness of fit between the child's temperament and the parental handling was the creation of a veritable child tyrant. Inevitably, however, Theodora found that the tactics of intimidation and manipulation that were so successful in achieving her immediate wishes within the family did not work outside the home. On the contrary, they boomeranged and made her school and social life stressful and frustrating, with serious alienation from her peer group. She could only respond with a projective defensive response, in which her problems and difficulties were blamed on everyone else.

In spite of this projective defense, Theodora was herself sufficiently distressed by the unfavorable course of her life to be motivated to reach out for the psychotherapeutic help offered her. With this motivation, buttressed by her high intelligence and many talents and by her parents' serious commitment to her welfare, her prognosis with therapy was favorable. And, indeed, treatment was highly successful, using a combination of direct psychotherapy and parent guidance.

Case 5

Zachary, age 17, had been brought by his parents who were deeply concerned about his future. Now in his junior year of high school, Zack had had an entire school history of marginal grades. Passing his subjects and being promoted from grade to grade had been achieved with a steady diet of parental admonition, rules, and disciplinary action over homework assignments, tutoring often several times a week, pep talks from teachers, and ominous warnings that failure to go on to a higher education was the road to a low level of employment and poverty. Zack was highly resentful of the interview, clearly being wary of still one more probing experience.

After telling Zack that I was aware of and interested in the disagreements between himself and his parents, and that I knew that he had problems in learning, I began by trying to find out what his actual interests and desires were for the future. "If everything could work out just the way you wanted, what will you be doing 10 years from now; when you are 17?" Zack's reply started "You think that———" I stated mildly, "I really am only asking you a question, I'm not trying to trip you up. Take your time—and tell me what you really want to be, not what you think you ought to want to be." Again, his answer was heavily laden with, "You think I don't care———." Finally, after a number of such comments had convinced me that they would go on this way indefinitely unless I really obtained Zack's attention to my genuine interest in his opinions, I said, "If you would listen to what I said, you could disagree with me better." Zack started in his usual way, then there was a double take—"What did you say?" I repeated my statement, then said, "I think you have been brainwashed so much that you expect all people to be saying the same thing. I haven't really said anything yet, I only want to be sure I understand your opinions. Let's start again." And when I repeated my query as to his aims, Zack began to try to put his sense of helplessness into words, with occasional lapses into the expectation that I would warn him of doom ahead, as everyone else did. As I caught him up on these projections of his own feelings on to me, he saw the point of what he was doing, and these lapses became a joke between us.

Zack declared that he wanted to be an artist, and inquiry showed that he had indeed persevered moderately in sketching objects and people and was deeply resentful that his requests to be given art lessons had been linked with his first succeeding academically, so that his wish had not been granted. I said, "Let's take a look at schoolwork from the beginning. From talking to you, I think that you are smart, so that can't be the reason for having trouble learning. And you have tried hard, so that's not the reason. There must be another." From this point on, we explored in detail his early school learning experiences. It became clear that he was a late reader and had been plagued by reversals of letters and their sequences, and by poor marks in spelling. Increasing discouragement then led to a growing avoidance of academic work. Homework had clearly poisoned his life. Since his parents' philosophy was that he get his homework out of the way before going to play, and since it dragged on throughout the afternoon and evening, in fact he was cut off from recreation on school days altogether.

The evidence pointed to an undiagnosed learning disability as the cause of Zack's problems, and this was confirmed by psychological testing. In his case, his temperamental attributes had served to ameliorate his psychological difficulties. His mood was predominantly positive, his intensity of expression was relatively mild, and he adapted quickly to new people and places. With these characteristics, he was quickly at ease in nonacademic situations and made friends easily. Outside of academic tasks, he showed moderate persistence and attention span and low distractibility, which were evident in his determination to pursue his artistic interests. His other temperamental attributes were not remarkable.

His parents accepted the diagnosis, with deep chagrin at their midjudgment of their son. A treatment strategy of remedial work was formulated, for which his temperamental characteristics became a valuable asset.

TEMPERAMENT DATA IN ADULT LIFE

In early childhood, the delineation of temperament individuality is relatively simple. The other major categories of behavior—abilities and talents (the *what* of behavior), and motivations and goals (the *why* of behavior)—are uncomplicated in their scope and expression, and easy to distinguish from temperament (the *how* of behavior.) As the child grows older, however, the task of identifying and categorizing these separate elements of behavior becomes more and more complex. Increasingly elaborate repertoires of abilities and talent mature, become evident, and increasingly influence the developmental course. Motivational patterns become conceptualized as brain functioning develops and matures, as life experiences become cumulative in their effects, and as coping and psychodynamic mechanisms become elaborated. Motivations, abilities, and temperament enter into increasingly complex interactional processes, so that individual items and patterns of behavior begin to reflect this interplay of influences. Thus, it may be relatively easy to determine whether slow achievement in task performance in a child, such as self-feeding and self-dressing, is due primarily to short attention span and low persistence, immaturity in neuromuscular or perceptual development, avoidance because of anxiety, or a simple combination of these factors. In an adult, by contrast, the isolation of the factor or combination of factors responsible for slowness in task achievement at work may be much more difficult.

The problem of identifying and rating temperament in the adult is further compounded by the increasing variation in activities of all kinds that emerges as individuals grow older. In the early years of life, there is similarity and comparability in the major activities and environmental demands and expectations at any age-period. There are, of course, variations depending on the sociocultural group, such as the age of toilet training, expectations for level of self-care, attendance at nursery school, the nature of the school environment, and so on. But for each group, protocols for temperament can be developed that cover the important areas of behavior and sequences of new demands and expectations. Scoring criteria can also be standarized with relative ease.

By the time an individual is an adult, however, similarity and comparability of behavior are increasingly replaced by differences and individual variation. Athletic activities, hobbies and other special interests, social life, special school schedules, and work experiences all become diversified in their form and content and prominence in the individual's life, and protocols and scoring criteria for temperament become quite complex for the adult as compared to the child.

The clinician, therefore, does not have a simple systematic interview protocol for the determination of temperament, as in the childhood years. The clinician must rather proceed with open-ended questions empirically and qualitatively. However, this process of inquiry is essentially similar methodologically to the process by which motivations and psychodynamic defenses are identified in any individual case. Whether it is for the identification of temperament, motivations, or psychodynamic defenses, behavioral data are required that will include the individual's expressions of attitudes, feelings, and thoughts, as well as his or her reports of concrete descriptive items of behavior. This is supplemented by the clinician's own observations of the patient's behavior in their diagnostic and therapeutic sessions. Inasmuch as any one situation or context from which data are gathered may be typical or atypical, information from a number of incidents and situations is required. Such a line of inquiry will usually provide the data for the delineation of not only temperament, or motivational patterns, or psychodynamic patterns, but of all three, as well as the relationship of each to the others.

Thus, for example, an individual reports that she reacts with intense anger to criticism and avoids situations where such criticism is likely, in the subject's estimation, to occur. The clinician confirms this report in his or her own observations of the patient's response to an implied criticism in the therapeutic sessions. This behavior may reflect the temperamental attribute of intensity of emotional reactions and initial withdrawal responses to uncomfortable new situations. Or it may reflect a vulnerability to criticism based on some neurotic need for perfection, coupled with a defensive strategy of avoiding situations in which possible imperfections may be revealed. To determine which factor or combination of factors is operating will require data on the subject's intensity of reaction and initial type of behavioral involvement in a variety of situations in which the patient is clear that she is not being and will not be criticized. Pertinent information in this regard can come not only from the patient's reports, but also from the clinician's observation of the patient's behavior in their various sessions together.

To take another example, an individual may report that she has difficulty sitting still and concentrating on work because of the conversation and movements of other people working in the same office. This problem may reflect the temperamental attribute of either distractibility or high activity level with restlessness while sitting still for any length of time, or both. Or the worker may have anxiety regarding work competence, or may be preoccupied with the judgments superiors will make on the finished products, and as a result the subject may be unable to concentrate effectively on tasks. Data on level of distractibility and activity in other situations—social, athletic, spectator experiences, and so forth—as well as ability to concentrate when competence is not being evaluated, will serve to make the differential diagnosis.

It is our impression that temperament and its functional significance in the adult, as well as in the older child and adolescent, are most often overlooked because of a one-sided attention to motivational factors. As a result, the misjudgment of behavior as exclusively motivational in origin is an all-too-frequent occurrence in clinical practice, on the part of both patient and practitioner. Patients constantly formulate explanations of the obscurities of their own behavior, and that of other people with whom they are involved, in terms of some underlying intention. This reflects a common human tendency to assume that any behavioral phenomenon is the result of some purpose and goal. Even the functioning of animals and plants is commonly designated by reference to motivation. A bee "seeks" food in a flower, a caged bird "wants" its freedom, the roots of a plant spread out "in search" of water. All too often, when the therapist challenges the patient's interpretation, it is not to call into question the motivational bias, but to present an alternative purpose and goal as the "correct" explanation. This is not to question in any way the vital significance of goals and purposes in shaping human behavior. The challenge is rather to the automatic assumption that all is motivation, that one need seek no further to explain the meaning of any item of behavior. It would be just as one-sided and inadequate to ascribe all behavior to the nonmotivational factor of temperament. Both purpose and temperament, as well as talents and ability, shape behavior. In some cases one factor may be most significant, in other cases it may be another, and in many instances all three play a part in a mutually influential interactional process.

It is indeed impressive, and we have experienced this many times in clinical practice, once the possibility of the contribution of temperament to the patient's behavior is considered, how often the same data which had been given an exclusively motivational explanation, can be re-interpreted and re-evaluated. And once this is done, additional lines of inquiry come easily to mind that can establish accurately the origins and dynamics of the patient's troublesome behavior.

TEMPERAMENT DATA FROM QUESTIONNAIRES

The clinician obtains historical data on past and current functioning primarily by direct interview techniques with the patient, the parents, or both. In a face-to-face interview, it is possible to explore in detail those areas that appear, from the informant's initial responses, to be most relevant to the problem under consideration. Nuances and subtleties of attitudes, feelings, and ideas can also be identified, as well as contradictions among different statements and reports, all of which may provide valuable clues to the clinician. Finally, in a direct interview, any confusion or misunderstanding that the informant may have as to the meaning of a specific question can be identified on the spot and corrected.

These advantages of the interview method apply to the gathering of temperament data equally as with other aspects of the behavioral and physical history. It is for the reason that we ourselves used a direct semistructured interview technique with the parents of our longitudinal studies, and derived our temperamental categories and patterns from an analysis of these interview protocols (see Appendix A). Interview methods, however, are time-consuming. This is especially true for research purposes, which usually require the conversion of the narrative interview record and the qualitative clinical judgments into quantitative ratings that can be subjected to statistical analyses.

For these reasons, a number of questionnaires have been developed to rate temperament at various age-periods and have been and are being widely used at many research centers. These questionnaires have the advantage over the interview method that the data can be obtained quickly and scored quantitatively immediately. For research purposes, this economy of time in administration and ratings makes the questionnaire technique practical in any study involving a large number of subjects. For the clinician, concerned with an individual patient or family, these advantages of questionnaires do not outweigh their limitations as compared to the direct interview method. There may be occasions, however, when a clinician may wish to make use of a temperament questionnaire, such as in a clinical research study of a special population. Out of the many different questionnaires those developed by Dr. William Carey and associates for the various age-periods of childhood, by Dr. Richard Lerner and associates for the adolescent period, and by ourselves for the 3- to 7-year-old age-period and for early adult life, follow the NYLS categorical scheme most clearly.[1] No temperament questionnaires have as yet developed for the later age-periods of adult life.

---

1. These questionnaires, together with instructions for scoring, can be obtained by writing directly to Dr. Carey, Dr. Lerner, or ourselves. Dr. Carey's address is: Dr. William B. Carey, 319 West Front Street, Media, Pennsylvania 19063. Dr. Lerner's address is: Dr. Richard M. Lerner, College of Human Development, Pennsylvania State University, University Park, Pennsylvania 16802. Drs. Stella Chess and Alexander Thomas's address is: New York University Medical Center, Department of Psychiatry, 550 First Avenue, New York, New York 10016.

OTHER SOURCES OF TEMPERAMENT DATA

In some instances, the clinician may find it desirable to supplement
the temperament data that has been obtained from the parents and
child by querying teachers or other adults familiar with certain aspects
of the child's behavior. For example, the parents may be so anxious,
or so much in conflict with each other, that only limited objective
descriptive details of the child's behavior that appear reliable can be
obtained from them. The playroom session or direct interview with the
child, in some cases, may be sufficient to clarify the vagueness, ambiguities, or contradictions of the parents' history. In other instances
however, the data obtained from the child may only partially illuminate an important issue, such as the character of the child's adaptability to new people and new demands over time. In these cases it may be
very useful to obtain a teacher's description of the child's behavior in
the specific area or areas that require further clarification. Occasionally, another adult, such as a relative or close friend of the family who
has been in a position to observe the child's functioning in detail, may
be available to give an objective description of specific aspects of the
child's temperamental style. Also, if the child has had psychological
testing, the psychologist may be able to provide useful information on
activity level, approach/withdrawal, adaptability, intensity, quality of
mood, distractibility, and persistence and attention span, as these
attributes were manifested during the testing situation.

In adults, the clinician may also find it desirable in some cases to
supplement the data obtained directly from the patient, whether it
pertains to temperament or other aspects of behavioral functioning. If
another person is available for interview who is close to the patient,
such as a spouse or long-term friend, this may provide a valuable
source of additional information for the clinician.

It should be borne in mind that any individual's temperament,
just as with motivational patterns, talents, or general personality
traits, may not be expressed identically in different life situations or
with different people. These different aspects of psychologic organization, in other words, show both consistency from one situation to
another, and modifiability by the special influences exerted by certain
environmental settings. Thus, a child may be intensely reactive temperamentally, but may show this characteristic more openly in a permissive home environment than in a formal structured schoolroom. Or, a
youngster's positive mood may be more evident in a playgroup or in
school than in a stressful home setting characterized by violent paren-

tal bickering. For this reason, the clinician may obtain conflicting reports from different sources of information, and will have to assess the significance of the contradictory data. Such an assessment can in itself provide valuable clues for a diagnostic evaluation, such as the indication that the home or the school is an etiologically significant source of stress.

SUMMARY

A central theme of this chapter is that clinicians do not have to engage in a special esoteric hunt to identify extremes of specific temperamental characteristics that may influence significantly the origins and evolution of the behavior problems for which they have been consulted. Rather, such temperamental data become evident in the course of the clinician's diagnostic and therapeutic activities, just as other procedures serve to illuminate other functionally significant aspects of the patient's psychologic organization and environment. Further specific questioning will usually be needed to confirm initial impressions and to determine the full extent of the influence of temperament on the patient's psychologic development. In this regard, the analysis of the role of temperament is essentially the same as that of any other functionally significant variable.

The clinician may also draw upon a number of sources of data, as detailed in this chapter. This makes it possible to correct ambiguities or distortions resulting from consulting any single source, and thus enables the clinician to make a comprehensive and accurate evaluation of the patient's temperament.

CHAPTER 10

Prevention and Treatment: General Considerations

In the previous chapters of this volume, we have commented on a number of issues of prevention and treatment, as they applied to specific cases and specific types of interactional patterns. In this chapter we will recapitulate and expand on these comments to make for a systematic presentation of the clinician's sensitivity to the issue of temperamental individuality in the prevention and treatment of behavior disorders.

An initial caveat is in order, which is implied and even explicitly stated in earlier chapters of this book and in our previous writings. In no way are we suggesting that clinicians or educators who use the concept of temperament actively with their families, patients, or students will have found a magical formula for the effective prevention and treatment of all the problems that come their way. In some cases temperament, as it interacts with environmental demands and expectations, plays a major and even decisive role; in other instances, temperament is of substantial importance in combination with other influential factors; in still other cases, temperament plays a minor or even insignificant role. And even in those individuals in whom temperamental issues must be considered seriously by the clinician, the specific dynamic interplay among temperament, other characteristics of the person, and the significant features of the environment will vary from subject to subject. This should be no surprise, as the same formulation applies to all other characteristics of the individual or the environment. The developmental effect of intellectual level, whether subnormal, average, or superior, or of a special talent or skill, or lack of it, or of the same parental attitudes, practices, goals, and ambitions for their children—all exert their influence differently with different children.

Behavioral outcomes are multidetermined and no single rule can fit all circumstances and all sequences.

GOODNESS OF FIT AS A CARDINAL PRINCIPLE

The goodness of fit concept does provide clinicians with a general model which they can apply to the multidimensional and multidetermined behavioral patterns in their individual patients. The clinician's analysis of the specific nature of the mismatch between the child's temperament or other characteristics and the demands and expectations of the environment gives the information necessary to formulate a strategy for prevention and treatment.

PARENT EDUCATION

As with so many other issues pertaining to the child's health, parent education regarding the nature and meaning of temperament can be a valuable preventative measure. With regard to their child's temperament, it is helpful for parents, and especially for parents with their first child, to know the following key facts: (1) Babies are born with different styles of behavior, just as they are born with different physical temperament. (2) These behavioral differences show themselves in various ways—in the regularity of sleep and feeding schedules, in the way the baby reacts to anything new, in how quiet or active his muscular movements are, how easily the baby adapts to any change, how much he cries, how loud the cry is and how expressive the baby's smile and laughter are, how sensitive the baby is to loud noises, bright light, and rough clothing, how easily he can be distracted, and how persistent in sticking to any activity. (3) The differences in any of these behaviors are all normal, even though some may make for easier management of the child's daily routines, while others make for more difficult management. If the parent is worried that the baby's behavior is so extreme that it does not seem normal, then the child's doctor should be contacted. (4) The parents should not try to change their baby's typical style of behavior to one they would prefer or that would seem to be more desirable for the baby. Such an attempt can only put the infant under great stress. On the other hand, as children grow older, it may be possible for them to understand their own behavior and on their own to modify the undesirable aspects of their particular respective temperaments. (5) Parents should not expect that they can find one simple set of rules that will work best for all children. Child-care practices that are effective with some children may not be so with others, depending on their temperament. If the parents are in doubt as to the best approach for their child, they should consult their pediatrician or nurse, or ask the child's grandparents or other experienced parents whose judgment they can trust. But parents should beware of advice that is given as a cookbook recipe, in the form of rules that are "guaranteed" to work with any child. (6) Above all, parents should not assume that if their infant cries more than other babies, or if they are having any other difficulties with their caretaking activities, that this must mean that they are incompetent or psychologically disturbed parents. This is sometimes the case, but it is much more likely that, with the best intentions in the world, they have not worked out on their own the best approach to their child with his particular temperamental characteristics. Or, it is also quite possible that even if they are sensitive and competent caretakers, that, even with the best of handling, their child will sleep irregularly, cry more than other babies, and have a difficult time adjusting to any new situation.

Not all parents require a systematic review of all these issues from the clinician. Those with temperamentally easy children may find their caretaking responsibilities relatively so easy and pleasant that they may not require any reassurance. They may even take all the credit for their infant's benign course, and in such cases the question arises as to whether the clinician should challenge this judgment of the parents. There is certainly no hard and fast rule in this regard. If the parents have had any substantial degree of uncertainty or anxiety regarding their competence as caretakers, it may be wise for the clinician to allow them to bask in what seems like the dramatic evidence of their success in the parental role. And actually the parents are not entirely wrong in the credit they give themselves. Even with the temperamentally easy child, a smooth and positive developmental course depends not on the child's temperament alone, but on the interplay between the child's characteristics and the parents' attitudes and practices, as well as other environmental influences. However, the easy quiet adaptability of the easy child is not always optimum under all circumstances. Therefore, the clinician should be alert to this possibility, and if a problem arises, to be ready to identify for the parents the role played by the child's temperament. Otherwise, such parents are all too likely to swing from self-congratulation to self-condemnation for being "responsible" for the child's disturbance.

Parental distress and self-doubt may arise in another way in such parents with a first easy child whose self-esteem is bound up with the outward and immediate evidence of their success as parents. If their second infant is, by contrast, of difficult temperament and "unhappy" and "dissatisfied" so much of the time, such parents may either decide that they are really not good parents, that their "success" with their first baby was a fluke, or else conclude that this second baby must be pathologic in some way. If they have read the popular psychoanalytic literature, they are even likely to decide that they must be rejecting this second child, based on some deep unfathomable unconscious reason. Here, again, it is important for the clinician to step in quickly to reorient the parents.

Other parents, even those with temperamentally difficult infants, may have enough objectivity and self-confidence, especially if buttressed by their own personal observations of the wide range of behavior in normal infants, so that they work out empirically on their own what the best caretaking tactics are for each of their children. Here, the clinician's role is an easy one, primarily to confirm the parents' observations and conclusions. Even here, of course, there may be special situations or unexpected stressful events that leave the parents bewildered and uncertain as to the best way to manage the issue. If this happens, the clinician can certainly be helpful in identifying for the parents the reason why their child, with his given temperament, is behaving in an apparently unpredictable and undesirable manner, and in advising them as to the best strategy for handling this special situation.

Then there are the parents who struggle unsuccessfully or with only partial success in achieving a goodness of fit with one or another aspect of their child's temperament. Usually, when they seek professional counseling the parents present the problem in terms of specific behavioral symptoms that are worrisome—the child keeps them up at night with frequent night-awakening and crying; he cries whenever they take him to a store to get new shoes or new clothes; the teacher reports that the child does not participate socially with his classmates; they can't take him on an automobile ride lasting more than an hour because he gets so restless and fussy, and so forth. Here the clinician must first determine whether these symptoms reflect some type of psychopathology, such as an organic brain syndrome or a pathologic hyperative syndrome. If, however, it is clear that the difficult behavior is the result of a poorness of fit between the child's temperament and parental handling and/or other inappropriate environmental influences, then a strategy of parent guidance with or without direct treatment in addition is indicated. The specifics of therapeutic modalities, where temperament is one of the major issues, are detailed in Chapters 11 and 12.

THE PEDIATRICIAN AND THE PEDIATRIC NURSE

The pediatrician and the pediatric nurse are the professionals who are usually in the best position to educate parents appropriately as to the concept of temperament and its significance for the child's development. They are the clinicians who get to know the parents and their children under circumstances of health and illness, of smooth behavioral functioning by parent and child, and of periods of disturbed behavior on the part of either or both. The role of the pediatrician in parent education and counseling with regard to temperamental issues is reviewed comprehensively by Dr. Carey in Chapter 14, and only a few additional comments are indicated at this point.

As Dr. Carey indicates, affixing a label to the child should be avoided if at all possible. This is true whether the designation specifies a temperamental category or constellation, or some other behavioral pattern. A label all too often develops a life of its own. A statement to a parent that "you have a normal child, but he is a distractible child" may appear to the speaker to mean the same as saying, "You have a normal child, and he has a tendency to shift his attention from what he is doing if somebody new comes on the scene, or he sees a new toy or gadget at the other end of the room." But the label "distractible child," by its very shorthand quality, can fix in many parents' minds the idea that their child is somehow different in some permanent inherent way. The label, whether it be "distractible child," "high-activity child," "slowly adaptable child," and so on, may have a positive effect in clarifying for the parents a number of different and hitherto puzzling aspects of the child's behavior. With this conceptualization, the parents may then be more receptive to the suggestion that if they change their attitudes and handling of the child in certain specific ways, this will be very helpful to the youngster. On the other hand, they may reify the designation, regard it as a diagnosis of abnormality just because the behavior can be given a label, begin to explain all the child's behavior on that basis ("There he is being distractible again," "He always adapts so slowly"), even when some or many items of the child's behavior do not warrant the label. A self-fulfilling prophecy is then in the making, in which the behavior begins to be influenced by the label.

This dilemma of what to tell the parents is especially acute in the case of the temperamentally difficult child. We picked the term "the difficult child" as an apt designation for one group of infants in the NYLS sample. As we took sequential narrative histories from their parents regarding the behavior of the children in the various routines of daily life, as well as their reactions to special situations and events, it was dramatically evident that these infants were the most difficult group for their parents to nurture and manage. This was not due to any pathology in the children or any gross mismanagement by their parents, but rather to a specific combination of temperamental attributes. Not wishing to manufacture one neologism or another to designate these children, we chose the label that described their impact on their caretakers—"the difficult child." We, and others, have found this designation to be helpful to many parents struggling to manage their intensely reactive babies with irregular sleep and hunger patterns, who also were distressed by most new stimuli or situations and then adapted only slowly. It tells the parent that their special difficulties are not their fault. It also tells them that their child is basically normal and with patient quiet and consistent handling will flourish as well as any other youngsters.

But any label that is used to bring together a set of separate behaviors into one conceptualization, no matter how useful and even necessary this is, will always present problems of precision of meaning and breadth of its implications. Children can be difficult for caretakers to manage because of other temperamental qualities at one age or another. Also, not all parents are bothered by the same aspects of the difficult child's behavior. Some are especially distressed by the child's loud and prolonged crying, but not by his slow adaptation; other parents have the reverse reactions. Parents who lead highly structured and scheduled lives themselves may find their child's irregular patterns very disruptive; other parents with loose and even irregular schedules of their own may not find their baby's irregularity a problem. Furthermore, the difficulties in management that the difficult child presents are difficulties in our culture, with its specific standards, values, and goals in child-rearing. In other cultures, with different child-rearing approaches and expectations, parents may not find this particular constellation of temperamental characteristics to present the same difficulty as it does in our culture (Korn & Gannon, 1983; Super & Harkness, 1981). Finally, it can be argued that the label "difficult child" is a pejorative term, and that, no matter how it is explained to the parents, they may interpret it as a judgment that there is something basically wrong with the youngster. Or, they may lay all the caretaking burdens and problems that may arise on this label. "After all, how can we do any better. The doctor has told us he was born a difficult child."

The issue is not with the concept itself of the temperamentally difficult child. This formulation has proven its value in clinical practice and in developmental research studies (Thomas, Chess, & Korn, 1982). The question is rather if, when, and how parents should be told that they have a difficult child. Certainly, no useful purpose is served by such a statement if the parents are functioning effectively as caretakers, do not feel that their child is excessively difficult to manage, and the child himself is showing a positive developmental course. As Carey (1982) has reported, a number of parents rate their child as difficult on discrete items of behavior, but yet perceive the child as generally average or even easy. We have observed the same phenomenon in some of the difficult children in the NYLS. Whatever the reason for this discrepancy in parental reports of their child's behavior and their overall perception, as long as the child is functioning well, no good can come from telling the parent, "Look here, from your own description, you really have a difficult child and not an easy one."

If the parents of a difficult child come for consultation because of a problem in only one or two areas of caretaking, here the clinician can discuss the one specific temperamental issue and what is required for a goodness of fit, without using the overall label of a difficult child. If, however, the problem behavior is more extensive, and the parents are caught up in unfavorable reactions of guilt, anxiety, or resentment, with the danger of an escalating pathogenic parent–child interaction, then the situation is different. In order for parent guidance or other therapy to be effective, the clinician will have to spell out the diagnostic evaluation, which will necessarily include an explanation of the concept of difficult temperament. It is always helpful in such cases to emphasize the positive aspects of the child's temperament, and not only its contribution to the development of the problem behavior. "He cries loudly, but this same intensity gives him a quality of lustiness and zestfulness when he is happy; he adapts slowly, which can make for problems, but this also means that he won't be a pushover with other children."

These same considerations are applicable to the issue of other temperamental labels as well as that of the difficult child. These labels should be avoided if possible when discussing the child's behaviorial style characteristics with the parents. This can be done especially when the particular temperamental attribute is not extreme, and the problem at issue is still at an early stage. One can then use phrases such as "Your child has a tendency to be uncomfortable in a new situation, but if you give him enough time he will get over it without any harm done," or "Your youngster learns quickly, but he does best if he can take a short break periodically." However, as with the difficult child, if the poorness of fit between the child's temperament and the parents' handling is severe and the child's functioning has already been significantly impaired, then the therapeutic management will require spelling out the specific details of the child's temperament. In such a situation, the parents have in fact been labeling the child, but pejoratively, whether they are reacting to the youngster as "stubborn," "willfully disobedient," "lacking in will-power," and the like. The clinician has the task of persuading the parents that they have been mislabeling their child, and to change this to the correct label.

OTHER APPROACHES TO PARENT EDUCATION

It is our definite impression that an increasing number of clinicians are discussing issues of temperament in childhood from preventative viewpoints with the families under their care. This impression stems from numerous anecdotal personal communications. These have not been as yet reported in the professional literature (though there have been numerous articles in popular magazines and newspapers), except for our own publications and those of William Carey (1981, 1982).

Several child psychiatrists and pediatricians have been utilizing group sessions with parents (including fathers as well as mothers). This should be a most useful strategy especially for first parents, which reassures them that their child's apparently idiosyncratic behavioral style is not so unusual, and gives them useful hints from other parents who have handled similar behavioral difficulties successfully.

In at least one natural childbirth class for parents during the pregnancy period that we know of, the leader of the group includes a discussion of temperament and its significance during the last trimester of the pregnancy. This is an especially favorable time for such an orientation for parents expecting their first baby. The six issues we have enumerated earlier in this chapter under the subheading Parent Education can be discussed at a time when parents are not confused, anxious, or defensive about any unexpected behavioral pattern that may arise after the actual birth of the baby.

Dr. James Cameron and his associates (Cameron & Rice, in press) have developed an original approach to the issue of preventative parent counseling with regard to infant temperament. A selected group of parents filled out the Carey Infant Temperament Questionnaire (Carey & McDevitt, 1978) when their infants were 4 months of age, and temperament ratings established based on the questionnaire responses. The infant's pediatrician was provided with a copy of the temperament profile. The parents were divided into two-groups—"no guidance" and "guidance." No counseling was undertaken for the no guidance group. The parents in the guidance group were given anticipatory guidance, tailored to the temperament ratings. That is, they were advised as to the problem behavior areas that were most likely to develop in subsequent months, and advised as to the optimal method of handling such problems. Follow-up when the infants were 8–12 months of age suggested that the predictive value of such counseling was sufficient to warrant its use in clinical settings. The parents' response to this program was generally positive, especially for first-time parents or those with active, slowly adaptive infants. This strategy of preventative anticipatory intervention appears especially suitable for large-scale pediatric units, such as public health clinics or group health maintenance organizations, and further trials of its potential usefulness appear justified.

STAFF EDUCATION

Burks and Rubenstein (1985) have reported a program utilizing the concept of temperamental individuality in a St. Louis children's institution which provides residential care for children who cannot be taken care of by their parents or by the foster-parent system. In this program, which they have just initiated, group sessions are held with all the staff who are in contact with the same group of children. The goal of these sessions is to give the staff an orientation to the issue of temperamental individuality, demonstrate to the staff how they can recognize each child's temperament and then use this knowledge in their therapeutic and educational work with the children. It is too early in the program for Burks and Rubenstein to have any definitive findings to report, but their initial impressions are optimistic.

THE GOALS OF PREVENTION

As suggested in a number of previous chapters, especially Chapters 2 and 3, the parents should not use their knowledge of the child's temperament to insulate him against all situations of stress and discomfort wherever this is possible. Goodness of fit does not necessarily mean an absence of stress for the child. New demands, new opportunities, and new expectations arise inevitably as the child grows older, as do unexpected and unanticipated events and challenges. The struggle to master the new may in some instances and for some children be an easy effort without any appreciable stress. In other instances and for other children, the struggle for mastery may be difficult and stressful. However, if the new demand is consonant with the child's characteristics and capacities, then expanded mastery, developmental progress, and a heightened sense of self-esteem will occur, and the struggle will have constituted a healthy experience for the child. For the parent to attempt to insulate the child from such situations or to dilute in some fashion his struggle for mastery, will deny the child the opportunities for expanding social competence and self-confidence, and for sharpening his own techniques for coping with difficult challenges.

Thus, for example, if the parents of a slow-to-warm-up child restrict involvement with new situations—special excursions, birthday parties with strange children, transfer to a new and more desirable school, vacations at unfamiliar places, and so on—because they make the youngster uneasy and uncomfortable, this may minimize periods of distress for the child. But the price the youngster pays for this comfort is very high. He loses the chances for learning from new situations and experiences, fails to gain the confidence that such challenges can be mastered even if he or she is shaky at first, and is denied the opportunities to work out effective ways of coping with his initial discomfort with the new. Or, as another example, if the parents of a distractible child arrange homework time so that he will not be diverted by any extraneous stimuli, the youngster will probably complete the homework more quickly. But he will not have learned how to remind himself when distracted, how to be aware that this is happening, and how to pull attention back to an assigned task that has a deadline.

The issue of goodness of fit, therefore, does not rest on the absence of stress. Quite the contrary. Absence of stress, as in the examples above, may constitute a serious poorness of fit. New demands and stresses, when consonant with developmental potentials, are constructive in their consequences. It is *excessive* stress, stress that results from a demand made on the child which he is not capable of mastering, that leads to poorness of fit and maladaptive functioning. To take the examples in the previous paragraph, it is goodness of fit when the parents schedule new experiences for the slow-to-warm-up child one or at most a few at a time, and give the child time to adapt before letting him go on to another demanding new situation. It is poorness of fit when parents either try to restrict the child's involvement with the new altogether, or demand that he master a number of new expectations simultaneously and quickly. Similarly, it is a goodness of fit for the parents of a distractible child to remind the youngster that he has been distracted and it is now time to return to the homework. It is poorness of fit when they either try to insulate the child from all distractions, or, if he is distracted, to derogate and penalize him, and demand that he or she should be oblivious to all extraneous stimuli when doing homework or other important tasks.

CHAPTER 11

Parent Guidance

For the treatment of behavior disorders in childhood—comprising the diagnostic categories of adjustment disorder, conduct disorder, and anxiety disorders in the American Psychiatric Association (1980) *Diagnostic and Statistical Manual of Mental Disorders* (3rd ed.) (*DSM-III*) classification scheme—parent guidance holds a preeminent position both because of its effectiveness and efficiency. These are the disorders in which a significant degree of disturbance in behavioral function has resulted from a poorness of fit between the child's temperament and/or other characteristics and the demands and expectations of the environment. While in some cases the poorness of fit may involve other characteristics of the child, such as excessive demand for academic achievement beyond the youngster's intellectual capacities, in most cases it is a poorness of fit with the child's temperament which is a major or even decisive factor in the unfavorable course of psychologic development.

When it comes to serious childhood psychopathology, such as autism, childhood schizophrenia, or organic brain syndromes, parent guidance may also be of significant therapeutic value in ameliorating certain symptoms or abnormal behavioral patterns, though not with the same degree of effectiveness as in the children with behavior disorders (Arnold, 1978). In these more serious syndromes, temperamental characteristics may serve to exacerbate the problems created by the basic psychopathology. In such instances, counseling of the parents can be helpful by guiding them to minimize the poorness of fit between the child's temperament and environmental expectations. (See the discussion of this issue in Chapter 16, "Temperament and the Handicapped Child.")

THE PARENT AS A THERAPEUTIC ALLY

The basic goal of parent guidance as a treatment strategy for children with behavior disorders is to change specific aspects of the parents' actual functioning with their child. It does not attempt to change directly any covert parental attitudes or defense mechanisms that presumably might be causally related to their overt behavior and attitudes. Such an approach assumes that parental functioning that is detrimental to a child's psychologic functioning does not necessarily reflect the presence of deep-seated anxieties, conflict, or pathologic goals in the parent that must be changed by psychotherapy or other means before the child's disturbed behavior can be changed for the better. The parent's handling of the child may be pathogenic for various other reasons—ignorance or confusion as to the best approach to a child with a specific constellation of temperamental characteristics; anxiety, guilt, and/or resentment if the youngster's behavior does not correspond to the pattern that is presumed to be the only healthy one; unrealistic demands that do not take into account limitations in the child's characteristics and capacities; or bad advice from relatives, friends, or professional experts. This approach to parent guidance also assumes that even if the parent does have some significant degree of psychopathology, that this does not necessarily prevent him or her from making the specific changes in the behavior that has been proving detrimental to the child. As Anna Freud has put it, she "refuse[s] to believe that mothers need to change their personalities before they can change the handling of their child" (1960, p. 37).

We can put it that parent guidance aims to make the parents therapeutic allies in the treatment of their child, rather than to evaluate them as potential or actual adversaries because of their unfavorable effect on the child's psychologic welfare. It is the rare parent who does not really wish his or her child a healthy, happy and productive future, no matter whether the parents' current behavior is serving to promote or undermine this goal. It is this common concern of the clinician and parent for the child's welfare that makes it possible to enlist the parent as a therapeutic ally. And inasmuch as the parent's influence on the child is continuous and intimate from day to day, any significant degree of favorable change in the parent's attitudes and behavior is likely to have a powerful therapeutic effect on the child. When such a positive change is achieved, the necessity for long and expensive direct treatment of the child is avoided. And in cases where direct psychotherapy of the child is required, simultaneous parent guidance may expedite significantly the course of the child's treatment.

GUIDELINES FOR PARENT GUIDANCE

For parent guidance to be effective, it has to be individualized to each particular child and set of parents. Counseling in general global terms, such as a sterotypic prescription for "tender loving care" (TLC), is inadequate and may even be counterproductive. What is necessary, rather, is the identification of the specifics of the poorness of fit in each individual case, that is the specific features of child and environment which, in interaction with each other, are producing a poorness of fit and consequent psychopathologic development. (In line with the aims of this volume, the discussion of the child's characteristics will focus on temperament, though other attributes of the child, such as perceptual, cognitive, or motivational patterns, may also enter significantly into an unfavorable interaction with the environment and the development of a poorness of fit.)

The identification of the specifics of the poorness of fit in any individual case requires a systematic clinical study, as detailed in Chapter 9. Once this analysis is completed, the clinician can then undertake an informing interview with the parents, in which the concept of poorness of fit is spelled out. Whether the term itself is used with the parents is not vital. What is important is that they grasp the idea that the child's problem is not just within the child or within the parents. The child is not "bad" or "abnormal," and neither are the parents. It is the match between the parents' handling and the child's own characteristics that is at the root of the problem. The specific nature of the mismatch is then described in specific simple terms that can be readily understood by the parents. An outline of the overall plan by which this poorness of fit can be changed to a goodness of fit is then described, but the parents are counseled to start by changing only one or two items of behavior. They may make their own choice as to which items to select, or the clinician may suggest several. What is essential is that the parents understand clearly the nature of the behavior or behaviors that they are to change, that the new behavior be detailed in concrete descriptive terms, and that they appreciate the immediate consequences that may result from their altered behavior.

Thus, for example, a set of parents came for consultation because of their concern over their 4-year-old daughter Lisa's inability to make friends and her increasing social isolation. They had started her in nursery school several months before in the hope that this would help her, but the contrary had happened. Lisa cried each morning when her mother left her at the school, and the teacher reported after several weeks that she seemed unhappy and held back from participating in the group's activities. The teacher's judgment was that the girl was "immature and not yet ready for school," and advised that she be withdrawn, which the parents did. They described Lisa as "timid" and "fearful" when they took her on an outing or to a new vacation spot. They were especially bewildered by her behavior, as it contrasted so dramatically with the zestful quick involvement of their two older children in any new social setting. Feeling helpless in the face of their daughter's distress, they had tried to make life easier for her by keeping her away as much as possible from new situations where she would have to meet unfamiliar children or adults. But, at the same time, they knew this was no solution. How would she manage when she had to go to school? Would she never make friends? Was there some basic defect in her character that required psychiatric treatment? Only with one issue had the parents acted differently. Two years before they went out for the evening, leaving Lisa with a competent but strange babysitter. The girl cried bitterly when they left, and stayed up fussing until they returned. However, with this issue the parents felt they could not appease her, even though they felt guilty over this "selfishness," because otherwise their own social life would be compromised. They went out once or twice a week and used the same babysitter. To their astonishment, Lisa's crying grew less and less as the weeks went by, until finally she greeted the babysitter cheerfully, waved goodby with a smile to her parents as they left, and spent a pleasant evening until she went to bed at her regular time.

The clinical workup, including the parental history and Lisa's behavior in the playroom, showed a typical slow-to-warm-up temperamental pattern, with no evidence of psychopathology. The parents were assured that neither they nor Lisa were "to blame," and that only a change in handling was required. The concept of slow-to-warm-up temperament was explained to them in simple terms, using several examples from the parents' history, such as her initial negative reactions to several foods followed by gradual acceptance. Their experience with the babysitting issue was highlighted as the model for a new approach to Lisa. She was not to be isolated from everything new, for their fears over her future social incompetence would come true.

On the other hand, if they demanded too many new adjustments all at once, Lisa would be overwhelmed and would in fact become a fearful timid youngster. And they should use the experience with Lisa's baby-sitter as a model. In other words, they should expect that Lisa would become upset and unhappy with a new situation or new demand, but with repetition and quiet firm reassurance that it had to be this way, Lisa would slowly adjust until finally what was new and unpleasant became familiar and enjoyable.

The parents were dubious at such a simple diagnosis and remedy; at the same time that they were reassured by the evaluation of the absence of any need for direct psychotherapy. But they were ready and willing to follow the parent guidance strategy as outlined. They picked Lisa's participation in the neighborhood playground as their first effort. Sure enough, the first time Lisa clung to them and wanted to go home, and when the parents insisted that she must stay, she stood silently at the periphery of the group looking utterly miserable. The parents had to steel themselves just to sit quietly on a nearby bench and appear to ignore her. After an hour they took her home, and were surprised at her pleasant account of the other children's activities, in which she had not participated. On a second visit to the playground 3 days later, Lisa still did not participate, but appeared less unhappy and did not demand to be taken home. The next time she made tentative advances to take part in the ongoing game, and within a month's time she was an active, cheerful participant in the group, only fussing when told it was time to go home. The parents then enrolled her again in another nursery school where the same progression from the negative to the positive took place. Over the next year she became a gregarious, socially competent youngster with more than enough good friends. She did remain uncomfortable when facing any new group, but could accept her parents' prediction that this distress was temporary, and would begin to disappear after a few encounters with these strange children, adults, or places. Finally, she was able to say, "I guess I'm shy, but I'm not timid or afraid."

This was an ideal case for parent guidance. The clinical evaluation was clear, the symptoms were of recent origin, no complicating defense mechanisms had been elaborated, and the nature of the poorness of fit was evident, as were the changes in the parents' functioning that were required to alter the poorness to a goodness of fit. The parents were cooperative, and had no special psychologic needs or conflicts of their own which were antagonistic to Lisa's best interest. They grasped the concepts of temperament and goodness of fit quickly, and even though these were formulations quite different from what they had previously read and been told, they were ready to carry out this new therapeutic strategy completely as recommended. And the guidance sessions required were few in number—the original informing interview, a follow-up discussion 2 weeks later, another one the following month, and a final follow-up after 6 months.

In Lisa's case, as in all efforts at parent guidance, it was important, and sometimes imperative, that *both* parents participated in the guidance sessions. The mother and father did not grasp the concepts of temperament and poorness of fit with the same immediacy and logic. Each had different questions to ask about the specific changes to be initiated, and even had different interpretations of how they were to proceed. The confusions could be corrected with both parents present and attentive. With only one parent present, he or she would have had to carry the message home to the other parent, without the therapist's authority or skill in identifying and correcting misconceptions. And when this happens, the stage is set for parents to work at cross-purposes, so that the guidance strategy is carried through half-heartedly or even in a distorted way. Also, with both parents present, it is possible for the therapist to recognize that one parent may be resistant and even hostile to the guidance procedure and probe further for the meaning of such a negative response.

But, of course, parent guidance does not always go so easily or smoothly. Penicillin doesn't always work dramatically. Sometimes the problem is longstanding, and the original child temperament–parent handling and poorness of fit becomes complicated by the secondary elaboration of defense mechanisms by child or parent, or both, which produce additional disturbances and symptoms. Sometimes, an additional factor is present, such as unrecognized dyslexia or neurologic problems, that exacerbates and distorts the original poorness of fit issue. Sometimes, problems and symptoms of poorness of fit have developed, such as in the youngster's social life, over which the parents have little influence even if they change their own functioning. And, sometimes, the parents themselves are imprisoned by psychologic insecurities, rigid standards, goals, or moralistic values that make them unwilling or unable to make the changes that will relieve the youngster of excessive and inappropriate demands and expectations.

Let us detail one such case, in which various complicating factors made for only limited success with parent guidance, as valuable as even the modest success was.

THE BOY WHO RAN OUT OF THE OFFICE

Several years ago a father and mother came to consult one of us (S. C.) regarding their 10-year-old son Archie, who was their oldest child. The parents were in despair. The boy's behavior kept the family in continual turmoil and frustration, and with all this, he himself was clearly very unhappy. The recital of problems went on and on, but most basic was Archie's constant arguing, and his loud negative response to any request or demand. Every family excursion turned into a shambles, and even many ordinary routine events at home became contentious confrontations.

The father, a most competent and successful man in his profession, was full of anger at Archie's disruptive behavior. Most of all, he resented the degree of difficulty and distress that the boy's constant arguing gave to his wife. His anger led to many episodes of physical punishment of Archie, which were not only to no avail, but turned the father, in his own words, into an "abusing parent." For this, he was full of rage and guilt at himself, because he could not reconcile this behavior with his self-image as a humane and decent adult, and with his easy, enjoyable relationship with his daughter and younger son.

Archie's mother was in deep despair and at her wit's end. The boy frequently accused her of picking on him. In a way, she saw this as an accurate picture, as she did indeed scold and pressure him more than she did her other two children. However, her daughter and younger son were ready to carry out household routines with reasonable amiability and promptness, so there were few actual arguments with them and practically no confrontations. In fact, they complained, with reason, that Archie was often allowed to get away with his refusals when they were not.

With the 2 other children, special treats—such as relaxation of television rules—usually went smoothly. However, with Archie, any dispensation of a family rule led to subsequent loud argument by him that the limitation was now suspended forever. For this reason, the parents found themselves avoiding, to their great frustration and bitterness, many special excursions and other treats for the whole family, which were spoiled by the unpleasant aftermaths.

Most of all, these parents were troubled that Archie had so little enjoyment of life. He regularly got into arguments with playmates, and then returned home with complaints of how they picked on him. When his play was within earshot of the parents, both agreed that it did end that way, but that Archie was picked on because of his own behavior. He disputed ordinary decisions, held up the game, refused to let others use his bat or glove unless he got his own way, and the end result was that he was excluded from the game and unwelcome the next time.

There were problems in school also, although on standardized tests Archie usually achieved above average grades. Homework was a cause of daily contention. Archie argued that he should be allowed to watch television first and then do his homework, or that he could do both at the same time. He asserted that he had no math homework, or had forgotten what his English assignment was, or had remembered at bedtime that he did, after all, have a science test the next day. His teachers reported that he was contentious in class, or else withdrew his attention and seemed not to know what was going on. His above-average results on standardized tests was a puzzle to them, as there was little evidence from his daily academic activity that he was in fact learning much.

On the other hand, the parents also reported that there were occasions when Archie acted as if he were an entirely different personality. He could be solicitous for his mother's welfare, volunteered for and carried through special tasks, and showed a lively sense of humor and ebullient spirit, which charmed the rest of the family. At such times, the parents hoped this was the "real Archie" showing itself. But as time went on, these attractive features and episodes grew less and less frequent, and the parents began to dread that the "real Archie" was characterized by his argumentative, contentious, disruptive, and negative behavior.

Over the years the parents had consulted a number of psychiatrists, starting when Archie was 3 years old. The first reassured them that Archie was essentially a normal child, but that play therapy was required; also psychiatrists told Archie's parents that they should use more TLC in handling their son. Unable to explain play therapy to a 3-year-old, and failing themselves to comprehend its focus, Archie's parents took no further action at that time. A consultation several years later, as problems multiplied, was handled with widely spaced discussions because of the psychiatrist's busy schedule. These were "helpful," but discussions were focused on a search for early trauma as the causative factor, and no such factors were identified. Along with a recommendation for psychoanalytic treatment, this psychiatrist supplied several names of specialists. Archie's parents consulted each, and in turn felt that the approach did not fit the actual situation. Prolonged intensive psychotherapy 4 times a week was the prescription. Archie had firmly declared after each single session that he would not go again. How then would there be results with a child attending only as a result of physical coercion, even if were possible to get him there? As to TLC, they felt that they had approached all their children with tender love and care, and that their other children were thriving; therefore, if Archie was not, another factor must be at work. And, in any case, how could they manufacture an additional dose of TLC? It was not like a prescription to be filled in a drugstore. They waited it out again, trying their best on their own.

The parents had only been spared a consultation with a psychiatrist who was in favor of the extreme brand of family therapy. Otherwise, they would have been told that Archie's symptoms showed, not that he was sick, but that the family as a unit was sick. Archie, in such an ideological scheme, would only become the family scapegoat, only the vehicle through which the family pathology was showing itself. Treatment for the whole family as a unit would be required. If Archie then refused to come, that was too bad, but the rest of the family— father, mother, daughter, and younger son—still would have to come, and their treatment would heal the family's sickness, and with this Archie would have a chance to blossom. Who knows how the parents would have responded. In their distress they might have agreed, and spent innumerable hours with the psychiatrist searching for hidden pearls of pathology in themselves and their other two children. Or they might have thrown up their hands, hopeless about themselves, about Archie, and about psychiatrists.

Their last encounter with another psychiatrist had been several weeks before coming to see me. He had been highly recommended, talked to them and to Archie, who came reluctantly and rebelliously, and then made the familiar pronouncement that Archie required psychoanalytic treatment 5 times a week. The parents could only wonder how an experienced and presumably wise professional could make such a completely unrealistic recommendation. If Archie's 1 visit was achieved practically by main force, how would he conceivably come 5 times a week for months or years, and if he were forced to come each time against his will, what good would it do.

The parents were ready to give up. But they knew they, and their other 2 children, couldn't go on with Archie as he was. More importantly, even if they managed to survive, they just couldn't stand by and watch Archie, with all his positive potential, go down the drain, and go through life as a miserable, angry, friendless human being.

They had heard that I (S. C.) might have a different approach, and so they came, but with a deep skepticism regarding psychiatry mixed with their fervent hope that there must be an answer somewhere. The parents came first, my usual procedure, so that I would take a developmental and clinical history and obtain my impression of their attitudes before I did a psychiatric evaluation of the child himself.

For his appointment, Archie came under protest and was brought virtually by force. When brought into the playroom, as soon as his father left, he dashed out of the room, through the waiting room, out through the lobby, and on to the street. His father ran after him, and only caught up to him just short of the end of the block. Brought back, protesting all the way, he spent the rest of the time, while his father stood guard, complaining that there was nothing wrong with him, and that he wasn't going to use my playthings or tell me anything.

It might seem that this session with Archie was completely wasted, with only the information that he could be completely rebellious and resistant to any direct treatment, something I already knew from the parents' story. To the contrary, I learned a great deal about Archie from this dramatic, negativistic encounter. It was clear that he had made a distinct affective relationship with me, that he expressed this directly, openly and vividly, and that his emotional state was appropriate to his thought content. His language use was excellent and grammatical, his thinking was coherent, and his motor coordination, at least in running, was smooth and effective. His reality testing for his age was also not deviant.

Thus, there was no evidence of organic disorder or childhood psychosis. And, from my interview with the parents, and my observation of their behavior with Archie in my waiting room, I had found no evidence that the boy's disturbance could be due to parental hostility and rejection, or some other type of pathogenic set of attitudes in one or both parents. They were thoughtful and concerned, eager to do their best for Archie, frustrated that their efforts had failed, and worried over his future. Their anger at Archie was clearly reactive to his difficult behavior, and if anything, they were more angry at themselves for their outbursts of rage at their son, than they were angry with him. Furthermore, their two other children were thriving. And I certainly did not subscribe to the thesis of all too many psychiatrists and psychologists that behind every disturbed child there must be a bad parent—and if the parents appeared normal, this only meant that their "pathology" must be deeply hidden in their "unconscious."

So, how did I explain the origin and evolution of Archie's severe problems? Here is where the developmental history, as I obtained it from the parents, was crucial.

The history showed no organic risk factors. This was the mother's first pregnancy, which was uneventful. Delivery was at term, there were no complications, and birth weight was within normal limits. Developmental landmarks were achieved smoothly and at the expected times.

The parents themselves did not appear to be the cause of Archie's difficulties. The pregnancy had been planned, and both husband and wife looked forward eagerly to becoming parents. Their marriage was congenial, without other serious stress or conflict—an impression gained in the first interview with them, and confirmed in the many subsequent discussions with them. There was also no indication that either parent had any pathogenic demand or attitude with regard to their son, such as overprotection, unrealistic goals, rigid control, manipulation, and the like.

What did come out clearly in the developmental history was the special features of Archie's temperamental traits. From earliest infancy onward he showed to a marked degree the typical features of the temperamentally difficult child. In infancy, his hunger and sleep cycles, as well as the time of bowel elimination, were irregular and unpedictable. He cried more than he smiled, his crying was intense and loud, and often no clear reason for the crying could be found, thus making it less possible to comfort him. Almost every new event—introduction to new foods, change in place of bath, arrival of a stranger, taking him to a new place—evoked a negative response with loud crying. Only after many exposures did he accept the food, bath, person, or place. In family gatherings, whether as an infant, toddler, or young child, sooner or later he was making a commotion. At the same time, when he was engaged in an activity or relating with a person with whom he had made a positive adaptation, Archie's same intensity of reaction made him a charming, ebullient, and helpful youngster—but only in such limited settings.

The parents were completely unprepared for the behavior of their infant son. They had expected that their love and enjoyment of their baby and their total positive commitment to his care and welfare would be reflected in his contentment and easy management. This would be true with most infants, but not with a temperamentally difficult youngster. So these parents could not understand why Archie cried so frequently and so loudly, why he fussed at taking most new foods, and why it was so difficult to get him on a regular feeding and sleep schedule. Although basically consistent people, they shifted from one measure to another to bring happiness to the baby. For a while they held him each time he cried. When this became an almost full-time procedure without having any visible effect on Archie's behavior, they decided to let him cry it out. This too seemingly had no positive results. They dredged their emotions for possible unconscious reasons for rejection. As they added to the family, it was with surprise and relief that they found that their daughter, and later their younger son, behaved quite differently, closer to the way they had originally expected Archie would behave. Their faith in their parenting abilities was renewed, except that this did not help them with Archie.

As he became older, Archie's interactions with peers and siblings all too often ended in commotion. Here, again, the parents shifted from one strategy to another, hoping for some quick decisive remedy. At first, they used the "let him work it out" approach. When this didn't work, they tried to intervene, especially the mother, who was with Archie most of the time. She tried to figure out the sequence of Archie's negative behavior, and tried to help Archie learn some social graces, such as waiting his turn at the slide, and refraining from biting during his quarrels with other children. She found herself defending him all too often when she suspected that, had the other child been hers, she would have been blaming the ruckus on Archie.

Thus, overall, these were parents who had wanted their child, were committed to his care, could provide a comfortable and relaxed home, and were intelligent adults who loved each other and wanted to love their baby. Because of this, they expected Archie to respond quickly and easily to this very favorable atmosphere by becoming a cheerful, friendly, and adaptable infant and youngster. When the opposite was the case, they were bewildered and shifted quickly from one child-care strategy to another, hoping for some sudden solution. This did not happen; on the contrary, matters grew worse, until the whole family atmosphere was terribly strained by the turmoil Archie was perpetually creating. Their helplessness and despair led to outbursts of rage and punishment against the boy, which only fed his contentious and negativistic behavior. A typical if extreme poorness of fit sequence was in this way established. In other words, the parents expected their baby to respond and adapt quickly in a positive manner to their approach to him. When the opposite occurred, their frustration and resentment led them into behavior that exaggerated Archie's intense negative responses, and these in turn exacerbated the parents' disturbed feelings and behavior.

The therapeutic plan had to rely exclusively on parent guidance, since Archie was completely inaccessible to direct psychotherapy. Even if direct treatment of the boy had been possible, parent guidance would still have been essential in such a case. The origin of Archie's problems and the process of increasingly negative interaction between the boy and his family, peers, and teachers, as I had analyzed it, was outlined to the parents. Furthermore, I gave them my optimistic judgment on the possibility of reversing these pathogenic sequences and experiences. The parents were pessimistic, to put it mildly, but also felt that this approach deserved their fullest cooperation.

Basically, the therapeutic strategy involved picking one issue at a time where the parents could challenge Archie's irrational behavior, take a stand, and carry it through quietly but persistently to the end. The first issue chosen was the casual weekend excursion, in which the boy would typically start by stating loudly that he didn't want to go where the majority wished, but had no alternative to suggest. After much turmoil he would finally go along, but sooner or later on the trip would make some new fuss over some extraneous issue. The parents were instructed to respond to his refusal to go on the trip by quietly accepting his decision and leaving him at home. They knew he could be safely left, and would probably watch television. This they did, and within a month the issue was settled. Archie either stayed home quietly or came along quietly. When it came his turn to select the place for the excursion, in fact he had no unusual preferences. Once this issue was accomplished, the parents were told to confront his unreasonable requests and fussing on the trip with a quiet ultimatum to either subside or be taken home. The first few times he was taken home by one parent, who then kept busy and disregarded Archie completely. Following this, the turmoil on trips subsided immediately with the ultimatum, then disappeared, and the boy began to enjoy the excursions with his typical intensity, and the family found him an asset rather than a spoilsport on their trips. Also their spirits began to lift.

And so it went, step by step. The parents carried through each issue calmly but with determination, with uniformly positive results. As a result, after 8 months of these parent guidance sessions, held weekly, the routines of daily living with Archie were greatly transformed. Whether it was his dressing and breakfasting on schooldays, his acceptance of his share of household chores, or his obedience to the

family's television rules, Archie's behavior became reasonably if unen-
thusiastically cooperative, with only occasional token efforts at resistance. His relationships with his parents, brother, and sister also
became increasingly friendly.

So far, so good. But this did not mean that further treatment was
no longer necessary. Quite the contrary. Archie's peer relationships
were still frequently difficult and contentious, and in this area the
parents did not possess the leverage to restructure the consequences of
his behavior as they could at home. At school, his negative reactions to
new situations and slow adaptability were interfering seriously with
his mastery of new academic subjects, as they came along in the school
curriculum. His parents had arranged for private tutoring, but Archie
resisted this additional demand to learn what was new, and his academic achievement now lagged substantially behind his potential as a
youngster of superior intelligence.

Most important of all, it was essential that Archie gain insight
himself into the nature of his temperamental pattern and the impact
his difficult behavior had on others. Only with such insight could he
learn to control and modify his first undesirable outward responses to
new people, new situations, and new demands, and achieve instead the
behavioral responses leading to healthy mastery and positive social
relationships. Without such insight, his improvement would be limited to the specific situation in which his parents had been able, with
the help of the parent guidance sessions, to restructure his behavioral
patterns.

With these long-term goals in mind, direct psychotherapy with
Archie was necessary, and this had been indicated to the parents as our
weekly discussions went on. The key question, of course, was whether
Archie would now be willing to come for treatment, or would he
again, as on his first visit, simply try to run away and refuse to
cooperate. Two indicators suggested that Archie's attitude might be
changing. On a number of occasions, when his parents instituted a
new approach to another item in his contentious behavior, he re-
marked "I bet Dr. Chess told you to do this." When his parents replied,
"Yes, she did," he had no further comment. Secondly, on several
occasions, as the months went by, he mentioned spontaneously to his
parents that people were treating him better and he was feeling less
unhappy.

Therefore, after the 8 months of parent guidance sessions, and just
before the summer vacation, another appointment was arranged for
Archie. This time he came into the office cheerfully, with no trace of

his original hostile and negativistic response. He spent the session reporting on his excellent academic performance, which I knew to be a highly exaggerated and one-sided account. Of course, I did not confront him with the facts, and suspected that he was trying to avoid facing openly the seriousness of his academic problems. He was seen a second time before the vacation started, so that when we resumed in September a positive adaptation to a weekly routine of therapeutic sessions would already have been initiated.

In the first year (September to June) Archie came faithfully for weekly sessions. Parent guidance was also continued on a weekly basis. Mainly the mother came, but periodically, when indicated, Archie's father also participated actively. During this period the major concentration was on Archie's academic problems, though attention was also given to his peer relationships. The extent of Archie's difficulty with any new school subject, and indeed even any new type of assignment, was indeed extraordinary for a boy of his superior intelligence, motivation for learning, and clear delight when he mastered any new academic demand. He literally appeared bewildered and confused with a new learning task, so that he could not understand what was expected. By contrast, once the new academic demand had been mastered, further assignments in the same direction presented no difficulties. This problem could only be explained as the reflection of his temperamentally based intense negative reactions to the new, intensified by a mild degree of dyslexia, evident by specific difficulties with reading, writing, and spelling.

Archie had developed an extensive pattern of defensive reactions to these academic stresses. He not only wanted help from his parents, but demanded that they do his work for him, and raised a commotion when they refused to meet this latter expectation. With his tutor the same pattern was present, though not as marked. He also procrastinated doing his homework, sometimes said he didn't have any, exaggerated his school accomplishments, and minimized his failures. In class he often clowned.

The therapeutic strategy for the parents in dealing with this issue involved primarily a graduated series of demands that Archie himself take increasing responsibility for his schoolwork, coupled with a confrontation of his defensive avoidance maneuvers. His mother insisted that before she would help him with homework for a new type of assignment, first he must read the material several times, and then make a first draft himself. Initially he reacted violently against this demand, then he began producing short paragraphs and these gradually lengthened to respectable 4- to 5-page drafts. Proud of these accomplishments, he took full credit for them. His homework assignments were verified strictly, if necessary by checking with the school, and television was interdicted until his homework was completed. His tutor concentrated on the dyslexia issue, and refused to do his homework for him.

With this concerted approach, supplemented by my discussions with him in which I raised the same issues, Archie's academic performance improved gradually and steadily, and the number of violent confrontations over these issues dwindled by mid-year.

As to Archie's problems with peer relationships, the parents were, of course, not in a position to intervene decisively and specifically when these difficulties arose. They were just not on the scene. Fortunately, Archie's improvement in other areas of functioning had sufficient spillover into his behavior with his age-mates that he did succeed in making several friends. The parents then invited these friends for weekends to their vacation home, and were able to spot a number of issues, such as Archie's lack of sensitivity about sharing, about his responsibilities as a host, about the need to take his friend's preferences into account, and the like. His parents approached these issues with Archie not in terms of criticism of his social ineptness, but as an opportunity to learn the accepted rules of social relationships. This he accepted grudgingly at first, which turned to positive interest as time went on.

The next September, the frequency of sessions was cut back, with sessions once in 2 weeks for direct therapy with Archie, and the same schedule for concurrent parent guidance. The old academic difficulties were again in evidence with a new class, new teacher, and new subjects. The parents were disheartened, and worried that this pattern would go on forever. As they said to me, "What will happen to Archie when we and you are no longer around to guide him?" I pointed out that many of the issues that had bedeviled them and the family only 3 years ago were no longer problems—Archie's brother and sister sought him out for games and advice instead of avoiding him, family excursions were usually pleasant, and the hassles over family routines and rules were no more than with many other normal youngsters in other families. Archie's teachers also now saw him as a pleasant and charming schoolboy, and only occasionally difficult. Actually, these positive changes were now so much a matter of fact in the household that the parents had lost their perspective on what had happened. I told them I saw no reason why further progress should not occur. Actually, initial positive change and the gratification this brings to a youngster, usually makes it easier to deal with whatever problems still remain.

Archie's defensive avoidance responses with regard to schoolwork diminished more swiftly in this second treatment year, and by Christmas time he was beginning to function with healthy mastery and academic success. His attitude toward me also changed. He began to banter and joke, took my challenges in good humor, even when they bothered him, and the charm and vitality his parents had initially reported to appear only or rare occasions was much in evidence.

In this second year of treatment, I set two major goals. For Archie, and this was most important, he now needed to gain insight into his own behavioral style, the effect it had on others, and how he could learn to recognize and control its unfavorable manifestations and consequences. For his parents, the issue was for them to recognize when and how their own responses to Archie's antagonistic and angry behavior fed and escalated these destructive reactions. In other words, when they got into a hassle with Archie and he finally blew up, this was not simply a case of a reasonable demand triggering Archie off, so that his short fuse sputtered until his hidden time bomb exploded. Rather, their request or demand led to an initial negative reaction on Archie's part, this made them angry, especially given all their past history with him, Archie then reacted to their anger with increased resistance and antagonism, this increased their anger and frustration, and so on to the final blow-up. It was not a question of appeasement of Archie—this would have been disastrous—but rather a quiet and even friendly firmness, while they stuck to their guns. And every once in while, Archie might even have a reasonable request, though presented unreasonably.

This analysis startled the parents—"We never thought of that"—but they understood the rationale quickly. They had to agree that as mature adults they should be capable of modifying their reactions when desirable more than a 12-year-old youngster.

As to Archie, this kind of insight is difficult for most preadolescents. Their self-image as an independent individual who can control and modify her own behavior to achieve goals is at best only in its formative stage. I put it to Archie in the simplest terms, "What happens is that something makes you feel rotten, then you behave rotten. The other people don't like that and they aren't going to know that its because something is bothering you. So they give it back, and treat you rotten. Then you feel more rotten and blame in on them. I think it's a shame that you should feel badly so often, and I have an

idea how we can change it so you are the boss. If you can learn to spot
what makes you feel rotten in the first place, then you can stop yourself
from starting the whole thing off by keeping your cool. Then people
will be decent to you, as you deserve. Anyway, if you feel rotten, why
take it out on them?"

To this formulation, documented with specific examples, Archie
listened at first with polite attention, but without understanding. At
the following session he could not recall what I had suggested, but
once I started the recital, he took over and finished the words—the
beginning of familiarity with the idea. The next time, Archie trium-
phantly had a successful try-out to report. This had to do with school
work, failing to understand an explanation and catching himself
about to be fresh to the teacher, but asking instead for a private
explanation after class—which he got, with praise from the teacher.

Arrangements were made for treatment to be resumed after the
summer vacation. This was done, but as the weeks went by it became
increasingly evident that a severe change for the worse was evident. It
became clear that he had achieved no real insight in his discussions
with me over the previous year, but was simply parroting back my
formulations. His few friendships were superficial and episodic, and
in spite of his earlier positive reports in this area, he remained essentially socially isolated. He resisted going to school, and after several
months, he refused to go at all. When challenged by me, even in the
mildest terms, he became increasingly antagonistic, and finally broke
off his therapy with me entirely. In effect, he ran out of the office
again.

In discussion with his parents, no stressful or traumatic event had
occurred that in any way could account for this change in Archie. It
was, however, impressive that the positive changes that had been
accomplished in his behavior at home with his family in the first year
of parent guidance remained intact. With only an occasional blow-up,
he was amiable, friendly, and cooperative at home, and spent a good
deal of his time reading.

In reviewing the history, it seemed to be clear that Archie's difficulties when he first came for treatment went beyond a simple poorness of fit resulting from inappropriate handling of a child with severe
difficult temperament. To cope with the stresses and problems generated by this poorness of fit and, perhaps, intensified by a mild dyslexia,
Archie had developed an increasingly rigid pattern of denial and
avoidance. This was dramatically displayed in the way he ran out of
the office on his first encounter with me, and later on with his school
avoidance. The same defenses were more subtly employed in his thera-

peutic sessions with me, when his reports of various successes and his mimicry of my formulations were done so cleverly as to deceive me. Given this complex psychopathologic pattern, the effectiveness of parent guidance in helping Archie's mother and father to achieve long-lasting changes in those areas within their control was indeed impressive.

Archie spent the past year (prior to our writing this chapter) quietly at home, reading a great deal, and participating cooperatively in various family activities. Finally, during the summer, he approached his parents on his own, told them he had been thinking, knew he had to go back to school, and recognized that he needed further therapy to accomplish this. Because I had in the interim retired from any private clinical practice, this was arranged with another therapist. It was also clear that Archie would do better with a new therapist with whom he had not already become entangled in defensive reactions of denial and avoidance, as he had with me. Given this latest development, I feel there is geniune basis for guarded optimism regarding his future progress.

PARENTAL PSYCHOPATHOLOGY
AND PARENT GUIDANCE

The prognosis for parent guidance is usually strongly influenced by the presence of significant psychopathology in one or both parents. Whatever its nature and causation, pathologic ideas and behavior make it difficult to give the child's welfare the high priority it requires, and impose a rigidity and inflexibility on the parent's behavior that makes it difficult or impossible for the parent to make significant positive changes in his or her interaction with the child. Direct therapy of parent or child, or both, or some form of family therapy is then usually required. Rigid parental moralistic standards that make for inappropriate and excessive demands on the child tend to have the same negative prognosis, even if they cannot be considered as evidence of psychopathology as such.

There are, however, exceptions, in which the parent's insight into his or her own psychopathology, combined with concern for the child's welfare, made it possible to transform a poorness of fit into a goodness of fit, with beneficial consequences for the child's developmental course. The following two case vignettes illustrate this possibility.

A young woman elementary school teacher, Miss R., had consulted one of us (A. T.) some years ago because of anxiety symptoms and increasing feelings of inadequacy as a teacher, a career that she had started 2 years previously. A series of discussions with Miss R. revealed that she made unrealistic perfectionist demands on herself, and that this had been true since her adolescence. In her personal life this neurotic pattern made Miss R. uncomfortable and tense in many social situations, but had not interfered significantly with her functioning. As a teacher, however, she set impossible demands on her pupils, as to behavior, completion of all assigned tasks, and immediate compliance with the schedule and her other demands. The inevitable shortcomings in her pupils' quick and complete responses to her expectations generated increasing self-doubt and anxiety in herself. Miss R. reacted by putting increased pressure on her pupils, who reacted negativistically, which then increased her own anxiety and pressures, so that a vicious circle was created in which she lost control of her class.

Once this dynamic sequence was identified, the young woman was able to grasp its meaning and its consequences. With much urging, Miss R. took the step of relaxing certain of her unrealistic expectations and demands on her pupils, and, to her amazement, found that this resulted in an immediate and appreciable improvement in the class's behavior and performance. Success bred success in this case. She now eagerly applied this new model of functioning to other aspects of her classroom work, and soon found herself with the reputation of one of the best of the new teachers in the school.

Therapy was discontinued at this point at Miss R.'s request. She did recognize that although she had achieved remarkable improvement in her professional work, that her basic neurotic perfectionist pattern had been by no means mastered. But she felt she could keep it under control, and that it did not seriously affect her other areas of functioning.

However, about 5 years later, she returned to consult me again. In the interim she had married, was now Mrs. S., and, when she became pregnant, she gave up teaching. Her marriage and social life were proceeding smoothly, but she was deeply concerned about her young son, who was now 6 months old. Her pediatrician had assured her repeatedly that the youngster was physically normal, but Mrs. S. was anxious almost to the point of panic at his behavior. He slept and fed irregularly, refused to take solid foods, and cried often and loudly. And this behavior had been the case from his earliest weeks. "What's wrong with him? I must be a terrible mother, look how different he is from all my friends' babies!" This was her repeated refrain, and the picture of anxiety and self-doubt Mrs. S. presented was an almost exact duplicate of her appearance on her original visit to my office several years back.

It was clear from her actual description of the baby's behavior, leaving out her self-recriminations, that Mrs. S.'s child had a typical difficult temperament pattern. A few additional questions established that she was attempting to make changes by forceful pressure, just as she had done with her classroom pupils in the past. She tried to force solid food down her baby's mouth, only to have him spit it out. She tried all kinds of ingenious devices to get him to sleep and feed regularly, all to no avail. She alternated between trying to ignore his loud crying and trying to stop it by picking him up and soothing him. The father apparently accepted his wife's judgment that it must be her fault, and left the problem to her.

I first reassured Mrs. S. that I saw no evidence from all she had said, and all that I knew about her, that she was a "bad" mother or that she had an abnormal child. I explained the concept of individual differences in temperament, asking her to recall different types of children's behavioral styles that she had observed as a teacher. Then I formulated the concept of the difficult child, showed her a description of this pattern in one of our books, at which she exclaimed, "But that's just like my baby."

I then suggested that her neurotic pattern had become intense and destructive again. Mrs. S. had demanded of herself that she be a "perfect" mother, the evidence for this was to be a "perfect" baby, and when her son turned out otherwise, she became increasingly self-derogatory and anxious, and tried to deal with this reaction by forcing her baby to behave "normally." But the more she pressured, the more intensely negative he became, the more her anxiety increased, and the same type of vicious cycle was in the making as had occurred originally as a teacher with her pupils.

Mrs. S. agreed that what I said made sense, especially in view of her own past history. But could the explanation be so simple? After all, she had read so much about all the complex and subtle factors in a mother's attitudes and behavior, especially if unconscious, that can influence a young infant's behavior. I told her, let's put my explanation to the test. Start with one solid food he has rejected and give him just a taste. Then give him a little more the next day, more again the following day—always without forcing it—and wait until he took the food easily and with enjoyment. Then repeat the procedure with a second food, and then a third. In the meantime don't worry about his irregular schedule, just feed him when he appears hungry. If he still cries, hold him quietly until he subsides, but without any special maneuvers to make him stop.

Mrs. S. returned a month later, literally amazed at the change. She had followed my advice scrupulously, and by now her child was taking a half-dozen solid foods with gusto. With this improvement in his diet his sleep and feeding schedule were becoming regular. I now suggested that when the child awoke at night crying, that she change him if wet, offer him a bottle, and put him back into the crib and leave him to fuss himself back to sleep. Again, Mrs. S. a month later reported success; her baby was now sleeping through the night regularly.

All seemed well. However, a year later, Mrs. S. came in again, looking as harassed and anxious as ever before. What now? Progress had been smooth until a few months before, when she started taking her boy to the neighborhood playground. As soon as he saw the strange children and parents and the unfamiliar play materials he started shrieking and insisted on leaving at once. She had repeated the attempt a number of times, always with the same result. She was sure the other mothers had marked her down as some kind of a monster if her child behaved that way—and she was probably correct. A few questions elicited the information that each time Mrs. S. had tried to force her boy into the group, even literally pushing him, and growing more and more anxious as he protested loudly.

I reminded Mrs. S. of our previous discussions, and my prediction that he might behave negatively in new situations in the future, but would adjust if given time and not pressured. But this was different, Mrs. S. insisted. This was not just a matter of feeding or sleeping schedules, but of his social behavior with other human beings, which was such an essential part of any person's life. To reassure her, I arranged for a clinical evaluation with a child psychiatrist, who found no evidence of any psychopathology. Again, Mrs. S. was finally willing to follow my advice. She took the boy to the playground, gritted her teeth while he stood on the outskirts, and then took him home. After repeating this routine for several days he was then willing to try the swings for a few minutes; the next day he was at the edge of the sandbox, and within 2 weeks he was a vigorous and zestful member of the playgroup.

Two years later, Mrs. S. asked for another appointment. What now, I thought? But this time she came in beaming instead of wringing her hands anxiously. "I came to tell you," Mrs. S. said cheerfully, "that I am now fully convinced you were right." What had happened?

She became pregnant again, she said, and had another baby boy a year ago. "And he was entirely different from my older boy from the beginning. He only cried when he was hungry, and then it was a soft cry. He took to each new food at once, he enjoys going to new places, he has slept through the night since he was 2 months old, and he has loved the playground from the beginning. I now believe what you told me about temperament, and that it had nothing to do with my being a bad mother." And her older boy? "He's doing fine and has lots of friends. When he started nursery school 6 months ago, it was a repeat performance. It took him over a week to join the group." "And," she shrugged her shoulders, "I did get a little anxious, but I didn't push, and now he's one of the liveliest boys in the group."

Another mother consulted one of us (S. C.) because her 4-year-old only son, Jeremy, was clinging to her and whining, and she knew it was her fault. And she was right. Since adolescence she had had a severe diffuse anxiety state with phobic tendencies. She had tried psychotherapy, but after a few sessions quit because the discussions made her anxiety intolerable. Her son was an easy child temperamentally and took to each new situation cheerfully. His mother, however, anxious as she was, hovered over him, kept asking him if he was all right, and didn't he want to go home. With this interaction, a pattern developed in which Jeremy adapted well and easily in his mother's absence, but as soon as she appeared he began to whine, he would hold on to her and make special demands which she eagerly tried to carry out. The father was supportive of his wife's psychological difficulties, but insisted that she had to change.

Clinical evaluation confirmed that Jeremy was a normal boy who explored the playroom toys eagerly and appropriately as long as his mother was out of the room. As soon as she appeared, he began to whine and complain. The dynamics were clear and simple—as a temperamentally easy child Jeremy had made one pattern of adaptation in the outside world (a healthy one), and quite a different one with his mother (a very unhealthy one).

A strategy of parent guidance was outlined which required his mother to efface herself when Jeremy was at school or at any social visit to a friend, so that he did not know she was there until it was time for him to go home. This the mother carried through, though she reported that each such occasion was an agonizing experience for her. Jeremy's behavior improved, he became more assertive and relaxed with new groups, and his clinging to his mother diminished. Finally, he announced that when the bus brought him home from school and stopped in front of their apartment house, he didn't want her to be standing there waiting for him. "None of the other children's mothers wait for them, why should you?" He was perfectly capable of marching into the house and up the elevator. His mother was terrified at this idea, and came rushing in to consult me. I told her Jeremy was right, he should feel as independent as the other youngsters, and there was a doorman to see him in safely.

Jeremy's mother agreed most reluctantly, and that evening told him she would no longer wait for him at the apartment entrance. However, the next day she managed "by accident" to be coming home from shopping just as the bus discharged Jeremy at his door. When he saw his mother approaching, he went into a wild tantrum and could not be comforted for hours.

With this the mother learned her lesson. Her anxiety state did not lessen, but she never again hovered around to "protect" him unnecessarily. What she realized was that she was not "protecting" him, but trying in vain to assuage her own anxiety. I urged her to attempt psychotherapy again for herself, given her proven ability to control her anxiety with her son, but this idea she resisted completely.

DETAILS OF PARENT GUIDANCE

In many ways, the NYLS parent sample represented an optimal group for the use of parent guidance as a therapeutic procedure when children suffered from a behavior disorder. The parents were interested in concepts of child development, as evidenced by their cooperative involvement in the study, they were child-oriented, and, with very few exceptions, gave a high priority to the healthy physical and psychological development of their children. Also, they knew that we had a wealth of information available on the children and that their child had had a careful clinical evaluation to identify the nature and cause of her behavior disorder. Finally, the behavior disorder was usually identified early in its development, because of the ongoing relationship of the parents with one or another of our research staff members. Thus parent guidance, in contrast to the frequent situation in clinical practice, could usually be instituted quickly before secondary consequences of the disorder had been elaborated, such as negative feedback from others, and/or the development of fixed neurotic psychodynamic defenses. This comment is in no way intended to minimize the importance of parent guidance even when such unfavorable consequences of the disorder had already crystallized, with their own unfavorable developmental consequences. Rather, in these latter cases, even when successful, parent guidance usually required many more sessions than with the NYLS group, the results were sometimes not as dramatic, and the guidance procedures more often had to be supplemented by direct treatment of the child or parent or both. But, whatever the situation and whatever other treatment is required, whenever parents are willing and able to participate positively in a parent guidance procedure, this should always be included as a major therapeutic effort.

In the NYLS sample, parent guidance was recommended as the primary therapeutic approach in all the children identified as suffering from a behavior disorder. In one child, the severity of symptoms was such that concurrent direct psychotherapy was also recommended. In another case, the parents decided to arrange for psychotherapy for the child on their own, rather than to proceed with parent guidance.

As indicated earlier in this chapter, the rationale of the guidance program was explained to the parents in terms of the concept that their youngster's psychologic development rested on a goodness of fit between the child's characteristics and the parents' attitudes and practices. The existence of a behavior disorder then signalled the fact that in one or another area or areas of the child's life a poorness rather than a goodness of fit was operating. This poorness of fit was then identified in detail in terms of the child's temperament, and of the particular aspects of the parents' handling which, in interaction with the child's characteristics, were producing excessive stress and disturbed development. Where other relevant factors also existed, such as inappropriate school expectations, these were also pointed out.

The parents were assured, and repeatedly so, that the poorness of fit formulation in no way meant that they were "bad parents," and that the same behavior on their part with another child with different attributes might have had entirely different consequences. Similarly, the child's disturbed responses to their well-meaning efforts did not indicate that the youngster was "sick," "bad," or "willfully disobedient." It was a question of lack of knowledge, misinformation, and confusion, rather than any intent to harm the child, that had led to the poorness of fit and the behavior disorder development.

The parents were then given specific suggestions and advice for changing the undesirable attitudes and practices. References to concrete specific incidents in the child's life were made to illustrate each recommendation. (The material in Chapter 3 on the types of parental responses to children's specific temperamental characteristics, and the various case illustrations in that and other chapters, offer many examples of poorness of fit between child and parent, and the types of change in parental functioning that are desirable in these instances.)

In most cases of behavior disorder in early and middle childhood, poorness of fit involved some feature of the child's temperamental characteristics combined with inappropriate parental handling as a major issue. Other factors did play a significant role in certain specific cases, such as parental denial of a child's intellectual retardation or difficulties in learning due to dyslexia. Whatever the issue, the basic strategy of parent guidance was similar. The central issue was always the delineation of the *specific* nature of the poorness of fit in the interaction between child and parent or peer group or school in each *individual* case, and advice tailored *concretely* to that *individual* situation. Where the pathogenic child–environment interactional process concerned relationships with peers or teachers, rather than the parents themselves, it was still possible in most cases to outline a strategy for the parents whereby they could intervene in some positive fashion. This might include coaching the child patiently but as often as necessary as to the appropriate rules of behavior with friends, arranging for a remedial reading program, or conferring with the child's teacher regarding ways of altering or minimizing difficult behavior in the schoolroom.

An essential feature of the guidance program was a systematic follow-up schedule with the parents, following the initial session. Even with parents who were eager and able to carry through the schedule of behavioral change recommended to them, more than one discussion was usually necessary for this to be implemented fully. Several sessions at least were usually required for them to grasp adequately the concept of the child's individuality and its influence on the youngster's ability to cope with parental and other environmental demands and expectations. At these follow-up discussions, the parents' behaviors in a number of specific incidents which had occurred in the interim period were reviewed. This review, which was done in detail, was usually necessary for the parents to develop the experience of identifying quickly those situations in the child's daily life that required modification of their techniques of management.

The utilization of parent guidance in cases of behavior disorders in the adolescent period is significantly more complicated than in childhood. New influences begin to shape more and more the youngster's behavior, attitudes, and goals: the struggle to achieve a separate self-identity and psychologic independence from the parents, the pressures for conformity with peer group standards, the implications of sexual maturity, the beginning concern with long-range plans and ambitions. All these factors make for complex and changing patterns of interaction with the parents, and a poorness of fit may involve a number of factors simultaneously. Actually, in our experience, a major issue in counseling parents during this period is to underline the fact that, like it or not, they do not have the influence over, let alone the control of their son or daughter that they had a few years previously. Temperamental issues do continue to be a significant factor in many instances. Thus, for example, a dispute between parent and adolescent over issues such as curfew time, amount of financial allowance, use of the family car, and so forth, may create a scene of excited turmoil if the youngster is temperamentally intense, in contrast to a quiet discussion which may be possible with a child of low intensity. Or a dispute may be settled quickly if the adolescent has low persistence, but may become a prolonged argument if she is highly persistent. The parents' expertise in handling such temperamental issues from experience gained during their youngster's earlier years may enable them to mitigate the disagreements that arise in adolescence and to avoid unnecessary escalation, but at times may not produce the same degree of positive resolution as was possible during the childhood period.

PARENT GUIDANCE SUCCESSES

In our treatment of the NYLS behavior disorder cases in childhood by parent guidance, this therapeutic procedure was evaluated by qualitative clinical judgment as moderately or highly successful in approximately 50% of the subjects so handled. This rating included both the estimation of parental changes in the desired direction and the improvement in the child's behavior disorder. These two factors went hand in hand in a reciprocal relationship. When the initial efforts at change by the parents brought quick positive change in the child's functioning, this then acted as a powerful stimulus for the parents to continue and extend their altered behavior and attitudes. An average of only 2–3 guidance sessions were required for this successful outcome. The judgment of success was based not only on the immediate results, but also on the subsequent follow-ups, usually over several years or more. In a few cases, where parent guidance had produced positive immediate results, recurrence of symptoms in the child or new symptoms appeared months or several years later. Clinical evaluation at such time revealed that the child, in reaching a new developmental level, or in the face of some new special situation in her life, had expressed the original temperamental characteristics in a new form. This the parents had misconstrued, and had responded inappropriately again, recreating a poorness of fit. It took only one or two discussions in such situations to clarify the dynamics of the new behavioral sequence, and to spell out effectively the changes to be made by the parents.

It is of interest that the percentage of successful results achieved with the temperamentally difficult children closely approximated those obtained with the temperamentally easy children, even though the former group were at much higher risk for the development of behavior disorders than were the latter group. Once the parents of the difficult children were reassured that they were not "bad" parents, that essentially they were as capable as other parents of managing their youngsters in a healthy fashion, that what was required was specific changes in their behavior and attitudes they were quite capable of achieving, and that once these changes were made their children would flourish and meet the behavioral standards of their community, it was as if a great weight had been lifted off these parents' shoulders. With few exceptions they responded eagerly—"Tell us what to do"— listened carefully to the guidance advice, and went home committed to carry out the necessary changes. This insured success when the behavior disorder was identified early in its development. In cases where the behavioral disturbance had persisted for several years or more, with the development of secondary neurotic self-defeating defense mechanisms and all their unfavorable consequences, as in the case of Archie cited earlier in this chapter, the effectiveness of parent guidance was not as dramatic.

As mentioned above, the NYLS parents were an especially favorable group for the utilization of parent guidance techniques, especially because of the wealth of information already available on them and their children when they came to us for help. However, we have also found parent guidance to be highly valuable in the treatment of behavior disorders in a middle-class clinical practice, though we do not have systematic follow-up data for this group. One difference was that these other cases often required more extensive observation and evaluation before the specific dynamics of the poorness of fit could be identified. Also, because in many cases the disorder had progressed for some time before the parents came to us for help, often after having tried other approaches fruitlessly, more of the children required direct therapy combined with parent guidance, in contrast to the NYLS group.

We have had a similar positive experience with parent guidance in the children's mental hygiene clinic in the pediatric department of Bellevue Hospital in New York City. These working-class, less highly educated mothers proved just as capable of grasping the concepts of temperament and poorness of fit and the logic involved in changing certain of their specific behaviors as were their more sophisticated, highly educated counterparts. As a matter of fact, it sometimes seemed that it was easier to deal with this group of mothers, since they did not have to unlearn the ideas they had absorbed by reading or listening to lectures by professional experts who had the same explanations and prescriptions for all cases.

PARENT GUIDANCE FAILURES

In the other 50% of cases in the NYLS, parent guidance was unsuccessful, as judged by the absence of change in both parent and child. In some cases, only one or two guidance discussions were attempted, because of the parent's refusal to consider that his or her functioning was undesirable to any significant degree. In other instances, lip service was given to our recommendations, or apparently earnest efforts made to follow the outlined program; but a number of subsequent discussions then revealed that nothing had changed. And in a few cases, parents were willing to come for a number of guidance sessions but made it clear that there was no acceptance of our judgments and suggestions. In fact, one father even stated, "I know exactly what you're going to say," then proceeded to give a caricature of the discussion in the previous sessions, and proceeded to go his own way.

These failures often reflected significant degrees of psychopathology, which resulted in rigid attitudes, standards, and expectations, which were not amenable to the therapeutic strategy of parent guidance. In other cases, they reflected similar inflexibilities due to self-righteous moralistic standards, which were just as impervious to the guidance recommendations. In a few cases—but only a few—it appeared that the parents were truly indifferent to their child's welfare, and came in with the attitude, "You're the doctor, it's your job and not mine to fix this problem."

Where parent guidance was unsuccessful, direct treatment of the child was recommended as an alternative. (In several other cases direct therapy was combined with parent guidance because of the severity of symptoms.) This direct treatment sample with uncooperative parents was too small to permit generalization. A few parents refused, while others agreed but in effect sabotaged the treatment by their continued pathogenic behavior and attitudes. In a few cases, however, it appeared that once the child was in treatment and began to show some signs of improvement, the parents were then willing to consider some changes in their own behavior that they had previously rejected.

Fortunately, the failure of parent guidance did not necessarily doom the child to an indefinite continuation and even exacerbation of psychological difficulties. This did happen in some cases, with disastrous consequences for the youngster's development (see Chess & Thomas, 1984, Chapter 14). In other instances, recovery from a behavior disorder occurred in spite of the failure of parent guidance. One child developed special talents which transformed her parents' basic attitudes toward her, other children were favored by unpredictable positive changes in their extrafamilial life, and others developed the ability as they grew into adolescence to distance themselves emotionally from the destructive interactions with their parents (see Chess & Thomas, 1984, Chapter 17).

Of special interest was the uniform failure of parent guidance in the NYLS group in 4 children who were temperamentally highly distractible and nonpersistent. These parents, typical for the NYLS sample as a whole, attached great importance to educational achievement for their children, and to success in professional careers or business for their sons. For both these goals, persistence, that is, "stick-to-it-iveness" was considered desirable and even essential, and the fathers prided themselves on their own possession of this desirable characteristic. With other temperamental patterns, the parents could be assured that with proper handling, while their children's temperament might not change, at least the behavioral manifestations that they found objectionable could be reshaped. It was different, however, with distractibility and nonpersistence. These parents had to be told that their child's pattern of incomplete attention to a task, and the frequent tendency to leave it unfinished unless reminded, could not be changed. Inasmuch as the parents had been creating excessive stress for the youngster by demanding that he alter just this aspect of behavior, they resisted any change in their judgment. "After all, if I can plug away at a job until it's finished, and so can other boys, why can't he? He must learn this, otherwise he will be a failure in life." Fathers used phrases like "he lacks character" to designate such sons, and the judgments quickly became self-fulfilling prophecies. As one such youngster finally put it, "Let's face it, my father is right when he says I have no character." It is significant that all these 4 children were boys, and expectations for task accomplishment still are significantly greater for boys than for girls, even when, as was often the case, the parents were pleased to encourage their daughter's career ambitions.

Our propositions to the fathers of these 4 distractible nonpersistent youngsters was that their boys could attain satisfactory and even superior levels of task achievement, and learn on their own to monitor their distractible tendencies when they were detrimental, but that they had to work in a way that was compatible with their own temperamental styles. The meaningful issue was whether these boys could learn to complete their tasks, which was an entirely feasible goal, even if they took several breaks in the process. It was task completion that was important, and not completion at one uninterrupted sitting. Also, distractibilty and nonpersistence were virtues at times. These children were sensitive to the nuances of the behavior and attitudes of others, and they did not tend to get so absorbed in a task that they became oblivious to their other responsibilities. But these formulations fell on the deaf ears of these achievement-oriented parents, for whom persistence and nondistractibility appeared as essential ingredients.

GROUP PARENT GUIDANCE SESSIONS

A very valuable parent guidance procedure has been developed by Dr. Stanley Turecki, a child psychiatrist at two of the major New York City medical centers (Turecki & Tonner, 1985). Dr. Turecki has established a program at Beth Israel Medical Center for parents who find their children difficult to manage for temperamental reasons. An initial screening is done to determine whether the child's difficulty is largely or primarily based on a poorness of fit between parental handling and the child's temperament. If this judgment is made, the family is accepted into the program. If the clinical evaluation indicates that the child's problem has some other pathogenic basis (dyslexia, organic brain syndrome, and so on), the family is referred to some other appropriate clinic.

This special difficult child program (i.e., referring to children with temperamental qualities that make their management difficult for their particular parents) emphasizes both individual parent guidance counseling and group sessions. At group sessions, parents bring up their specific problems, while other parents in the group may then join in the discussion and report similar difficulties with their children and how they have handled them. Many fathers as well as mothers attend the sessions and participate actively. The leader of the group presents possible solutions to specific problems and then throws the floor open for comments from the group. In this process the leader also elaborates as necessary on the meaning of specific temperamental attributes and the kinds of mismanagement that are most likely to occur with each. The parents also have the opportunity to ventilate their feelings of guilt and anxiety, which meets with reassurance and support from the group; "We've been through it ourselves, and it's not your fault." Where direct therapy for the child and/or one of the parents is also indicated, this is arranged.

Thus far, Dr. Turecki and associates have treated almost 120 children in this special program. They have identified impressionistically two main groups of children: (1) those who correspond closely to the typical pattern of the temperamentally difficult child, as we have defined it; and (2) a group characterized by impulsivity of behavior due to a combination of high activity level and high distractibility. This second group tends to show positive mood and moderate approach reactions, in contrast to the first group, but, like the first group, these children tend to be irregular and have low adaptability. Both groups tend toward low sensory threshold.

Dr. Turecki reports that the concepts of temperament and goodness versus poorness of fit are easily grasped by most of the parents, who comprise a mixed middle- and upper-middle-class and working-class population. His data are being analyzed systematically, and his findings promise to add a new and most useful dimension to the use of parent guidance therapeutically, as well as providing information on which kinds of parents find which kinds of children difficult to manage and for what reasons. We have received personal communications from several other clinicians reporting their utilization of group sessions with the parents of temperamentally difficult children (Wicoff, 1983), but without details as to their procedures or findings to date.

SUMMARY

Among some mental health professionals, parent guidance is contemptuously labeled as "Band-Aid treatment," at best only useful for alleviating superficial problems, while leaving the "deep" disorder untouched. This kind of appraisal is a reaction that carries over from the concept that the only "real" therapy is one that digs deeply into the presumed unconscious conflicts and defenses of the child and parent.

However, the test of any treatment is its effectiveness, not its depth. If a nasty purulent carbuncle of the skin can be cured by superficial incision and drainage, a deeper surgical procedure would be unnecessary and perhaps even dangerous. As we and others have utilized the technique of parent guidance for children with behavior disorders, as outlined in this chapter, we have found it to be safe and efficient, and in many cases to have eliminated the need for other types of time-consuming and expensive treatment. But, to be effective, parent guidance can not be slipped on like a Band-Aid. It requires a careful analysis of the origins and dynamics of development of the individual case, without trying to tailor each child to fit the Procrustean bed of the a priori concept that all instances of behavior disorders among children must have a similar origin. To be effective, the technique of parent guidance also requires that the clinician make his or her recommendations based on the analysis of the individual characteristics of the child–environment interactional process in each case, and not pull out a ready-made therapeutic blueprint which is presumed to fit all problems.

On the other hand, parent guidance, like any other treatment, is not a panacea. Failures do occur, or the approach chosen may be inappropriate, in which case direct treatment of parent or child, or both, may become necessary. We will consider this issue in Chapter 12.

Direct Treatment of Child and Adult

Throughout this volume, as well as in our other publications (see references to Chess & Thomas, and Thomas & Chess in reference list to this book), we have emphasized that in no way do we advocate a temperament theory that deals with healthy versus pathologic personality development. Rather, we see temperament as only one attribute of the individual, and stress that temperament must at all times be considered in its internal relations with the individual's abilities and motives and in its external relations with environmental expectations, opportunities, and stresses.

In the same way, we do not advocate an approach to psychotherapy based primarily on temperament, whether in children or adults. As detailed in Chapter 11, indirect treatment of a child with an adjustment disorder through parent guidance may focus on the temperamental issues that have played a significant role in the development of a poorness of fit leading to the disturbed behavior. If the parents can reorient their attitudes and functioning appropriately and quickly, the prognosis for a speedy recovery for the child is excellent. But, if the child's disorder has been severe and prolonged, secondary neurotic defensive mechanisms may have been elaborated. These not only interfere with the youngster's ability to respond positively to a favorable change in the parents, but may exacerbate existing symptoms or produce new ones. In such cases, direct treatment of the child becomes necessary. Or the parent, because of his or her own psychopathology, may be unable to carry out the changes recommended in the parent guidance discussions. Here again, direct therapy of the parent is indicated. If the parent is resistant to such a recommendation, the clinician may have to settle for direct treatment of the child alone, in the hope that this will prove helpful, even without the parent's active cooperation.

For the older child or young adolescent, parent guidance is sometimes useful, though generally not to the extent possible with younger children. Direct treatment is usually indicated. For the adult with a psychiatric disorder in which temperament is a significant factor, parent guidance is no longer applicable, and this is generally true also for most older adolescents. In these age-periods direct treatment is necessary.

The approach to direct therapy in which temperament is a significant factor will now be discussed for these various age-periods. The emphasis will be on individual psychotherapy, inasmuch as this has been the treatment modality which has been favored in almost all cases. Brief consideration will also be given to other treatment strategies. This discussion will in no way attempt a comprehensive systematic survey of psychotherapy or other treatment methods. Rather, in line with the purpose of this volume, prime attention will be given to the treatment of cases in which temperamental issues have been a significant factor in a poorness of fit which has led to the development of a behavior disorder.

TREATMENT OF THE PARENT

As indicated in the Chapter 11, pathologic parental behavior or rigid moralistic standards and demands that have contributed to the poorness of fit with the child's characteristics and capacities will, unless changed, lead to the failure of parent guidance. In such cases, treatment of the parent, for his or her sake as well as the child's, is necessary.

In other instances, a parent may require supportive psychotherapy because of anxiety and insecurity over the child's behavior, even though no behavior problem has developed. This was the case with one of the mothers of an infant in the NYLS, who displayed extremely difficult temperament from the earliest months of life onward. The mother was convinced that the boy's irregular sleep pattern, intense frequent crying spells, refusal to take any new food the first time, and slow adaptability to any change must somehow be her fault. Fortunately, her husband was clear that this was the infant's own style, and not his wife's doing, and was reassuring and supportive to her. We also emphasized that all the information we had and our own observations gave no indication of any disordered development. All this reassurance was helpful, but only partially so. Because of the persistence of a substantial degree of anxiety and guilt, the mother undertook psychotherapy, which proved quite helpful. The final recovery for her came as the years went by and her son's progress in every way proved satisfactory, and even superior, though his temperament did not change.

It is of interest that not all cases of severe psychopathology in a parent necessarily result in a poorness of fit with the child and the development of a behavior disorder. A father may suffer from a severe obsessive–compulsive neurosis which seriously interferes with his business and social activities, and yet be responsive to his children's needs, and reasonably flexible and appropriate in his expectations and demands from them. A schizophrenic mother may harbor an elaborate paranoid system of thinking, and yet, in effect, isolate this pathologic thinking and behavior from her relationship with her child, with whom she may be a positive and nurturing caretaker figure. Such a benign separation of the parental role from other aspects of life does not always or even often occur, so that the mother's paranoid thinking, for example, may involve her attitudes to the child to a degree which becomes even life-threatening to the youngster.

The recommendation of psychotherapy to a parent as necessary for the child's welfare meets, as one might expect, with many different responses. Some parents take the advice seriously and objectively, understand its rationale, and proceed to make the necessary arrangements. Others are reluctant and defensive, but can be persuaded, though their initial reaction is not a favorable prognostic sign. Others evade or refuse outright. Either the idea of facing their own problems is too threatening, or they are convinced, no matter what the evidence to the contrary may be, that the problem lies entirely in the child. Such parents are often self-righteous or moralistic, or else expect a successful service from the clinician which will not disturb the tenor of their own lives. Direct treatment of the child is then the only alternative, although the parents' attitude in such case does not offer an encouraging prospect for the child.

When the parent accepts the recommendation for his or her treatment, or for couple therapy, the clinician starts with the presenting symptom being the parents's difficulty in making the desirable changes in behavior and attitude necessary for the child's welfare. Clearly, the clinician must be familiar with the concept of temperament and its functional significance if he or she is to proceed effectively with the patient. As to whether the treatment widens to include other aspects of the patient's life, and if so, how the therapist handles these issues, as well as the question of particular therapeutic techniques—these questions are beyond the scope of this volume. What is essential is that, whatever the selection of therapeutic strategies may be, that the therapist should not lose sight of the importance of the presenting symptom—the poorness of fit between parent and child.

TREATMENT OF THE YOUNG CHILD

Psychotherapy with young children relies heavily on the use of the playroom. It is through play that the child communicates his hopes, fears, fantasies, problems, and coping patterns beyond what he is as yet capable of expressing through language. The therapist can identify the child's problem through watching and participating in the child's play, especially since the therapist starts with the history obtained from the parents and other relevant adults in the child's life. The therapist can then guide the direction of the child's play, using his or her own preferred techniques, so that the play goes beyond a repetitive communication of the same behavior and the same problem and becomes an activity in which new behaviors are attempted and rehearsed and new methods of coping with problems attempted.

Not infrequently, the same play strategy the clinician has utilized to identify the child's temperament can then become the basis of the therapeutic approach. For example, in the case of Martin (see Chapter 9), the clinician used a systematic play technique diagnostically which evaluated him as a slow-to-warm-up youngster. If Martin had required direct therapy, the same approach to the therapeutic play sessions could have been fruitful in giving Martin repeated experiences in adapting to the new in a relaxed nonthreatening environment.

For young children, one cannot expect that play therapy, no matter how effective it may be in an individual case, can be a vehicle of communication through which youngsters gain insight into the nature of their temperament and why it has certain consequences in certain situations and with certain people. The young child's cognitive level is not sufficiently developed to grasp such general concepts relating to self-image and the interactional nature of a specific behavioral interchange with another person or persons. What the clinician can hope to achieve through a series of acted-out scenarios in the play sessions, is to give the child a way of developing alternative habits of coping with specific situations and problems—quiet explanation of feelings instead of loud tantrums for the intense negative child when frustrated; ways of becoming part of a new group for the slow-to-warm-up child; methods of expending the need for physical activity for the high-activity child which do not interfere with what other people are doing, and so on. Of course, the effectiveness with which such new habits rehearsed in the playroom stick or not will depend largely on how they are reinforced, ignored, or discouraged by parents and others.

TREATMENT OF THE OLDER CHILD AND YOUNG ADOLESCENT

Middle childhood and early adolescence are periods of new and rich activities for most children in social functioning, mastery of new tasks, and expanding opportunities and demands for academic learning. These are also the age-periods in which a youngster begins to develop the capacity to conceptualize a self-image, a sense of his or her own identity. The older child begins to make judgments as to his values, abilities, strengths and weaknesses, and his immediate and long-range goals. With this self-evaluation comes a sense of how the child stands up as a person overall compared to his peers, and how confident he can be in facing the unknown and unpredictable expectations and opportunities of the future. It is a period in which this process of self-evaluation and self-conceptualization only begins to be set, and the process can be changed by subsequent events in the youngster's development. But it is an important beginning, and one that does not arise out of some mysterious, mystical sequence. Rather, a positive self-image grows out of successive successful experiences with social, task, and academic activities, accompanied by consistent positive feedback from peers and adults. A negative self-image, on the other hand, crystallizes out of sequences of negative experiences which appear to be, or actually are failures to live up to the expectations of peers and adults.

The therapist, of course, will not be called upon to treat the youngsters with positive self-images who are functioning well in the various areas of life. Rather, he will be asked for help with those who are doing badly socially or academically, or with other necessary activities, or all three, where frequently, neurotic defense reactions are aggrevating the problem and even producing secondary symptoms. A negative self-image is to be expected in such youngsters, though some may insist defensively, "There's nothing wrong with me."

In such cases of behavior disorders in the older child or young adolescent where there is a poorness of fit between the child's capacities and the environmental expectations, temperamental issues often play a significant role. Parent guidance will have been a failure, or at best only partially successful. Therapy at these older age-periods no longer utilizes play techniques as a primary approach, but rather turns to verbal discussions as with older adolescents or adults. Occasionally, a special play procedure may be useful. For example, if the youngster is interested in checkers or chess, and the therapist has some competence with these games, a game of checkers or chess may illuminate issues of competitiveness, specific temperamental attributes such as intensity, persistence, or distractibility, self-defeating responses to failure, patterns of communication, or some cognitive disturbance in approaching a challenging task. However, the therapist must be wary of incorporating such a game into the routines of therapy itself. A game that permits or even requires periods of silent contemplation while the youngster figures out stratagems of play, may easily become the central occupation of the therapeutic session. If this becomes part of the regular schedule of treatment, then the game loses its therapeutic value, and rather sidetracks the opportunities for active and direct discussions of the child's real-life problems.

Whether by such special techniques, or by the clinician's usual method of conducting therapeutic interviews, or both, the therapist explores the possibility of giving the patient insight into the nature of the temperamental characteristics and the kinds of situations in which these attributes create difficulties for him, and how this can be changed. (The therapist will, of course, be simultaneously concerned with the treatment of any other aspects of the youngster's disordered functioning that require attention).

Some older children or young adolescents can engage in the productive introspective process required to gain such insight, which makes for a favorable prognosis for treatment outcome. Many other youngsters at these age-periods, however, cannot engage usefully in this subjective process of self-examination, either because of defensive reactions (as in Archie's case in the previous chapter) or because of relative immaturity as yet in their capacity to conceptualize the meaning of temperament and how it applies to the specifics of their own behavior. Arlene, whose case was detailed in Chapter 6, is an example. In Archie's case, his defensive denial and avoidance patterns doomed the psychotherapy to failure. In Arlene's case, treatment was successful in providing guidance for her and her parents in specific situations which they followed appropriately, with positive results. By early adolescence Arlene had still not been able to conceptualize adequately the common factor in all these experiences, nor to generalize the tactics she used to master each one successfully. In such cases, one can hope that the cumulative effect of these successive positive experiences will lay the basis for the development of a positive self-concept as the years go by. If so, in later years such individuals may be able to formulate on their own the strategies necessary to cope successfully with the environmental demands that are temperamentally difficult for them. Other children, however, are not able on their own to make this qualitative cognitive leap to such a level of insight and self-awareness, and may require further therapy at a later age.

TREATMENT OF THE OLDER ADOLESCENT AND ADULT

The older adolescent or adult with a behavior disorder has not had the benefit of parent guidance, except in rare exceptions. Also, as indicated in Chapter 9, the task of identifying and rating temperament in these age-periods is complex as compared with childhood. Behavioral repertoires are elaborate; cognitive and motivational patterns are highly conceptualized and symbolized. The role of temperament in the origin and evaluation of the behavior disorder is deeply intertwined with other aspects of psychologic function. Also, the influence of temperament is highly variable; sometimes it is highly significant, and in other cases only of minor importance. But the same can be said of any potentially pathogenic factor. It is only by a comprehensive evaluation of a systematically gathered body of clinical data that the clinician can decide in any individual adult case what are the factors that appear primarily responsible for the adult's behavior disorder and require treatment.

Up to now, the major research studies and clinical applications of the functional significance of temperament have concentrated on the childhood period. Behavioral patterns are simpler to categorize, and specific attributes, such as temperament, are easier to rate in these early years. Also, manipulation of the environment to change a poorness of fit to a goodness of fit is almost always simpler and more effective in childhood or young adolescence than in older adolescence or adulthood. In our own NYLS sample, our last follow-up of the subjects of our studies when they were in their late teens and early 20s indicated this variability in the functional significance of temperamental factors, especially the correlation of difficult temperament with behavior disorder (Chess & Thomas, 1984), but we expect to obtain more extensive and systematic data in our next follow-up designed to evaluate our subjects in their mid- and late 20s. However, it is our strong impression, both from our NYLS data and from our clinical office experience, as detailed in Chapter 8, that temperamental patterns in adults are important in many instances in shaping the course of both healthy and pathologic development in adult life.

The most extensive clinical report on the significance of temperament in cases of behavior disorder in adult life, and on the development of therapeutic techniques for such cases is contained in the volume by Burks and Rubenstein (1979). Previous efforts by other investigators at categorizing and rating temperament in the adult have had limited usefulness. With few exceptions these other approaches have ignored the necessity for an interactionist view of development, or have formulated global and simplistic categories, or have failed to explore the place of temperament in the dynamics of psychologic development and behavioral functioning in the adult. Seen against this background, Burks and Rubenstein have undertaken an important, ambitious, and pioneering task. Out of their extensive experience in psychotherapy and counseling, they have spelled out an approach to apply their concepts of temperament to practical psychotherapeutic and counseling work. At the same time they clearly state: "We do not see temperament as the only, or even the most important, determinant of behavior. We stress temperament in order to consider the effect of this heretofore rather neglected component in the dynamics of human behavior" (p. 5). In their work they have emphasized the need of their patients and clients to recognize their own temperamental style, and to struggle with others for a basic acceptance and respect for their own behavioral styles as normal. The authors report many clinical examples where their therapeutic approach led to a favorable outcome, but emphasize that their clinical data require verification, elaboration, modification, and occasionally significant change through the application of appropriate quantitative methods of analysis.

Whatever the therapeutic strategies a particular clinician uses, self-knowledge and insight into the causes and consequences of his or her behavior on the part of the client is a basic therapeutic goal, except where the seriousness of the patient's disorder or the rigidity of his defenses makes this impossible. This kind of self-knowledge is not possible for the young child, but begins to emerge and crystallize in middle childhood and early adolescence, and matures gradually in most adults. One important therapeutic goal for the clinician is to help the adolescent or adult patient to develop this self-awareness and insight regarding his temperamental characteristics. However, by itself this is not sufficient, if this self-knowledge is distorted by self-derogatory judgments. The cases of Frances and Kevin, as detailed in Chapter 8, are cases in point. What is also necessary is the basic acceptance by individuals that their temperament is normal for them, and should be recognized as such by others. However, it should be realized that, although there are times when they can and should express their temperament freely, there are also occasions when such expression should be curbed, and even times when specific situations may require them to behave temporarily contrary to their basic temperamental style. The clinician's help is invaluable in helping individuals attain these insights.

TEMPERAMENT AND THE VARIOUS PSYCHIATRIC SYNDROMES

The functional significance of temperament in a psychiatric disorder is usually most evident in a simple adjustment disorder, and therapeutic efforts that take the role of temperament into account are most likely to be effective. For the more serious disturbances, such as organic brain damage, manic–depressive illness, or schizophrenia, just as in childhood autism, temperament is not a primary issue, and treatment issues must be directed elsewhere, as appropriate. Even in these more serious syndromes, however, once the primary disorder has been brought under the best possible degree of control, temperamental issues may be of significance in some cases. Thus, the temperamentally easy schizophrenic patient may find it easier to adjust to a new environment outside the hospital than may a similar case with difficult temperament. In such situations, well-timed advice and help by a mental health professional may facilitate the patients' abilities to mobilize and utilize their positive resources most effectively.

OTHER THERAPEUTIC APPROACHES

Our discussion of therapy for cases of behavior disorder in which temperament plays a significant role has emphasized the modalities of parent guidance and psychotherapy. Other treatment forms, such as behavior modification or psychopharmacology, have not been used systematically in any reported series of cases, though some may feel that parent guidance sometimes actually represents a modified form of behavior modification techniques. What is also at issue is the danger of applying the incorrect treatment because the significance of temperament is ignored. An outstanding example is the prescription of Ritalin or a similar drug for a child with temperamental high activity, in the mistaken belief that this represents a case of pathologic hyperactivity. Or the slow-to-warm-up child may be labeled as anxious because of his behavior in new situations, and one or another sedative drug may be tried.

CAN TEMPERAMENT CHANGE?

No behavioral attribute is immutable and immune to the influence of internal psychophysiological or external environmental influences. This is as true for temperament as it is for IQ. In Appendix B we elaborate on this issue of consistency and change in temperament over time. This question has only just come under systematic study, and reliable data are as yet very sparse. We certainly have no inkling as yet of what procedures, if any, can produce specific and predictable changes in temperament. In any case, it is the professional's responsibility to understand the child or adult's temperament as it is currently operating, what its functional significance is, and how the favorable aspects of any specific temperamental pattern can be maximized, and its unfavorable consequences minimized.

SUMMARY

In our discussion of treatment in this chapter, we have avoided the advocacy of any specific therapeutic system, whether it be psychoanalysis, other forms of psychotherapy, behavior modification, or some form of milieu therapy. We have, however, emphasized that treatment cannot be restricted to temperament alone, just as it cannot afford to ignore temperament. We have also reiterated the concept of goodness or poorness of fit as a useful model for analyzing the functional significance to temperament and in pointing the way to specific therapeutic strategies. With these caveats in mind, our overall thesis is that the clinician, no matter what his or her theoretical and therapeutic orientation, has the responsibility, among many others, of determining whether or not temperament plays a significant role in the ontogenesis and evolution of patients' behavior disorders. If it does have such a function, the clinician must then consider the various possible therapeutic approaches that may ameliorate the poorness of fit in which temperament plays a part.

PART THREE

Special Areas

CHAPTER 13

Temperament and School Functioning

With the onset of schooling, new and more complex stimuli, demands, and expectations begin to influence the child's psychologic functioning. The educational setting becomes a new center of struggle, adaptation, and mastery, rivaling and even surpassing the significance of the home and playground for the youngster's development.

The school makes a number of new demands, separately and in combination. Whether she begins in nursery school, kindergarten, or first grade, the child faces the simultaneous requirements of adapting to a new geographic setting away from parents and sibs, to strange adults in unfamiliar roles, and to a host of new rules and regulations. Peer group activities also frequently become more elaborate and challenging. And with the onset of formal learning, the child is expected to master increasingly complex cognitive tasks.

Success in academic and social functioning in school is influenced by many factors—the child's personal characteristics, family background, and the school environment. Temperament plays an important role in shaping the course of a child's adaptation to school, but its influence is part of a much more elaborate and varied interactional process, when compared to the relatively simple dynamic interplay in the developmental stages of infancy and the preschool period. Temperamental characteristics will help determine the individual child's response to a new and demanding cognitive school task, but so will her intellectual and perceptual capacities, level of motivation, psychodynamic patterns, home environment, teacher attributes, curriculum structure, and nature of peer relations. The same is true of the youngster's efforts to master the new and more complicated social issues that are encountered in the school setting. The complex interplay of these many factors will be evident as we focus in this chapter on the role of temperament.

The influence of temperament on school functioning can be categorized along two dimensions: the direct effect of the child's temperament on academic and social performance, and the effect of the child's temperament on the teacher's judgments and attitudes.

DIRECT EFFECT OF TEMPERAMENT:
THE INITIAL ADAPTATION TO SCHOOL

As indicated in earlier chapters, the youngsters with initial withdrawal responses to new situations, whether these are expressed quietly or loudly, is likely to find the first school experience a stressful one. However, by and large, for the subjects of the NYLS, whether entry into school was at the nursery school, kindergarten, or first-grade level, this stress did not result in significant maladaptive school problems. These youngsters, because of the socioeconomic status of their families, went to good schools with experienced teachers and relatively small class sizes. With the temperamentally difficult child whose initial stressful reaction to school was usually with loud and prolonged crying, the teachers were not likely to feel guilty, intimidated, or victimized as was the case with so many of the parents. As a result, these teachers were usually able to be patient, calm, and consistent with these temperamentally difficult children, so that a positive and even zestful adaptation to school gradually emerged. One can speculate that the story might be different in inner-city poverty area schools. With teachers harassed by the frequently inadequate resources and working conditions in these schools, the temperamentally difficult child may not find the sympathetic and patient approach the youngsters in the NYLS generally found in their schools. We do not have the data, however, to attempt to verify this speculation.

The slow-to-warm-up middle-class child also usually found the same patient and sympathetic teacher approach that helped to resolve constructively her initial stressful response to school. In a few instances in the NYLS group, however, nursery school or kindergarten teachers interpreted such a child's quiet withdrawal response, in which the youngster stood silently at the periphery of the play group, as anxiety, and suggested to the parents that the child or the family required psychotherapy. Martin, whose history is described in Chapter 9, was such a child. In such instances, a discussion with the teacher as to the basis for the youngster's behavior was usually sufficient to reorient the teacher's approach to the child.

Occasionally, school problems may arise with the youngster with initial withdrawal responses at later stages of their school careers. Two case vignettes from the NYLS will illustrate this possibility. One girl, Bernice, with a slow-to-warm-up temperament, was accelerated to the third grade at the end of the first grade because of her superior intelligence and quick learning. In the first months of the third grade her work was unsatisfactory and she appeared apathetic and disinterested in learning. The teacher judged that the acceleration had been a mistake and recommended to the mother that Bernice be put back to the second grade. The mother, who on her own had grown to understand her daughter's initial withdrawal reactions to new situations, told the teacher that this slow beginning was typical of her child, that the acceleration had confronted Bernice with new classmates and new academic subjects, and that if the teacher were patient, her daughter would soon begin to improve. The teacher reported this story several months later to our research staff interviewer, and added, "I thought this mother was just making excuses for her daughter, but I agreed to wait. And you know, the mother was right. Bernice has now caught up to the rest of the class, is alert, interested, and involved with the other pupils."

The other example is Carl, who in his early years had been one of the most extremely difficult children temperamentally in the NYLS. Whether it was the first bath or the first solid foods in infancy, the first birthday party, or the first shopping trip, each new experience evoked stormy responses, with Carl crying loudly and struggling to get away. However, the parents were not intimidated or threatened by these reactions and had learned that if they were patient, presented only one or a few new situations at the time, and gave their child the opportunity for repeated exposure, that Carl would finally adapt positively. Furthermore, once he adapted, Carl's intensity of responses gave him a zestful enthusiastic involvement, just as it gave his initial negative reactions a loud and stormy character.

The same behavioral sequence occurred with Carl's entry to nursery school, kindergarten, and the first grade. Fortunately, in each year his teachers were patient and flexible, and by the end of each school year his initial stormy behavior had changed, and taken on a cheerful and cooperative character. By the second grade, school was no longer a new experience for Carl, and his final positive adaptation in the first grade carried over to the new term, and the subsequent years of elementary and high school. He lived in the same community throughout these years, went through the neighborhood schools with the same schoolmates and friends, and new academic subjects were introduced gradually. His academic and social functioning were smooth and effective, and he developed a self-confident self-image, and came to view himself as an easily adaptable person.

When Carl went off to college away from home, however, he was suddenly confronted with a whole series of new situations—strange surroundings, an entirely new peer group, new types of faculty approaches, school schedules and curricula, and a complex relationship with a female student with whom he was living. His intense negative responses to the new, now again, after all these years, dominated his initial adjustment to school. He found studying difficult and made virtually no friends. He was bewildered by his behavior, felt "This just isn't me!" and came to consult one of us at the end of his first term. Other possible reasons for his difficulties were explored—dependency needs for his parents, sexual conflict, anxiety over academic demands, peer competition—but no evidence of any of these was elicited. It appeared clear that his difficulties in adapting successfully to college life stemmed from his temperamental pattern of initial intense reactions to the new with slow adaptability. This pattern had been strongly evident in Carl's infancy and early childhood, with the many successive and simultaneous new demands for socialization and adaptation of those age-periods, had then dwindled in significance in middle childhood and adolescence, when new demands for task performance and social functioning came gradually and less frequently, but then reemerged as an influential force shaping his behavior when he was faced with the many new academic and social situations coming simultaneously when he started college.

Only one discussion was necessary with Carl, and consisted primarily in clarifying for him his temperamental pattern and the techniques he could use for positive adaptation. Actually, Carl had already begun to take these steps on his own—cutting the number of new subjects, disciplining himself to study each subject daily for a specific amount of time, simplifying his involvement with the young woman, and making a point of attending peer social group activities, no matter how uncomfortable he felt. When seen again at the end of the academic year his difficulties had disappeared, and since then his functioning has been on the positive level of his high school years. We cautioned him that similar negative reactions to any unexpected combination of new experiences might occur in the future. His response was "That's all right. I know how to handle them now."

THE LATER ADAPTATION TO SCHOOL

Once the initial adaptation to school is achieved, other temperamental characteristics can influence the youngster's social and academic functioning in school. As in other life situations, it is usually the extremes of a temperamental attribute or pattern, which, although normal, are most likely to be significant factors in producing excessive stress for the child in the school setting.

Thus, both very high and very low activity levels can pose potential problems, depending on the teacher's understanding and handling of the pupil's behavior. The highly active child may become restless, fidgety, and tense if forced to sit quietly in the classroom for long periods of time. This behavior will interfere with her ability to concentrate on her classwork and make the child a nuisance to the teacher and to classmates sitting next to her. Experienced and knowledgeable teachers usually have little difficulty in identifying such pupils and their need for periodic motor release. Such teachers will adopt various strategies to give such youngsters additional physical activity, such as sending them on errands to other teachers or the principal's office, giving them responsibility for cleaning the blackboard or watering the classroom plants, and so on. Other teachers, unfortunately, who fail to recognize the highly active child as normal, will tend to seize on the all-too-popular label of "hyperactivity" and recommend the youngster for special professional help. All too often such children are placed on medication without the careful clinical evaluation that will definitively distinguish between high activity as a normal temperamental attribute and pathologic attention deficit disorder with hyperactivity. (The case vignettes of Karen and Brian in Chapter 9 indicate the criteria for making this differential diagnosis.)

The child with very low activity level sometimes becomes the butt of the teacher's impatience and her classmates' ridicule as the class "slowpoke." In the case of one girl in the NYLS, Kate, this slowness of movement was especially prominent and was combined with the slow-to-warm-up pattern. Kate was labeled "sluggish" by her kindergarten teacher, and her slow movements and slow adaptability misjudged as intellectual slowness. The teacher reluctantly promoted her to first grade, where the new teacher felt at first that this had been a mistake because Kate was so "slow and plodding." All too often, such a teacher's judgment becomes a self-fulfilling prophecy, as the pupil becomes discouraged and defeated in her academic efforts because she believes the teacher is right. In Kate's case, fortunately, this did not occur because of our intervention and counseling of the parents and teacher. By the end of the year it was clear that Kate was intellectually competent and was learning up to grade level. This positive judgment was passed on to succeeding teachers, and Kate had no further problems with teacher attitudes.

The highly persistent nondistractible child often seems to be made for learning. Parents and teachers only have to guide the youngster to maintain her steady and persistent effort to learn whatever is presented. Occasionally, however, parents who set high store by social peer group activity will worry that their persistent child gets so absorbed in a solitary academic activity at home and cannot be distracted that she refuses to join friends in play or socializing. Or the parents may have heard of the dangers of "overachievement" and conclude that their child's top standing in her class, surpassing that of "brighter" classmates, is an ominous omen of psychologic disturbance. Over the years we have seen this kind of adverse judgments in parents who came for consultation because they could not succeed in changing their child's behavior pattern. Some accepted the evaluation that the youngster was normal, with a promising future, even if she plugged away in school, and sometimes chose a solitary activity over peer group play. Other parents were so much the victims of the stereotyped idea that "overachievement" is pathologic and that the All-American boy or girl is always gregarious that they could not reorient their attitudes and cease their pressure on the youngster. In such cases, a self-fulfilling prophecy all too often took place, in which such children accepted the parents' derogatory judgment on their normal temperamental pattern, and became convinced that there was something wrong with them, so that a behavior disorder did develop.

Occasionally, problems in school functioning do occur for a highly persistent and nondistractible youngster if she insists on continuing an activity and the teacher demands that the youngster shift to the next scheduled activity with the rest of the class. Such forcible interruption of absorbed attention and effort, whether at home or in school, is typically a source of frustration for a very persistent child. If this frustration is expressed in tantrums or other explosive reactions, such a child can be labeled by the school as anxious or a disciplinary problem, and also be teased by his classmates as a "crybaby." Richard, one of the NYLS subjects, is a case in point. From earliest childhood he was consistently highly persistent and nondistractible in his temperamental characteristics. If interrupted forcibly from an activity in which he was absorbed, Richard's frustration was usually expressed in an explosive tantrum. His parents and older brother had learned not to let him start an activity that did not permit completion. The same was true with Richard's nursery school teachers, and his development in his early years was smooth and uneventful. In the first grade he attended a private school which was at that time imbued with the educational philosophy that first-grade children were not ready for formal reading or writing, and had to be first trained in various "reading readiness" activities. Richard, however, had begun to learn to read and write at home, and came to the first grade intent on pursuing these interests at school. Furthermore, even when absorbed in some other activity in the classroom, the teacher insisted on pulling him away when the program changed at intervals appropriate for the attention span of the other children. These repeated frustrations led to increasing tantrum outbursts, until the teacher informed the parents that they had an anxious and disruptive child, and that "family therapy" was required. At that point the parents consulted us. A clinical play session with Richard failed to reveal any pathology. His longitudinal records were reviewed and a detailed description obtained from the teacher as to the sequences of events that led up to his tantrums. On the basis of these data and the negative clinical findings, we concluded that Richard was suffering from an adjustment disorder due to school demands that were dissonant with his temperamental characteristics. The tantrums were alleviated by transfering Richard to another school where his persistent intense interest in academic work was not only permitted, but encouraged. Problems began again in the fourth grade, with several incidents in which his teacher arbitrarily frustrated his absorption in a project or other activity, with recurrence of his explosive tantrums. He was labeled a disciplinary problem, and became the butt of his classmates' teasing, which only increased his outbursts. Psychotherapy then became necessary. Improvement occurred, but there were recurrences episodically in subsequent school years, with the development of a depressive element to his symptomatology.

By contrast to the favorable adaptation to school of most persistent youngsters with low distractibility, the child who has low persistence and high distractibility is much more likely to have difficulties in academic achievement. Such a youngster typically learns in short spurts because of her short atttention span and frequent distractibility by extraneous stimuli as compared to other children. She can learn effectively, but only if teachers and parents recognize this pattern as normal for her, and do not demand that she sit for long periods concentrating on her homework or other tasks with undivided attention. All too often, however, such excessive demands are made, which the child cannot master. She is then labeled by parents or teachers, or both, as disobedient, resistant to learning, or lacking in character and willpower. Again, the child is likely to end up by accepting such derogatory judgments on her as valid, and they become self-fulfilling prophecies.

Most youngsters with the easy child temperamental pattern adapt quickly and smoothly to the academic and social expectations of school, just as they do to the demands of early socialization and peer group activity in the preschool years. In a few instances, however, if the parents impose special idiosyncratic goals and standards, these children adapt easily, but conflict and stress arise when they are faced with the different standards of the school setting. There were two such cases in the NYLS sample. One girl, Isabel, had parents who set special store by self-expression and spontaneity and the right of all persons to their own individuality and uniqueness. Isabel incorporated these parental standards and became a delightfully expressive and charming youngster, with many interests and activities. However, her disregard of externally imposed rules and of group modes of functioning alienated her from organized play activities, and seriously interfered with formal learning in the first grade. She ignored the teacher's schedules, and participated indifferently or not at all in the basic group classroom learning activities. She was spontaneously responsive only to an individualized relationship to the teacher or to any of her classmates. When she fell far behind in reading achievement, in spite of superior intelligence, her parents, who also prized academic achievement, were responsive to our counseling that they modify their approach to their daughter. Isabel, being the temperamentally easy child that she was, quickly learned appropriate patterns of group functioning, and her peer group adaptation and her academic achievement both changed dramatically for the better.

In the case of the other temperamentally easy child, Kaye, the outcome was not as favorable. Her mother was determined that her daughter should not be subjected to the rigid and arbitrary parental and school authority she herself had experienced as a child. Going to the other exteme, for the mother this meant avoiding, and even openly rejecting training Kaye in task performance. The girl became a charming and socially vivacious person, who used these attributes to sidestep demands on her. In the preschool years, these social techniques served

Kaye well with her playmates and especially with older children and adults. Unfortunately, as she grew older, her ineptness with task performance crystallized progressively into immaturity of functioning, made worse by her social diversionary tactics. This difficulty with task mastery interferred with her peer relations, and was especially disastrous in the school setting. Her problem in following instructions and focusing on formal learning tasks resulted in increasingly poor academic functioning. Unfortunately, Kaye's parents, in contrast to Isabel's, were unresponsive to counseling and guidance. As a result, Kaye's development through the school years was characterized by marginal academic achievement, a self-evaluation as being "stupid," and increasing social difficulties and loneliness.

The temperamental attributes of rhythmicity and sensory threshold do not appear to be significant influences on school functioning. It is possible that a youngster with a very irregular sleep pattern may have difficulty in getting out of bed at the same time each school day, or that someone with a very low threshold to sound and light may be disturbed by a noisy and brightly lit classroom. However, we have not seen these issues arise to any significant degree either with the NYLS sample or in our clinical practice.

EFFECT OF THE CHILD'S TEMPERAMENT ON THE TEACHER

In previous chapters, especially Chapters 2–7, we have spelled out the many ways in which the child's temperament may influence the parents' judgments, attitudes, and handling of the child. When they misinterpret the meaning of the youngster's behavior and their approach to the child results in a poorness of fit, the consequence for the child's behavior are unfavorable, and sometimes seriously so. In the previous sections of this chapter, we have indicated how the pupil's temperament may have this same kind of active influence on the dynamics and sequences of the teacher–child interaction. As a rule, teachers may be less subject to misinterpretations of the child's behavior than are parents. Teachers are less subjectively involved with each individual child than are the parents, and competent, experienced teachers have learned over the years empirically how to handle productively children with different temperamental patterns, even if they cannot conceptualize their insights and strategies. On the other hand, disinterested teachers, or those with rigid narrow mental sets of what is normal in a child, may be prone to label a child who is more difficult to manage than the average pupil as suffering from some psychological disturbance that requires outside professional help.

Overall, our experience with individual children with school problems has convinced us that a youngster's temperamental characteristics can play a significant role in creating unfavorable teacher judgments and handling. We suspect that the same may be true, though probably to a lesser degree, even at the college and graduate school level, though our case material in this regard is too sparse to make even tentative formulations.

However, our clinical impressions, as firm as they may be, require confirmation from systematic research data. We ourselves made a modest beginning in this regard, but the pioneering and authoritative studies have been done by Dr. Barbara Keogh and coworkers in the Department of Education of the University of California at Los Angeles. These will be described below.

Our own efforts in this regard involved first of all a study of a sample of 93 children (not the NYLS) in a suburban middle-class kindergarten (Gordon & Thomas, 1967). Two teachers, each highly experienced in this age-group, were asked to rate each child on a 4-point Quality of Participation Scale. This rating referred to the child's typical style of reaction to new situations and activities in the classroom, and corresponded to a characterization of a quick-to-warm-up versus slow-to-warm-up child. The teachers were also asked to estimate each child's general intellectual level on a 7-point scale. The children had not as yet been given psychometric tests, but a group IQ test was done the following September when the children were in the first grade. Because of this, the teacher's estimate of intellectual level could be compared with the IQ score done 6 months later. Discrepancies between the teacher estimates and the IQ scores were compared with their ratings on the Quality of Participation Scale. This analysis showed that the teachers systematically overestimated the intelligence of those children who plunged into new activities and situations quickly, positively and unhesitantly, and underestimated the intelligence of those who stood on the sidelines at first and then only gradually became involved in the new activity. These discrepancies were statistically significant. This analysis confirms the finding reported above in this chapter that, in several of the NYLS children with slow-to-warm-up patterns, teachers also underestimated these youngsters' intellectual capacities. Such teacher judgments always run the danger of becoming self-fulfilling prophecies, as the teachers communicate in one way or another their evaluations, and the children accept them as valid and begin to perform in school at suboptimal levels.

In another study, we analyzed the correlations between the temperamental characteristics of the NYLS subjects at 5 years of age and their academic achievement scores in reading and arithmetic at various points in elementary school (Chess, Thomas, & Cameron, 1976b). A substantial number of statistically significant correlations were found between the characteristics of withdrawal and low adaptability at 5 years and the later achievement scores. No significant correlations were found between temperament and IQ scores. The significant relationship appeared to be with the constellation of the slow-to-warm-up children, whose academic achievement was suboptimal, as compared to their intellectual capacities. In terms of the study of the suburban kindergarten group described above, this finding may be at least partially the result of a self-fulfilling prophecy created by teachers' underestimation of the intelligence of children with this temperamental pattern.

In the studies of Keogh and her associates Pullis and Cadwell (see Keogh, 1982), a shortened form of our Teacher Temperament Questionnaire (Thomas & Chess, 1977), was utilized to make it less time-consuming and more reliable. They subjected the questionnaires obtained from 35 teachers and over 300 children to reliability and factor analyses. The 8 temperament dimensions of our questionnaire (rhythmicity is not included in this questionnaire, inasmuch as teachers rarely have enough information to rate the children on this category) were found to factor out into 3 primary dimensions. The first, identified as Task Orientation, is made up of persistence, distractibility, and activity level. The second, called Personal Social Flexibility, comprised approach/withdrawal, positive mood, and adaptability. The third, Reactivity, included negative mood, sensory threshold, and intensity. The factor structure was stable across ages 3–6 years, and the 3 factors appear to identify patterns that are functionally significant in the school setting.

Keogh also shortened the questionnaire from 64 to 23 items, selecting items which were factorially consistent with the longer form. The consistency of her findings using the shortened form indicated that it is a feasible and economical substitute for the longer form. Using this shorter form, Keogh's research group examined the relationships between children's temperament, other pupil attributes, and teachers' decisions about classroom management and placement recommendations. There was a strong and consistent relationship between the pupils' temperament characteristics, especially Task Orientation, and teachers' classroom decisions (Pullis & Cadwell, 1982). After controlling for IQ, Pullis also found that Task Orientation and Flexibility related significantly to teachers' estimate of pupils' ability, the children with more positive temperament being rated higher than those with less positive patterns. In addition, as we also found (Gordon & Thomas, 1967), teachers overestimated the ability of children with specific temperamental characteristics (Keogh, 1982, 1984). Keogh concludes from her research unit's findings that variations in temperamental patterns make a significant contribution to a child's level of success at school. As Keogh (1982) stated:

> These variations in patterns are clear contributors to teachers' views of pupils' teachability, to the estimates they make of pupils' abilities, and to the kinds of expectations they have for pupils' educational performance. Recognition of the stylistic differences in children's behavior is important for teachers, as these variations are the basis of many instructional and management decisions. (p. 278)

A number of other investigators have also examined the correlations between the child's temperament and various aspects of the child's school functioning and teacher attitudes (see Pullis & Cadwell, 1982, for a summary of this literature). A substantial series of studies of this issue has been performed by Dr. Roy Martin and associates at the University of Georgia, which are summarized in Martin, Nagle, and Paget (1983). This group has developed a revised form of our Teacher Temperament Questionnaire, called the Teacher Form of the Temperament Assessment Battery, which has improved the psychometric properties of our original instrument, especially its internal consistency. In their first study, they found significant correlations between the temperamental variables of activity, adaptability, distractibility, and persistence with ratings of observed behavior in the classroom. In a second study, correlations between teacher attitudes and the child's temperament were identified. In their third study, reading achievement was correlated with persistence, low distractibility, high approach, and adaptability, while achievement in mathematics was correlated with adaptability and persistence.

SUMMARY

As Keogh has indicated (see above quote), the research findings to date justify the conclusion that a child's temperament can have a significant effect on her level of school functioning. Thus, it is important for teachers to recognize these differences in behavioral style in their individual students, so that they can make the optimal instructional and management decisions in each case. Keogh reports that "teachers who have participated in our research have reported that consideration of pupils' temperament has made them more sensitive to their own perception of individual children" (Keogh, 1982, p. 277). Most emphatically, this had also been our own experience. In our numerous discussions with teachers from many different schools over the years, whether in regard to youngsters in our research study or to individuals in clinical settings, we have found that, with few exceptions, teachers grasp quickly the concepts of temperamental individuality and goodness of fit. They find that they can apply these concepts to the practical problems of management of individual children in the classroom; many have been doing so empirically and by trial and error over the years of their classroom experiences. They tell us that shaping their management decisions to the needs of students with different temperaments, rather than being a burdensome exercise, makes their teaching activities not only more effective but also easier.

CHAPTER 14

Temperament and Pediatric Practice

WILLIAM B. CAREY

Other chapters in this volume are intended to acquaint clinicians of various professions and levels of training and experience with the manifestations and management of temperament in general clinical practice. By contrast, this chapter is directed specifically at pediatricians and other primary child health care practitioners such as general medical doctors and pediatric nurse practitioners. It should also be of interest to mental health professionals in psychiatry and psychology who are involved in research and consultations in the primary-care setting and in the training of pediatricians.

After a brief reminder of the general dissimilarities between pediatric and psychiatric practice, this chapter will be concerned primarily with a description of the particular ways in which the diagnosis and management of temperament are different in the pediatric care of children. The pertinent clinical interactions cover a wider range of the child's health, development, and behavior. Situations necessitating measurement of temperament include not only those involving clinical treatment of children with problems in functioning, but also routine assessment of well children. Temperament data are used in general educational discussions and specific counseling of parents of well children, in addition to problem solving in children with behavior disorders. Two subjects of particular interest to pediatricians will be discussed in greater detail: dealing with difficult temperament in well children, and the persistent confusion of attention deficit disorder (ADD) with temperament. A final section offers some suggestions on criteria for referral of problems by the pediatrician to the mental health specialist.

DIFFERENCES BETWEEN PEDIATRIC AND PSYCHIATRIC MANAGEMENT

As a background for the discussion in the rest of the chapter, let us first recall some of the general differences between management of children's development and behavior by the pediatrician as compared with the methods used by the psychiatrist or other mental health specialist. In the first place, pediatricians deal primarily with children showing normal behavior or minor deviations, and only occasionally encounter major problems.

One of the complexities of the pediatrician's role is that he or she must elicit from parents their various concerns and then determine which of them are worthy of further evaluation because of their objective severity or their annoyance to the parents. By contrast, parents generally arrive at the office of the psychiatrist or psychologist with a situation that they have already defined as a problem requiring special attention.

Since the problems dealt with by the pediatrician tend to be more minor and the degree of parental concerns less, the process of evaluation and programs of treatment are likely to be simpler and briefer. Counseling generally relies less on gaining insight into feelings and focuses more on offering education, reassurance, and offering specific suggestions (Schmitt, 1983).

However, pediatric interest and competence in developmental and behavioral issues varies greatly from an uneasy avoidance of them to a degree of competence approaching or even equaling that of a psychologist or psychiatrist. A multitude of factors in the pediatrician's personality, training, and experience determine whether his or her level of involvement in this area will be that of just meeting basic requirements, developing a special interest and competence, or becoming a full-time subspecialist (Dworkin, 1983).

The objective of this chapter is to provide useful information for pediatricians at all of these levels of functioning.

INTERACTIONS OF TEMPERAMENT AND CLINICAL CONDITIONS IN PEDIATRICS

The finding by the NYLS of a relationship between children's temperament and behavior disorders was only the beginning. Since the publication of their report (Thomas *et al.*, 1968), Thomas and Chess (1977) and other investigators (Carey, 1981) have continued to examine various other ways in which temperament and clinical conditions interact. A current review article (Carey, 1985a) has comprehensively presented the studies demonstrating temperament both as a factor predisposing to a variety of other clinical conditions and as an outcome of a number of clinical problems. This lengthy report is briefly summarized here because of its pertinence to pediatric practice. In fact, many of the clinical conditions described are more within the normal province of pediatrics than that of mental health specialists. The reader interested in pursuing further the individual factors mentioned here may wish to read the review article; the extensive list of references will not be included here.

More recent investigations have produced evidence that a child's temperament may be a *predisposing factor* to problems in virtually all aspects of his or her health: physical status, development, and behavior (see Table 14-1).

In the area of physical health, a pertinent finding is the relationship of activity and difficult temperament with accidents. Abrasive temperamental traits are strongly suspected as instrumental in evoking child abuse but proof has been hard to establish for methodological reasons. Among the functional physical problems with some evidence of a temperamental predisposition are colic (Carey, 1984a), functional abdominal pain, sleep disturbances, and enuresis. Rate of weight gain in infants may be in part related to how much the infants cries (Carey, 1985b), and failure to thrive is under investigation for the possibility of a similar contributory mechanism.

A child's developmental status appears to reflect not just the quality and quantity of the environmental input, but also the style with which the child exploits the opportunities presented. Active infants have been demonstrated to achieve milestones earlier, probably due to the greater energy expended toward these goals. Easy infants and children were shown to advance more rapidly, presumably by greater adaptive utilization of positively stimulating environments.

The child's general behavioral adjustment, as discussed extensively elsewhere in this volume, is a reflection of the fit between his temperament and the demands of the environment. These are both direct effects of the temperament on the interaction, and secondary effect by way of the changes in the parents behavior produced by the experience of living with the child. Similarly, in the educational setting there are direct effects of such characteristics as adaptability and persistence/attention span on the performance of school tasks and the secondary effects via the teachers' reaction to the child's behavioral style. Other areas of behavioral adjustment such as self-esteem and coping style (or "defenses") may well show an imprint of temperament when these matters are subjected to scrutiny.

A number of other areas of significant clinical interaction that may emerge from further investigation include functional constipation, obesity, and hypertension.

Quite apart from the role of temperament in predisposing to the incidence of various clinical conditions is the way in which it may affect the child's reaction to an illness once it is present. Intense, negative, and slowly adaptable children are likely to be hard for their parents to manage. They are quick to report their symptoms, which leads to faster diagnosis and treatment, but perhaps also excessive treatment at times. Mild, positive, and adaptable children, on the other hand, are less of a challenge to care for when sick. Their lower level of complaining is easier to live with, but may result at times in a delay in beginning appropriate treatment.

Beyond the areas of impact of the child's temperament on his own physical health, development, and behavior, one must not fail to consider also its effect on other members of the family and other caretakers. Anecdotal and research evidence supports the conclusion that living with a difficult child may significantly decrease parental self-esteem, mood, and marital harmony. The problems that other caretakers have with the management of such children may also diminish the parents' satisfaction with sitters, day care arrangements, teachers, and medical care.

Equally of interest to pediatricians are the possible variations in temperament occurring as an *outcome* of clinical conditions, both "risk factors" such as prematurity, in which no organic pathology may be evident, and established clinical problems such as deafness. The data on this issue are sparse but leave no doubt that the familiar concept of the psychosocial environment modifying the behavioral processes issuing from the genotype is far too simple. The child's temperament is probably also influenced to some degree by his physical and neurologic state and by the nonhuman environment. Many of the factors known to impinge on development may turn out also to affect temperament.

Prenatal correlations possibly of significance include genetic abnormalities, such as inborn errors of metabolism like phenylketonuria. The demonstration of low approach in two studies of Klinefelter's syndrome (the XXY constitution) should encourage other studies

TABLE 14-1. Comprehensive Diagnostic Formulation

		RELEVANT FINDINGS (STRENGTHS AND DEFICITS)	SERVICE NEEDS
Child			
Physical health	General somatic state Organic and functional Nutrition, growth, and physical maturation Neurologic status Sensory, reflex, motor, coordination		
Development	Capacities Motor Language Information processing Attention and organization Social skills Intelligence		
Behavior	Temperament (style) Clusters (e.g., difficult, easy) Traits (e.g., adaptability, attention) Performance (adjustment) Social competence		

Task performance (especially school)
Self-direction, care, esteem
Coping style
General mental and emotional state (e.g., anxiety, depression)

Interaction with environment

Input

Parental care (e.g., attitudes and expectations, feelings, management)
Sociocultural situation
Nonhuman environment

Outcome

Effect of child on parents and other caretakers
Complaints by caretakers

Summary of findings

Plans

To meet needs

For follow-up

Note. Table adapted from Carey and Levine (1983).

of chromosomal abnormalities. Other congenital abnormalities include multiple minor physical anomalies, thought to be related to low attention span in preschool children.

The role of pregnancy and perinatal stress in altering a child's temperament has been subjected to study only recently. Areas considered are: (1) obstetric complications such as prematurity, intrauterine growth retardation, asphyxia, medication, and trauma; (2) medical complications of the mother, such as nutritional status, toxins, drugs, infections, medical illness, and emotional state; and (3) other medical complications of the newborn such as hyperbilirubinemia and phototherapy. Studies of behavioral changes in newborns have usually not been extended to children at later ages.

Significant postnatal insults to the central nervous system might also have a place: nutrition, toxins, drugs, infections, and trauma. Handicapping conditions of the central nervous system such as retardation and cerebral palsy have not as yet been identified as factors affecting temperament. General medical illnesses brought to attention but without definite results include asthma, hypothyroidism, serous otitis, and anemia.

Research on clinical conditions possibly affecting temperament is in too early a stage to permit firm conclusions at present. So far, however, the most convincing evidence of effects on temperament has involved chronic conditions affecting the central nervous system such as malnutrition or toxins, rather than more transient ones such as abnormal delivery or head trauma.

MEASURING TEMPERAMENT IN PEDIATRIC PRACTICE

Techniques for measurement of temperament in clinical practice have been fully discussed in Chapter 3. In this chapter our focus narrows to describe the considerations unique to pediatric practice. This section is primarily concerned with the timing of temperament determinations; the following section will discuss the uses of the data gathered.

In routine checkups or by means of health maintenance visits, pediatricians obtain various kinds of screening data such as weight, height, vision, hearing, developmental status, and tuberculin testing. Certain other tests like sickle cell preparations and urine cultures are done only under special circumstances. It would be expensive and impractical to do all of these procedures at every visit. Similarly, although it might seem ideal to record new data on a child's temperament at every visit to the pediatrician, this would not be a realistic utilization of resources.

The substantial numbers of pediatricians now using temperament questionnaires in their practice have not been polled for their opinions as to what they regard as the best scheme. At this time I can only offer my own plan as one for other pediatricians to consider. I send an Infant Temperament Questionnaire to the mother of every infant in my practice when he or she is about 6 or 7 months old. A self-addressed stamped envelope is provided for returning it. A postcard is sent as a reminder if the form is not returned after 2 weeks. Roughly 95% of parents return the questionnaire properly completed. I make no extra charge for this service but other pediatricians may choose to do so.

The other questionnaires are available for use at older ages if problems arise but are not sent out regularly. However, some pediatricians may find that having routinely collected temperament data is helpful at certain stressful times such as with 2-year-olds, at school entry, or as puberty begins.

An example of selective use of a temperament questionnaire at a later time might be as follows. In the fall a mother telephoned that her son, who was almost 3 years old, was adjusting slowly to nursery school. Since he soon was to be coming to the office for the routine checkup examination we do on 3-year-olds, a Toddler Temperament Scale was sent to the mother to complete and return prior to that visit. Scoring of the scale showed a typical slow-to-warm-up pattern, which had also been present when the child was routinely rated at 6 months. His behavioral style as an infant had not been reported to be a problem, but became a source of concern with entry into nursery school. Counseling based on these data helped the parents to understand that he had not really changed but was having some presumably transient distress because of a major social adjustment. It was then easier to handle the mother's guilty feeling that her son's adjustment problem was due to her new part-time job.

We pediatricians must rely heavily on what parents tell us about their children in the process of diagnosis and management. Our opportunities to observe children directly are limited as to time and are often atypical as to quality. Extended interviewing can be arranged but is not usually necessary. Therefore, it is more efficient to utilize temperament questionnaires for getting a comprehensive, organized, and generally objective view of the child's temperament. Office observations and interview data are helpful to supplement the picture of the child's temperament and to get a better idea of its impact on the parents and other caretakers.

The 4 questionnaires designed by our group cover most of the pediatric age range, from 4 months to 12 years. One important period not specifically served by any questionnaire using the NYLS dimensions is the first 4 months. Researchers and practitioners will especially welcome a psychometrically sound scale for the first 4 months, when so much important interaction is occurring. The delay in the appearance of instruments for this interval has not been from a lack of interest but from a recognition of the technical difficulties in design. Behavioral style is of uncertain but possibly low stability during that time. Parents have less experience on which to base their observations. Some important differences, such as reactions to new foods and differentiation of strangers, are largely unreportable. Until scales appropriate for this early time are established, temperament data then should be obtained from interviewing and observations. Use of the Infant Temperament Questionnaire before the child is 4 months old cannot be counted on to provide reliable data.

Information on obtaining our group's questionnaires can be found in the Appendix at the end of this chapter.

USES OF TEMPERAMENT DATA IN PEDIATRIC PRACTICE

The clinical uses of temperament data in pediatrics have been described in some detail elsewhere (Carey, 1982). This section is a synopsis of that report.

Temperament data can aid pediatricians in fostering parent–child relationships on three levels: First, general educational discussions about temperament between pediatricians and parents help to provide a background of information, which increases parents' awareness and understanding of individual differences. Second, the identification of the temperament profile of the individual child provides parents with a more organized picture of his behavior pattern and of possible distortions in their perceptions of it. Third, the pediatrician may attempt to influence the temperament–environment interaction, when its dissonance has led to reactive symptoms, by suggesting alternative methods of parental management. The first two levels are almost entirely within the usual province of pediatric practice; the third one is shared with mental health consultants.

In general, educational discussion between the pediatrician and the parent the concept of individual differences is presented as a theoretical background or in relation to specific instructions about feeding, crying, sleeping or other caretaking practices. These discussions can be held at almost any time from before the child is born through adolescence. Their aim is to provide parents with the knowledge that there are behavioral predispositions, present at birth, and continuing over time with some stability and some change, that affect how children respond to the care they receive. Disagreeable behavior is not all directly attributable to inadequate parental care or brain malfunction. Child-rearing rules must be varied to suit individual reactions styles. For example, parents need to know that infants vary in the ease of establishing regular feeding patterns, the rapidity of acceptance of new foods, and the amount of noise tolerated during sleep.

For pediatricians and other primary health care workers to incorporate the concept of temperament in their thinking about children raises them to a higher level of understanding of the complexities of human relationships. For them successfully to communicate this view to parents in their practice is one of the most valuable steps they can take in providing parents with information on child development and behavior.

Identification of the specific temperament profile of the child means determining the child's temperament pattern and using it as a basis for shaping the counseling of the parents to meet the particular needs of the child. General discussions are of interest, but specific advice is usually more helpful.

Whether the temperament data are obtained from a questionnaire, or preferably from a combination with interview and observational data, the objective is not to attach a diagnostic label to the child. Such terms as "difficult" are better kept in the mind of the pediatrician and on the child's record, but data given to parents should only be in descriptive terms. Since these diagnostic labels are often poorly understood by clinicians and researchers, one should not expect parents to derive benefit from their use. Far better is the practice of giving parents the results of a temperament profile in such terms as "rather active," "somewhat intense in his reactions," or "she does a lot of fussing at this time."

Using this temperament profile, the pediatrician is in a position to aid parents in handling more skillfully the child's care when well and sick. An example has been given of the use of knowledge of a slow-to-warm-up pattern in helping parents understand and deal with their son's slow adjustment to nursery school. Also mentioned above was the way children's behavioral style in illness may exaggerate or minimize the symptoms and the importance for parents and physicians to learn to interpret them correctly.

Parents of difficult or slow-to-warm-up children often do not recognize the nature of the pattern. They may feel guilty, believing that their child is "immature" and "insecure" and that this is all their fault. Relieving parents of such unwarranted self-criticism is one of the most valuable steps available to the pediatrician in fostering positive mental health. The process of actually dealing with difficult temperament in children will be discussed in greater detail below.

The other main use of determining the child's individual temperament profile is the identification of major discrepancies between the parents' ratings and their perceptions. Infants rated as difficult may be perceived as easy and vice versa. The reason for these phenomena are discussed further in the next section of this chapter.

Finally, the pediatrician may attempt to influence the temperament–environment interaction. When there is a physical, developmental, or behavioral problem arising as the result of stress in such an interaction, and the clinician knows enough about these matters in general, and of the specific case in particular, it may be possible for him to influence the interactions favorably by suggesting alternative patterns of parental handling. If this is successful, the stress in the interaction should diminish and the reactive disorder should disappear. The other part of the therapeutic process is that the caretaker must learn to accommodate somewhat to the child's behavioral style, which is evidently less changeable and not abnormal in itself.

DEALING WITH DIFFICULT TEMPERAMENT

The concept of difficult temperament has been widely accepted and the diagnosis is evidently being made often in research and practice. It is surprising, therefore, that so little has been written on techniques suitable for its management. Thomas and Chess have on numerous occasions described in general the patience and flexibility required of the parents of such a child and the significance of poorness of fit in generating problems in behavior, but little can be found in previous publications as to specific steps appropriate for primary health professionals, particularly before any secondary clinical conditions have arisen. The principal reason is undoubtedly that there are no easy answers. A less obvious explanation is the problem in defining precisely this phenomenon with which we are attempting to deal. Before discussing some practical steps for management, we must clarify further the question of difficult temperament.

As has been explained in earlier chapters in this volume, the concept of difficult temperament emerged as the NYLS showed that children with the five temperamental characteristics (low rhythmicity, approach, and adaptability; high intensity; negative mood) were more likely to develop behavior problems than those without them (Thomas *et al.*, 1968). This impressive finding has led to a firm establishment of this particular set of behaviors in the minds of some, with greater invariance as to cultural setting, clinical consequences, and age than the original investigators intended or the data would justify. Furthermore, some researchers and clinicians have assumed that the only reason to collect temperament data is the rigid categorization of children into these diagnostic groups. Those of us who have developed questionnaires may be in part responsible for this process.

The NYLS population is an American urban, middle-class sample in which, up to age 10, the presence of behavior problems was a prime outcome measure. The possibility of divergent consequences in other cultures has been examined only to a small extent so far. The review earlier in this chapter of the involvement of temperament in other areas of clinical concern such as physical health, development, and school problems, demonstrates additional significance for all the other four traits: activity, persistence, distractibility, and sensory threshold. As children grow older from infancy into childhood, there are important changes in what is "difficult," such as the increased significance of low persistence and low attention span and the shift of distractibility from a desirable to an undesirable trait. A greater than 3-fold increase occurred between the 3.7% of mothers who regarded their 4- to 8-month-old infants as "more difficult than average" to the 12.5% of practically the same population who judged their 1- to 3-year-old toddlers thus (McDevitt & Carey, 1981). Moreover, if being "difficult" enables an infant to survive in a famine (DeVries, 1984) and being "easy" predisposes to failure to thrive (Carey, 1985a), the meaning of the terms has become blurred if used in an abstract fashion.

Although the emphasis of the chapter is primarily practical, one should carry this theoretical discussion a bit further. There are two possible approaches to solve the question of what constitutes temperamental difficulty. The phenomenon could be defined either in more general or in more specific terms. A more general conceptualization could be: any behavioral style characteristic or cluster of characteristics that make a child or group of children hard for their caretakers to manage and are thereby conducive to interpersonal stress and reactive clinical problems in the child. On the other hand, we might particularize into specific problem areas like social difficulty, educational difficulty, temperamental predisposition to child abuse, abdominal pain, and so on. Strengths of such predispositions would vary and their impact and management would depend upon the circumstances (Carey, 1986).

There should be no doubt as to the reality of difficult temperament. Bates (1980) has promoted the view that it is a "parental perception" rather than a characteristic of the child. However, evidence abounds to support the reality and clinical significance of difficult temperament and its measurability (Rutter, 1982; Thomas, Chess, & Korn, 1982). Cross-sectional studies such as questionnaire standardizations demonstrate that groups of parents agree that certain behavioral style characteristics make children hard to manage. The frequent discrepancies between parental ratings and their perceptions of difficulty and their varying opinions as to their child's most abrasive traits argue not for the opinion that difficulty is all in the mind of the mother but for the conclusion that there are both general and individual views as to which traits are most bothersome.

The following suggestions on dealing with difficult temperament use the term both in the established sense, that there is a set of behaviors that most parents find hard to manage, and in the broader sense that almost any temperament trait may generate stress in certain settings. These are some suggested steps for management based on my own clinical experience and from informal discussion with others: (1) recognition of the pattern by the clinician; (2) general counseling to give parents information, perspective, and confidence; (3) specific counseling to help parents achieve a more detached handling; (4) direct counseling of the child for insight and plans; and (5) environmental interventions for parental support.

1. Recognition of the pattern by the clinician. Difficult temperament characteristics may be identified by various techniques either in the course of a routine checkup visit or when concern about the child is being expressed by the parents. The initial appraisal should also include evaluation of other aspects of the child and the environment, especially the impact of the child on the parents, the vulnerabilities and liabilities of the parents, and any secondary clinical problems resulting from these factors. Advice should be withheld until these issues are clear.

If parental concern about the child stems from factors other than a "poor fit" with difficult temperament traits, the management takes a somewhat different form than that described here. As one example of this, if an obviously easy child is seen as a burden by a mother overwhelmed by social problems, the attention goes more to her personal needs.

On the other hand, if this assessment uncovers temperament characteristics that most parents would find difficult but these parents seem to be enduring them well, the clinician's investigation may stop at this point. Such tolerance or lack of complaint could be due to inexperience or denial, but are equally likely to be a reflection of strength and realistic explanations. The information about the child can be stored away for possible later use. Certainly the mention of diagnostic labels, which may be misunderstood or harmful, is inappropriate.

2. *General counseling—to provide parents with information, perspective, and confidence.* If the clinician has established some form of difficult temperament in the child and the parents are experiencing discomfort in the relationship, further steps are called for. The clinician's role should be to supply any needed background information on temperament differences in general and how they may affect and interact with caretakers. This particular child's pattern and his contribution to the interaction should be understood. Parental feelings of guilt, that they are fully responsible for the distress, must be relieved. Anger must be recognized and dealt with appropriately. Misplaced blame on foods or previous professional advice must be acknowledged. From all of this should emerge a new perspective.

Once this revised view of the situation has been established, the outlook for the future can be discussed. Parents should know that, although there are no simple answers as to management, experience has taught us that with appropriate steps difficult children generally do well eventually (Carey & McDevitt, 1978; Thomas & Chess, 1977). Such confidence helps to sustain parents through the turmoil of everyday life and may encourage them to make use of opportunities to express affection during cordial intervals.

Although it is not exactly the same, there are some parallels between the relationship of parent and difficult child and that between psychotherapist and difficult patients (Smith & Steindler, 1983).

3. *Specific counseling for concerned but detached handling by parents.* The aim of specific advice to parents should be to teach them better coping skills and to revise the child–parent interaction enough to reduce unnecessary stress for parents and child. That should make

life more bearable for the parents and should decrease the likelihood of secondary clinical problems arising.

As in other counseling, the parents' own ideas should be used and approved whenever possible (Schmitt, 1983). If the clinician suggests specific alterations, an important consideration is coordination of the strategy of the two parents and other significant caretakers. Furthermore, all of this must happen without violating the requirements of the siblings. A principal element in the management of a difficult child is the anticipation of stressful interactions, not the avoidance of them, but preparation that allows the parents to bring their best efforts to bear.

Of paramount importance for parents is that they strive to achieve some detachment from the abrasive behavior of the child so that self-defeating overreactions, especially to the intensity and negativity, can be minimized. Parents have to learn to be sensitive and responsive to the real needs of the child, rather than the flamboyant or distorted messages about them. The slowly approaching and adapting child needs parental patience and firmness, but not forcing into or evasion of novelty. Flexible schedules are helpful for the arrhythmic infant and for the older child with low persistence or high distractibility. A child with low threshold may require some shielding from excessive stimuli. The active child does better with acceptable outlets for his energy.

The emphasis of this section has been on helping parents to cope with difficult temperament rather than trying to change the temperament itself. We know that temperament can change over time and some of the reasons for this are beginning to be comprehended. However, very little is understood about how clinical interaction might achieve this. Some children with difficult temperament have undergone psychotherapy because of it, but no study has yet evaluated the efficiency of this process. One problem with such an investigation would be this author's observation that, when parents have taken such children for psychotherapy, the difficult temperament has frequently been misidentified by the therapist as other issues such as "a problem dealing with anger due to family dynamics" or as "hyperactivity".

Behavioral modification techniques have been proposed and tried for helping the noncompliant child (Forehand & McMahon, 1981). Such an approach may prove to be useful but first the proponents of this method must recognize that noncompliance does not always come from "maladaptive patterns of family interaction" and that their acknowledged 22% failure rate may be due to difficult temperament in the child rather than just problems in the parents and social situations.

The question of whether cerebral stimulants, now commonly used for ADD, are altering difficult temperament rather than correcting a brain malfunction, is discussed elsewhere (Carey, 1985a).

Therefore, at our present state of knowledge, specific counseling by pediatricians should be aimed at modifying the parental interaction with the difficult temperament rather than trying to change the temperament itself.

4. *Direct counseling of the child for insight and plans.* With older children, the opportunity may arise for direct discussion between the clinician and the patient. This counseling might involve the clinician's sharing with the child his or her insight into the problem and some suggestions for more effective management. The child who understands his own behavioral style and the stresses that it may promote in his relationships should be in a better position to avoid clinical problems. For example, the fourth-grade child with a slow-to-warm-up pattern, who experiences abdominal pain before important events at home and school, would be helped to recognize his behavioral style and to learn new ways of dealing with it.

5. *Environmental intervention for parental support.* The clinician can make a variety of suggestions that will help the parents beyond the immediate interaction with the child. Mobilizing assistance from relatives and friends for the task of child care may allow parents a chance to seek refreshment, and mothers a personal identity, outside the home. Day care arrangements may accomplish the same objectives. Evenings and weekends out of the house with spouse or friends can do much to restore a sense of perspective and well-being. Professionally organized parent support groups for this specific problem of dealing with difficult temperament have only just begun on a trial basis and may prove to be a major resource for parents in the future (see Turecki & Tonner, 1985).

Some criteria for referral of such children by the pediatrician to psychotherapists will be presented below.

THE PERSISTENT CONFUSION OF ATTENTION DEFICIT DISORDER AND TEMPERAMENT

The phenomenon variously called minimal brain dysfunction, hyperactivity, or attention deficit disorder (ADD) is probably the most confused area in pediatrics today (Carey, 1984b). From the point of view of a discussion of temperament, the main problem is that the low attention span and high activity (and sometimes other traits such as impulsivity) said to be diagnostic of ADD are also normal temperament variables. Yet no effort has been made by proponents of ADD to distinguish when they are caused by the presumed brain malfunction and when not. Two theoretical systems appear to be competing as explanations of roughly the same areas of behavior, but the two factions have not resolved their rival claims and are largely ignoring each other. Previous efforts at resolution of the confusion have had little impact (Carey & McDevitt, 1980; Carey, McDevitt, & Baker, 1979; Rubenstein & Brown, 1984).

The historical background of this confusion appears to be that in the 1960s as the inadequacies of the prevailing excessive environmentalism were becoming clearer, two different theories arose to explain the individual's contribution to the organismic–environmental interactions resulting in problems of behavior and learning.

On the one hand, some have contended that the source of problems is malfunction of the brain. A multitude of opinions was consolidated by the report of a special task force of the U.S. Public Health Service headed by Clements (1966) and by the American Psychiatric Association's (1968) *Diagnostic and Statistical Manual of Mental Disorders* (2nd ed.) (*DSM-II*). The most recent reformulation was as "attention deficit disorder" in the *Diagnostic and Statistical Manual of Mental Disorders* (3rd ed.) (*DSM-III*) (American Psychiatric Association, 1980). Attention deficit disorder has been called the "most common neurobehavioral disorder in the pediatric age group; it affects 5% to 10% of the school age population" (Shaywitz & Shaywitz, 1984). This widely read pediatric review of ADD describes it as an abnormal set of behaviors caused by brain injury or genetically determined malfunction of the brain. The child with this "syndrome" can be expected to develop problems of behavior and learning in almost any setting. *DSM-III*, on the other hand, takes no position on the etiology of ADD.

For some investigators and many of the general public, the real troublemaker is thought to be various foods and other substances ingested that set off the presumed brain malfunction. Space limitations prohibit further discusson of this controversial subject.

On the other hand, temperament researchers have proposed that problems of behavior and learning occur not primarily due to an abnormality of brain function, but are due to poorness of fit between the behavioral style characteristics of the child and the values and expectations of the social environment. In most social settings the "difficult" cluster is especially likely to promote disharmony (Thomas *et al.*, 1968), while in school low persistence (attention span) and low adaptability are particularly important (Carey, 1985a).

We are not dealing here simply with a matter of semantics. If the child and the environment are in conflict, it makes a major difference whether the problem is seen as something wrong with the child or as a inharmonious interaction in which the child is only one of the participants.

Despite the common use of the diagnosis of ADD, there is little evidence that there really is such a syndrome. There is neither adequate proof of concurrence of the supposed elements, nor is there sufficient difference of them from other phenomena to justify the use of the term "syndrome." High or low attention span may be found with high or low activity and with high or low distractibility. The diagnosis has little interrater, retest, or cross-situational reliability. The low attention span and high activity attributed to ADD cannot be distinguished from the same behaviors in other conditions (Rutter, 1983). Moreover, the low adaptability that may be the most prominent behavioral characteristic in school problems (Carey *et al.*, 1979; Rutter, 1983) is not reported as a part of the "syndrome" of ADD.

The persistent confusion of ADD and temperament leaves the pediatrician in a distressing quandary as to what diagnoses and treatments to employ. Several suggestions are offered here:

1. In the absence of proof of a syndrome of ADD it is not logical to continue to refer to it (Rutter, 1983). One cannot deny that some children have behavioral predispositions that put their success in school in great jeopardy. Our concern is with an appropriate assessment and identification of them.

2. In place of ADD or other vague labels one would do well to substitute a comprehensive diagnostic formulation (Carey & Levine, 1983), that requires the clinician to record under separate headings the child's (1) general physical and objective neurologic status, (2) developmental status or capacities, (3) temperament, and (4) behavioral performance or adjustment (see Table 14-1). Such a formulation also includes the child's interaction with the environment, the input of parental care and of the sociocultural and nonhuman environment, and the outcome, that is, the effect of the child on his caretakers and their complaints about the child.

3. More research is needed to clarify the confusing situation described above. Of special value should be more studies of normal populations to show how complex a matter adjustment and accomplishment in school really are. For example, what are the antecedents of low attention span, what are its components, and what concomitant behavioral traits (such as adaptability) push the inattentive child into academic troubles or rescue him from them?

To conclude this section, let us acknowledge that it seems likely that eventually a small group of children will emerge with a true syndrome that may be shown to stem from some form of cerebral malfunction. However, for the present pediatricians should reconsider the promiscuous use of the diagnosis of ADD. Many of the children now being given this label probably have nothing wrong with their brain function but are only experiencing a poorness of fit between their behavioral style and the requirements of their caretakers at home and school.

CRITERIA FOR REFERRAL

To complete this chapter, it remains only to make some suggestions as to how and when pediatricians should refer problems in the area of temperament interactions to a psychiatrist or other mental health specialist. The criteria presented here are limited to this area and not intended to cover the full range of developmental and behavioral deviations.

Helping parents deal with difficult temperament, that is, any set of temperament characteristics that they find abrasive, should be largely a pediatric task. For example, high activity or slow adaptability are variations of the normal pattern, can be handled in the primary-care setting, and should not be treated as deviations requiring referral to specialists. Only under the extraordinary circumstances of a seriously deteriorating parent–child relationship that cannot be managed appropriately in the primary care setting, should such a referral be necessary before secondary symptoms have arisen.

On the other hand, if there are secondary symptoms such as behavior problems resulting from the stress of a poorness of fit between the child's temperament and the handling of the caretakers, and if the pediatrician has not been able to alter parental behavior sufficiently to ameliorate the problem, the time has come to turn to the more expert help of the mental health specialist. The precise point at which a referral should occur is hard to state; much depends on the counseling skill of the pediatrician, the nature and severity of the problem, and the quality and availability of the specialists. Some pediatricians may wish to transfer immediately the responsibility for a problem that other pediatricians could manage successfully with a level of skill equal to that of the available psychotherapists.

There are advantages to the pediatrician's retaining the management of the problem whenever possible. The pediatrician's long acquaintance with the child and parents often means that he or she can proceed more rapidly without having first to establish a relationship and construct a picture of the background. The quality of the interactions may be better understood and in less danger of being misinterpreted and incorrectly diagnosed than it might be by a stranger to the situation.

The case of an 11-year-old boy may serve as an example of the interplay of parental management and pediatric and psychiatric counseling. As a young infant his irregularity, loud crying, and slow adaptation made him a challenge even for his capable parents. His difficult temperament was confirmed by an Infant Temperament Questionnaire completed when the child was 6 months old. However, with consistent pediatric management and parental competence the boy developed no secondary behavior problems. When he began nursery school, the teacher reported that he showed aggression with peers on the playground but had no problem during learning periods. The parents felt able to manage the boy's temper until a fight at school resulted in the child's breaking of his opponent's arm. The apparently severe degree of antisocial behavior in the child and distress in the parents justified a referral to a psychiatrist at this point. The therapist assuaged the parents' feelings and was able to help the child to reduce his aggressiveness in a few sessions. The therapist's attention then turned to the boy's underlying behavioral style, which he diagnosed as "minimal brain dysfunction," and recommended that this condition be treated by a special diet. This suggestion put the pediatrician and psychiatrist at odds as to the diagnosis. Psychotherapy had served its purpose and was discontinued. The close contact between pediatrician and parents, and a regular diet, were resumed. The boy continued to have difficulty adjusting to new situations and coping with change, but has generally done well at home and at school. When last heard from, he had just received an award as the outstanding student in the fifth grade.

Pediatricians cannot change many of the biological handicaps and negative psychosocial influences with which some children are burdened. However, with increased knowledge of temperament and its interactions, we can help parents deal constructively with childrens' difficult temperament and the problems resulting from disharmonious interaction of it with the social milieu. Referral of children with behavior problems to a mental health specialist should be necessary only when the reactive problem requires more time or skill than the pediatrician is able to offer.

SUMMARY

This chapter presents a description of the ways that children's temperament is important to the primary-health care professional, and especially the practicing pediatrician. In addition to the more familiar differences between psychiatric and pediatric management, the pediatrician finds in dealing with temperament a wider area of clinical interactions, more diverse situations for measurement, and a greater range of uses of temperament data than does the mental health practitioner. Temperament is involved in clinical interactions both as a factor predisposing to physical, developmental, and behavioral status, and as an outcome of prenatal, perinatal, and postnatal conditions. Measurements of temperament are performed not only when there are problems in functioning but also in the routine assessment in well children. Temperament data are not just used for problem solving, but in general educational discussions and specific counseling regarding normal children. Two special problem areas for pediatricians have been discussed in this chapter: the management of difficult temperament without secondary behavior problems and the confusion of ADD with temperament. Referral to mental health specialists should seldom be necessary for children displaying difficult temperament alone, only for those children with secondary problems stemming from temperament–environment interactions that are beyond the ability of the pediatrician to manage.

APPENDIX. INFORMATION ON OBTAINING TEMPERAMENT QUESTIONNAIRES

The addresses from which our 4 temperament questionnaires may be obtained are listed below. Since these instruments were developed with minimal financial support, please send a prepaid contribution of $10.00 for each scale to help us cover expenses. The forms may be photocopied as much as you wish from the one you receive.

1. Infant Temperament Questionnaire (4- to 8-month-old infants)—revised in 1977 by W. B. Carey and S. C. McDevitt
   William B. Carey, MD, 319 West Front Street, Media, Pennsylvania 19063
   Telephone: (215) 566-6641
   Reference: (1978). Revision of the Infant Temperament Questionnaire. *Pediatrics*, *61*, 735-739.

2. Toddler Temperament Scale (1- to 3-year-old children)—developed in 1978 by W. Fullard, S. C. McDevitt, and W. B. Carey
   William Fullard, PhD, Department of Educational Psychology, Temple University, Philadelphia, Pennsylvania 19122
   Telephone: (215) 787-6022
   Reference: (1984). Assessing temperament in one to three year old children. *Journal of Pediatric Psychology*, *9*, 205-217.

3. Behavioral Style Questionnaire (3- to 7-year-old children)—developed in 1975 by S. C. McDevitt and W. B. Carey
   Sean C. McDevitt, PhD, Devereux Center, 6436 East Sweetwater, Scottsdale, Arizona 85254
   Telephone: (602) 998-2920
   Reference: (1978). The measurement of temperament in 3-7 year old children. *Journal of Child Psychology and Psychiatry*, *19*, 245-253.

4. Middle Childhood Temperament Questionnaire (8- to 12-year old children)—developed in 1979-1980 by R. L. Hegvik, S. C. McDevitt, and W. B. Carey
   Robin L. Hegvik, PhD, 307 North Wayne Avenue, Wayne, Pennsylvania 19087
   Telephone: (215) 687-6058
   Reference: (1982). The Middle Childhood Temperament Questionnaire. *Journal of Developmental and Behavioral Pediatrics*, *3*, 197-200.

All 4 scales assess the NYLS temperament charactcristics by eliciting parent responses to about 97 behavioral descriptions. Total internal consistency was .83, .85, and .84, respectively, for the first 3 scales; 1-month retest reliability for these scales was .86, .88, and .89, respectively. For the Middle Childhood Temperament Questionnaire (MCTQ), the median category internal consistency was .82 and the 2½-month retest reliability was .87. Some external validity data are available.

CHAPTER 15

Temperament and Nursing Practice

A considerable body of literature has developed in recent years pointing to the importance of children's temperamental individuality in pediatric nursing practice. (Mercer, 1981; Millor, 1981, 1984; Moller, 1983; Roberts, 1983; Ventura, 1982). This is equally true for nurses whose role is expressed as nurse practitioners, public health nurses, and those functioning in well-baby hospital clinics, schools, and private pediatricians' offices. It is certainly also an important element in the nursing of hospitalized sick babies and children. This chapter will summarize this literature and also report some of our own relevant clinical observations. For a fuller discussion, the reader is referred to the articles and textbooks cited here.

In the pediatric nursing textbook, *Nursing care of infants and children*, Whaley and Wong (1983) present a description of the 9 temperamental characteristics of the NYLS, and the 3 clusters of easy child, difficult child, and slow-to-warm-up child. The relationships found among these temperamental patterns and behavior disorders are reported, as well as the finding that a good fit of parental management and child temperament counteracts a high risk of vulnerability. The authors illustrate the practical usefulness of the concept of temperament as a pediatric nursing tool in their discussion of the temperamental issues in the management of the life-threatening failure to thrive syndrome. References to the importance of temperament are also made in several other nursing texts (Brown & Murphy, 1981; Chow, Durand, Feldman, & Mills, 1984; Heagerty, Glass, King, & Manly, 1980; Hymovich, 1982; Tackett & Hansberger, 1980).

Well-baby care generally takes place in community health stations or pediatric offices. Patterns differ, however, around the United States, depending upon the rural or urban site of care, the programs of the state or city, the realities of danger in traveling within high-crime areas where in fact the need may be greatest, and the geographic distances to be covered to reach a clinic. Some programs focus on problem situations in which either mother or baby may have been at risk for illness or survival during the pregnancy, labor or delivery, or during the neonatal period. In some countries, but not often in ours, visiting nurses routinely help out well mothers with well babies at home in the initial period of life.

Unless the pediatrician, whether in a clinic or private office, has made a project of demonstrating his or her personal availability for discussion, and has made it clear that no parent's question will be thought too stupid or too trivial for attention, it is often assumed that the doctor is too busy to hear a seemingly unimportant question. If rapport has been established with the nurse, as is usually the case, this is the person to whom parents turn with their concerns regarding behavior. They are used to the fact, after all, that the nurse will frequently give directions as to the next step with medication, and will decide whether a health question can be answered with or without consulting the doctor. Parents wondering whether or not to be concerned over some behavioral habit, or worried over the possibility of slowness in development, or finding the child unexpectedly difficult to handle in some respect, are likely to seek out the nurse first. Either the nurse will give them the answers, or will decide that the issue merits the pediatrician's direct examination and advice.

TEMPERAMENT IN WELL-BABY CARE

Routine care of well babies may cover the same general areas of nurturing whatever the geographic area, ethnic group, or socioeconomic class. However, an individual parent caring for a specific infant needs individualized directions and advice: this is part and parcel of well baby care. The amount of feeding, the number of feedings to give each day, whether these should be by the clock or by infant self demand, when and how to introduce solids, how often and how much is proper for the baby to sleep—these and other aspects of baby care vary within the normative range from baby to baby, and parent to parent. Pediatric nurses generally take such individualized functioning into account in delivery of care. The particular temperamental style of the baby is sometimes but not always routinely included among these aspects of individuality nurses do review with parents (Blosser, 1979; Brown, 1977; Mercer, in press; Roberts, 1983; Ventura,

1982; Whaley & Wong, 1983). Certainly, aspects of child temperament will arise in the questions that come to the nurse, whether he or she recognizes them or not.

In Chapters 4–8 of this volume, there has been discussion, developmental period by period, of temperamental style among children and their practical implications for child care. Chapter 14, by Dr. Carey, also takes up temperament as it relates directly to pediatric care. When, in well-child care, parents report having a difficult time in feeding, dressing, introducing school attendance, and similar ordinary childhood events, nurses are in a position to review this particular child's behavior in the context of temperament as revealed by both present and past behaviors. They can help the parents to understand the concept of a goodness of fit between the child's behavioral style and parental handling, whether they use this term or not. The pediatric nurse is also in a position to help parents settle upon a manner of child-rearing that fits their own personalities and life-styles, while taking into account whether the child in question is an easy child, slow-to-warm-up, or difficult, high- or low-active, high- or low-distractible, high or low with regard to threshold to sensory stimuli, an approacher or withdrawer to new situations, quickly or slowly adaptable, high or low in persistence and attention span, and whether the child's biological rhythms are regular or irregular.

With her knowledge of the child's temperamental individuality, the nurse can start the parents on a manner of handling that will help youngsters achieve socialization and task mastery at their own pace and in their own style, but yet to become able to fit in with the mores of society and accomplish the demands it makes upon them. This can be exemplified in the issue of needless power struggles that should be avoided or nipped in the bud. Let us take the instance of a child with high persistence who has become involved in a task considered potentially dangerous or otherwise disapproved of by parents—or an approved task that time and other plans require bringing to an end. Disregard by the child of instructions to stop the activity may be seen by the parent as willful disobedience, especially if this has been a repeated sequence of events. The parent then considers the child's failure to obey an action meriting some disciplinary consequence. The child finds herself punished again and again for behavior that she has not intended as disobedience and in fact may have had little awareness of the passage of time or the tenacity of her own persistence. If allowed to go on, this antagonistic parent–child interaction can easily mushroom into a behavior disorder. At this early stage, before significant damage has been done, it is the pediatric nurse whom the parents are often most likely to consult. Once the nurse has been able to redefine the central issue as the child's temperamental quality of persistence rather than a conscious and determined defiance of parental authority, a cooperative program can be planned. Child and parent can then be joined in the attempt to avoid confrontations by looking ahead. Parents can even make the issue into a game, as they outpersist the child when her actions must be terminated. Thus, a controlling parent has been converted into a parent in control.

Or, with another child, an after-school activity is available which is considered by the parents to be highly desirable. The child balks, yet it is the type of recreation that has been of interest in the past. An unsuccessful attempt is made to coerce the youngster into attendance, but she becomes tearful, develops a bellyache, or uses other maneuvers to avoid going. Discussion with the nurse brings out what the parents have really known but overlooked. Their daughter has almost uniformly exhibited similar discomfort at the introduction to some new event, because she is temperamentally slow-to-warm-up. This evaluation can be a pointer that the nurse uses to suggest a different strategy which will give the child the opportunity to experience the program to determine whether she does in fact enjoy it. It can be arranged that she go with a friend; a promise may be given that if she attends 4 times and decides she does not like it, she then has the freedom to decline without risking her parents' disapproval. She is reminded of similar situations in the past when she "just knew" she would hate it but then loved it in the end and, also, of other times when she did dislike a program and was allowed to drop it without parental counterpressure. This approach turns the new event from an adversarial situation into one of cooperation; respect for the temperamental style of the child has altered the beginning parental concern that they were harboring a child tyrant.

It is the nurse who is likely to hear about such problems in their early stages, when it is easier to restructure the activity and prevent unnecessary child–parent confrontation and growing dissonance between the two sides. It is the nurse who can, in many such situations, quietly reinterpret for parents the child's seemingly ungrateful, or oppositional, or anxious behavior as the expression of a style that is quite normal, that is present in other children, and that has its assets as well as the liabilities that brought about the parents' worries.

As children enter upon new developmental stages, and as new and more complicated demands are made upon them, parents frequently

forget the steps that had been necessary in order for their child to
master the earlier demands. Once again, it is the nurse who may be
called upon for help. She is in a position to note basic similarities in
present temperamental patterns to those shown in the past, although
the precise present situation may be different. She can then utilize the
former problem and the success of its solution to show how, for
example, the child who sailed through grade school, except for the
first weepy weeks or days each term, is really now facing a similar
demand with regard to a new junior high school. Once again, the
youngster needs time to attain the familiarization that will permit her
to perform successfully and to enjoy the new school experiences—
although the strategies to be employed must take into account both the
child's present developmental stage and the specific circumstances of
this particular junior high school. Clearly the answer will not be, at
this age, to have mother stay in the classroom for a few days, as was
done before. But it might be for parent and child to tour the school
together in advance so as to find out exactly where each room is prior
to the first hectic days of school opening, to rehearse together the new
situations that are likely to arise, as well as other strategies.

Should there be questionable features of the child's behavior, it is
the nurse who will be in a position to note these and to call them to the
pediatrician's attention. And if a poorness of fit appears to be building
up, a growing antagonism or distance between parent and child, again
it is the nurse who will be likely to witness the spontaneous undesirable interactions between parent and child as they sit waiting for the
doctor, and to note the need for intervention while the situation may
yet be in a nascent stage.

TEMPERAMENT AND THE SCHOOL NURSE

The school nurse is in a key position to identify problems related to
temperament. School children referred to the nurse for one physical
symptom or another may, of course, be suffering from some acute or
chronic illness. But the symptom may also be the expression of excessive stress resulting from the child's inability to cope with the social or
academic demands of the school setting. Such a poorness of fit, of
course, does not always involve temperamental issues. There may be
an unrecognized learning disability, a physical handicap that the
teacher has minimized, or a tragic home situation that has overwhelmed the youngster. But not infrequently the poorness of fit and

excessive stress may be related to school demands which are dissonant with the child's temperamental characteristics. The various possibilities have been discussed in Chapter 13. If the child's stressful state shows itself in poor academic performance or deviant behavior, this usually comes to the teacher's attention. But if the reaction takes the form of a physical symptom, the school nurse is the one more likely to be involved. And in most cases, the youngster may find it easier to confide in the nurse than in the teacher. The latter is likely to represent an authoritative and even forbidding figure, while the nurse traditionally is likely to be viewed as a nurturant and sympathetic figure.

TEMPERAMENT IN THE NURSING CARE OF SICK CHILDREN

When ill, some children show little or no change in their temperamental behavior qualities as compared to when they are well. The infant with predominant positive mood, with an approaching and quickly adapting style may in fact be at risk of having her degree of illness underestimated because she remains cheerful, even if a trifle less ebullient than usual. The difficult child may not appear to be more difficult than usual. Since it is hard to take seriously all the child's complaints when usually they are of minor import, the complaints that signal actual discomfort and illness that require prompt attention may go unheeded at first. On the other hand, there are youngsters who behave differently when sick than when well. After several bouts of illness, these changes in style of behavior for sickness versus health are identifiable if they are consistent. It is not unusual for a parent to become aware that his or her child must be ill because she is less boisterous than usual, or more fussy, or is more cooperative than is her wont.

For the nurse, it is important to be aware of such alterations in behavioral style during illness. Also, during the actual care of the sick child, it is the temperamental characteristics as they present themselves at that time that the nurse has to manage for the most effective benefit to the child. The sick youngster who needs bed rest, but has high motor activity, can, by turning and twisting and doing acrobatic stunts, make the restful value of the time in bed quite questionable. For this child, periodic brief respites from full bed rest may in the end make for higher achievement of actual restfulness. On the other hand, if the nurse escalates admonitions and restrictions, the patient's cooperativeness may be lost. The child for whom anything new is a stress may be relaxed by several sessions of rehearsing before any new procedure is done. This may provide considerably greater peace of mind for the child, and a cooperative atmosphere for nursing procedures. The quiet child with high imagination and mild intensity of expressiveness can be a silent worrier who needs active reassurance lest she imagine the occurrence of frightening disasters. Time given to reassurance, although hard to take out of a nurse's busy schedule, may in the end prove more time-saving than dealing with a demoralized and panicked youngster, let alone the anguish this prevents. The awareness that a child is of high intensity of expressiveness, and gives as much energy to a minor complaint of discomfort as to a major one, can help the nurse first to identify the seriousness of the grievance before she gives it her attention. By contrast, the quiet child may be lying silently in terror, convinced that life-threatening events are coming. Reassurance for such a child is vital, but will come only if the nurse is alert to the fact that the amount of outward agitation is not always a true measure of the amount of inward turmoil.

A few examples of the importance of a nurse's sensitivity to a child's inner feelings and reactions can illustrate these points. One of us, as consultant to a pediatric in-patient unit, was called to see Heather, a 5-year-old girl who was recovering from a plastic surgery operation on her scalp. The surgical procedure had gone smoothly, and the child had seemingly comprehended all that had been explained to her. However, though a friendly talkative child before the operation, postoperatively she had become a somber youngster who spent much of her time watching herself in a mirror or weeping quietly without explanation. While the psychiatric consultation request had come officially from the hospital pediatric resident, in fact it had been initiated by the nurse who was troubled about this child's conduct. One year previously, Heather had been badly burned in a tenement fire and the right half of her scalp had healed with scars and no viable hair follicles. The plastic surgery operation was to be done in two stages. In this initial stage, the hair of the back portion of the healthy scalp was turned and stretched so as to cover the back half of the scarred side. Thus, the hair, while thin, eventually, when the front half of the scalp had been similarly repaired, would cover the child's entire head. This had been carefully explained to Heather ahead of time, but now she was depressed instead of being jubilant during the healing process.

It required about a half hour for me to gain Heather's confidence after my reassurance that I was not contemplating some further surgical activity. We spent some time chatting about little girl concerns, and in fact she had somehow transferred herself onto my lap during this talk. Finally, when I asked her to explain about her scalp, she expressed her bewilderment and fear. The carefully explained "in a few months" had been translated by her 5-year-old sense of time into "tomorrow," and she had awakened from the anesthesia expecting to see hair already sprouting. Instead, she found that her healthy side was now shaved-something that had either not been told to her or passed over lightly. Thus, in place of the new sightliness Heather had expected, she was now completely bald and wondering whether this was to be for always. Low-keyed in expressiveness, her misery was shown only her sorrowful demeanor and self-preoccupation. I knew that the staff would have been glad to expand their explanations, but I found that Heather had been afraid to ask questions because she feared that the answers might contain still more unpleasant shocks. I explained the facts again and again. But repeatedly, Heather, only partly heeding, kept asking, "But will it grow tomorrow?" I explained that when she wakened next morning, her hair would look the same as today, but by Thanksgiving (it was early September) she would see a little soft fuzzy hair, and by Christmas there would be still more. I stated that, after she was 6, the other side would be done, the same as this, and that by the time she was 7, she would have hair all over her head.

Clearly, Heather's time sense was still not in tune with the reality, but she finally began to comprehend that in the end she would not be bald. At this point, I located the nurse who had initiated the consultation and, with Heather's permission, explained what her misapprehension had been. The nurse was greatly relieved to know the cause of Heather's misery, and made a bargain that Heather would ask her about anything that she didn't understand. I added that I was sure Heather wouldn't remember all we had spoken about and would want to hear it several times or more from her nurse. And, indeed, when I returned 2 days later to check, I found that Heather was once again her pleasant, outgoing, original personality and had asked "her" nurse for explanations repeatedly. Had Heather been a temperamentally difficult 5-year-old, she might have shown her distress by rambunctious aggression; had she been older she might have comprehended the true situation and been ready to ask for reassurance more easily. Had she been a persistent child, she might have been asking repetitive questions virtually all day long. In all of these instances, effective nursing is assisted by understanding the youngster's temperamental individuality and taking it into account in nursing practice.

An example of the disruption of nursing care that can be created by the reactions of a highly intense youngster, together with the self-protective response of the staff, is to be seen in the case of an adolescent recovering from a leg amputation as a result of sarcoma. As in the previous case, the psychiatric consultation had been initiated by nurses, in this case by the nursing staff as a whole. They were distressed at their own reactions, having become aware that they were avoiding entering the room of this boy since a rather unsettling incident several days previously. And they were chagrined, since the youth clearly needed human contact in view of the catastrophic circumstances to which he now needed to adapt.

The episode in question had occurred almost a week previously. In the immediate postoperative period Eddie had been cooperative, although clearly upset about his physical state. Previously a good athlete, he had been active in high school sports, although not an outstanding team player. Nevertheless, at age 15, much of his group interactions occurred in relationship to athletic events. All this would now be changed for the worse. The nursing staff had empathy for the boy, and were in the habit of dropping in briefly to check and chat. On one occasion, just as a nurse entered the room, she was hit by a flying glass, hard enough to be stunned and to require an x-ray to make certain that her concussion was not accompanied by a fracture. No one had spoken to Eddie about this incident, and he was given routine nursing care.

In their own minds, the nurses were convinced that Eddie had deliberately thrown the glass and tried to injure the nurse. They reasoned that the boy was intensely emotional, which was true, that he was angry at the world for losing his leg, and that he had taken out this anger at the nurse. But now, several days later, the nursing staff had come to realize that while they were resentful that Eddie had not expressed remorse, they themselves had reacted by spending as little time attending him as possible. This did not seem to them an acceptable nursing attitude, and as they had discussed the need to give the boy more attention, their apprehension and avoidance had emerged in their minds as being not only Eddie's problem, but their own need for consultation as well.

Eddie, it turned out, was highly relieved to have a third party enter this situation. He accepted my assurance, after my mental status examination, that I was not pronouncing him "crazy," and he was glad to talk about what had occurred. His first query was about the nurse he had struck with the glass, whom he had not seen since. He was vastly relieved to learn that she had not in fact been injured. "No one will talk to me so I couldn't say how sorry I was, and I couldn't find out how she was. I thought she was dead and I had killed her." The "flood gates" then opened. Eddie had, to his own surprise, seemingly accepted his leg amputation and was making plans as to how he would accommodate to his crippled state. His friends had been phoning and visiting, his parents and brother had been talking also about positive actions to be taken. But, one day, he suddenly became aware of the enormity of his problem, and in a burst of rage against fate, he had flung the glass that was in his hand against the wall opposite his bed. This wall was just at the entrance to the room, and by chance the glass was pointed at the door. Just as he threw the glass, a nurse entered, and the glass struck her head. She fell, other nurses came, and from that moment on Eddie had been isolated by the staff, alone with his thoughts. Now he had not only his personal tragedy, but he also imagined himself to be a murderer.

Given permission, in a sense, by my interest, Eddie now explored his personal situation. He was an intelligent boy, and had gone through the options and results of use of prostheses that would come with training and time. But in the conscientiously optimistic conversations he had had with physical therapists, family, and friends, he had not felt able to voice his despair over his unintended attack on the nurse. Used to complaining loudly about trifles, Eddie was at a loss as to how to express his feelings about this enormity. For once, aware of the distress of those around him, he had been trying to curb his spontaneous intensity of expressiveness and refrain from adding to the concerns of others. But I, as a stranger who was not personally concerned but ready to explore, was acceptable as an outlet. He needed an opportunity to give full expression to all his despairs and apprehensions. He was ready to meet his new world, he had courage, but he also was very, very worried about the hard road ahead. He found himself repeatedly thinking in the old terms, then realizing with a jolt that he would not be capable of participating in so many things which he had heretofore taken for granted. Once this outpouring was over, I then met with the nursing staff. They had no idea that Eddie thought that he had caused the death of the nurse his glass had hit, but realized that in fact no one had talked to him about it. They now realized that his seeming indifference to his action was in fact a composite of lack of opportunity to state his remorse, and shock at what he thought he had done. They were ready and most desirous that rapport once again be established with the youth. Once a three-way discussion had been held with myself, Eddie, and one nurse, Eddie and the nursing staff were ready to have open discussions, giving him an opportunity to air his worries in place of his previous attempt to keep them to himself. Here again was an illustration of the sensitivity of the nursing staff to its failure to meet its own standards, its determination that the situation be understood rather than merely patched over. Once they understood what had happened, they could resume their fully supportive and compassionate nursing practice, with understanding now of the patient's temperamental individuality. A nursing poorness of fit had now been restored to a goodness of fit.

While these examples take up unusual situations, they are not actually out of the mainstream of nursing practice with the sick child in which the child's temperament plays a significant role. More routine aspects of pediatric nursing care of sick children are less dramatic, but, as others have noted with regard to nursing functions related to day care and child abuse (Blosser, 1979; Brown, 1977; Katsura & Millor, 1978; Mercer, in press; Millor, 1984; Moller, 1983; Ventura, 1982), the temperamental style of the child has messages for daily management. In the routines of care of hospitalized children, this is equally important. The temperamentally easy child may be so gentle in expression of distress that the nurse or doctor can overlook symptoms of importance, unless one remembers that a mild overt expression of unhappiness in such a child is so vastly different from her usual behavior as to signal possible symptoms of importance. Conversely, the temperamentally difficult child with high intensity of expressiveness may give complaints about minor irritations that are quite as loud as the reactions to major pain or discomfort. This also presents a challenge to the nurse to investigate the cause of the child's distress on each occasion, and not shrug it off as "there she goes again." The complaints may be almost always minor, but not necessarily always. It is necessary that the nurse not overlook a genuinely important signal for nursing action with such a child by checking on other indications of trouble beyond the child's statement. The youngster with a low threshold to pain may, in fact, need more nursing attention than the one with high threshold. On the other hand, the high-threshold child may refrain from bringing to attention a new pain or other symptom that merits concern, simply because it does not cause substantial subjective distress. The outgoing youngster may confide every thought and feeling quite cheerfully, certain that everyone about is a friend, the slow-to-warm-up child may be too shy to report intimate events and keep them until visiting day, when they are reported privately to family. This child needs to be asked specifics, and also needs to have parent–nurse cooperation, so as to be sure that the parents report physical and emotional events to the nurse whom they see as a friend.

Knowing different children's individual temperamental styles may be a great help in guiding the handling of such procedures as giving injections or changing bandages. With a temperamentally difficult child, after giving a single explanation, it may be best for both child and nurse that the procedure be done quickly, leaving further explanation to be done while the child is no longer anticipating a worrisome action. When it is necessary to repeat this procedure or do another, the nurse can then make reference to the previous action and its lack of hurtfulness—or to its exact degree of pain with regrets that it is necessary; then again quick action. For the easy child, careful step-by-step explanations will bring full cooperation, and the procedure can be accomplished efficiently and more comfortably, bringing trustfulness for future nursing needs.

Even the hospital management of children not requiring intrusive physical procedures can benefit from awareness of the child's temperamental style. An illustration of two nursing attitudes with the same child and their effect is the following:

Julio, age 10, was an inpatient whose periodic severe asthma had once again occurred. Hospitalized for immediate treatment, he was now undergoing tests to determine the offending agents. A persistent child, Julio also had low pain threshold, and was quite apprehensive about the coming tests. The daytime head nurse had little patience with Julio's anxious questions which she answered basically by saying the doctors knew what was best for him. In contrast, the nurse of the afternoon shift had a good relationship with the boy, who responded by being especially helpful. He was, after all, ambulatory and bored with staying in bed. Early one afternoon there was a request for an urgent psychiatric consultation regarding Julio, with a specific statement that he was disturbed, aggressive, and trying to run away from the hospital. A call to the pediatric resident indicated that he had in fact not seen the child, but was passing along the nurse's urgent request. It was not possible to come immediately, and when I arrived on the unit an hour later the shifts had changed, and the nurse now in charge was surprised that a consultation had been requested because she found no fault with the boy. Together we read the previous nurse's note. It indicated that Julio had wanted to go out into the hall. This happened after he had interfered with her nursing duties with the other children and was showing rising agitation and frenetic questioning. The nurse thought Julio was emotionally disturbed and in need of transfer to a psychiatric unit. The afternoon nurse stated that when she arrived Julio was indeed agitated and worried. He wished to phone his mother, and as the phone was in the hall, he had been trying to reach it over the protests of the previous nurse. The current nurse explained that Julio's mother was very helpful, and the nurse considered that he needed these telephone reassurances. Since Julio was very responsible, she explained, she allowed him to go to the telephone by himself. He always returned promptly as he had today. After all, he was overly sensitive to pain, the house staff had not always warned him in advance about needlesticks and and other minor procedures, so that his apprehension had some basis in fact. And when worried, the other children on the unit, as is not unusual, had magnified his fears with horror stories about what was in store for him.

Thus we have two Julios; one an agitated, aggressive, emotionally disturbed boy, and the other a responsible, worried but basically cooperative youngster, able to make warm and trustful relationships if given the little extra reassurance he needed. To the morning nurse Julio was a problem, in contrast to the acutely ill children remaining in their beds and passively accepting nursing care. His need for physical activity, not now being acutely ill, his oversensitivity to pain, and his persistent questions intruding upon the day nurse's time were handled dissonantly given Julio's temperamental needs, with resultant escalation of his anxiety into panic.

SUMMARY

Nurses are on the firing line all day long with sick children and with the worried parents of healthy youngsters. To care for an apprehensive and bewildered sick child, and to reassure and counsel a distressed parent, an experienced and sensitive nurse knows how important it is to understand the individual differences in behavior that different children show. We have been impressed innumerable times over the years at how well nurses understand the concept of temperament, whether they use the term itself or not, and how well so many of them apply the concept in their daily work with children and their parents. Systematic studies and discussions of temperament are now appearing with increasing frequency in nursing journals and textbooks, as indicated earlier in this chapter. This body of literature promises to add significantly to our knowledge of the theoretical and practical significance of temperamental individuality, not only for nurses, but for all professionals with responsibilities for the care of children.

CHAPTER 16

Temperament and the Handicapped Child

Goodness of fit between child and environment is especially crucial for the handicapped child, whether the handicap takes the form of mental retardation, brain damage, deafness, blindness, or other chronic disturbances of physical or psychologic functioning. At best, the handicapped youngster finds the mastery of the usual environmental demands and expectations that arise in the course of normal developmental sequences more stressful and difficult than does the nonhandicapped child. If, simultaneously, there is a significant poorness of fit between the child's temperament and the environment, then excessive stress and suboptimal and psychopathologic outcome becomes likely. On the other hand, certain temperamental attributes, such as easy adaptability or persistence, may serve to ameliorate the adjustment problems of some handicapped youngsters. Furthermore, each type of cognitive, physical, or other handicap may modify or change the type of management that is optimal for a specific temperamental constellation, as compared to that of the nonhandicapped child. For these reasons, it is especially important that those responsible for the care and education of the deviant child identify his temperamental characteristics. Once this is done, the approach that will be optimal for that child, within the limitations imposed by the specific handicap, can be formulated and implemented.

DIFFICULT VERSUS EASY TEMPERAMENT AND THE HANDICAPPED CHILD

As we have noted in earlier chapters (see especially Chapter 3), difficult temperament constitutes a high risk factor for behavior disorder development even in the nonhandicapped child, depending on the nature of the expectations and demands made by caretakers, teachers, and peers. For the handicapped child, this risk factor is often intensified, even in the face of relatively benign handling. Thus, for example, many handicaps, such as deafness, blindness, neurologic dysfunction, or mental retardation, may make the positive adjustment to a new situation, whether at home, in the playground or at school, difficult and stressful, and a source of apprehension. If, in addition, such a child has the temperamental characteristics of intense negative reactions to the new with slow adaptation, then many if not most new situations are likely to become the setting for violent outbursts, severe tantrums, and even disorganization of behavior. It will require truly unusual patience, empathy, and quiet consistent handling on the parents' part to nurse such a child through these tumultuous and potentially disruptive episodes, so that they are transformed into positive rather than pathogenic experiences.

One of our NYLS subjects, with brain damage and difficult temperament, had parents who were not capable of giving her the positive handling she needed. As a result, her developmental course took on an increasingly severe pathologic direction through her childhood years. This girl, Barbara, though she was the product of a full-term pregnancy and uncomplicated delivery, showed signs of neurologic dysfunction in early childhood. Her motor coordination was noticeably inadequate, and, as language developed, she showed a tendency to be echolalic and repetitive. Neurologic examinations from age 4 years onward consistently revealed alternating hyperphoria of the adducting eye in lateral gaze, choreiform movements of the arms and body when the arms were maintained in extension, and clumsiness of gait. The diagnosis of mild dyskinesia with hyperactivity was made. Psychometric testing at 3 and 6 years confirmed the findings of neurologic dysfunction with considerable perceptive–motor problems. Her IQ scores ranged from 91 to 106, but there was wide scatter in both verbal and performance scales, and her responses during testing were perseverative and distractible.

Temperamentally, Barbara was highly active and irregular, she tended to withdraw from new situations, adapted very slowly, and her mood was predominantly negative. She also showed high distractibility and low persistence. Thus, she was a typical temperamentally difficult child, with additional adaptive issues related to her high activity level and distractibility.

During her infancy, Barbara's parents attempted a permissive child-centered approach, which would have been appropriate for a temperamentally easy child with no organic difficulties. However, with Barbara, given her hyperkinesis, arrhythmicity, poor motor coordination, and explosive tantrums when frustrated, such an approach was doomed to failure. In addition, her slow adaptability and perseverative tendencies converted many of her initial responses to the routines of daily living into fixed and elaborate rituals. The mother attempted unsuccessfully, to maintain a reasonable consistent approach to her truly extraordinarily difficult daughter, but the father resorted to highly punitive approaches which only increased Barbara's intense negative reactions and her ritualistic behavior patterns as well as adding anxiety and fears to her symptoms. The parents were not receptive to the possibility of direct treatment for her, and parent guidance sessions were ineffective in changing the father's approach.

By age 6, Barbara was socially isolated, unable to function in a normal school situation, and was increasingly dangerous to herself and to other members of her household with her destructive, perseverative, and impulse-ridden behavior. Residential treatment became necessary, and was continued at several different centers until she was 18. With this treatment regime her behavior improved, her symptoms ameliorated, and she made educational advances. However, each time she went home on a trial basis, there were explosive outbursts of rage against both parents over the most trivial of incidents. Clinical evaluations in middle childhood and adolescence failed to reveal any evidence of a thought disorder, and the original diagnosis of organic personality syndrome with adjustment disorder was maintained.

After graduation from high school, Barbara moved to a youth residence hotel and then a small apartment of her own. Her life since then has been one of turmoil, with the most extreme fluctuations in mood, behavior, and functional levels. She has held a number of office jobs, at which she impressed her supervisors by her competence. With each job, however, she became anxious over any new stress or demand, missed work, and eventually quit or was fired. She was married at 22 to an obviously disturbed young man, they quarreled constantly and violently, and the marriage ended in divorce after 2 years. Psychotherapy and pharmacotherapy have had very limited effect in stabilizing her behavior and violent mood swings.

By contrast to Barbara, Bert, another NYLS subject with early evidence of brain damage, was temperamentally an easy child, with fairly high persistence and moderate activity level. In his case, the etiology of the brain damage appeared to stem from a premature birth with a stormy neonatal course, characterized by respiratory distress accompanied by periods of apnea and dyspnea. His attainment of developmental landmarks, such as sitting, walking, and expressive language, were retarded, and gross motor coordination was awkward and clumsly. Psychometric testing at 4 and 6 years of age, however, gave him a score of 110, which was considered minimal because of the wide scatter and his language lag.

In his early years, Bert's parents were essentially permissive in their approach, but frequently failed to establish clearly defined limits. When irksome management problems resulted from lack of clear parental structures, they were responsive to parent guidance, and modified their approach. Bert, with his positive mood and easy adaptability, responded quickly and positively.

Bert's persistence and easy temperament also stood him in good stead in his social relationships and school functioning through childhood and into adolescence. When he was misunderstood in his initial efforts at verbal communication, he patiently and persistently repeated his statements until they were understood. In the early school years, when other children teased him about his peculiar speech, he worked conscientiously and cheerfully to improve his enunciation. Several clinical evaluations failed to reveal any evidence of significant behavioral disturbance.

Up to this point, the differences between Bert and Barbara's developmental courses were striking. Though Bert's functional handicaps due to neurologic dysfunction were substantially greater than Barbara's, his easy temperament and persistence enabled him to cope directly and master the many difficult adaptive demands of his preschool and early school years. Barbara, by contrast, with her low persistence and difficult temperament, responded to the same social and academic demands by giving up, exploding with intense tantrum behavior, and substituting perseverative rituals for productive mastery. All these difficulties in functioning were further compounded by her parents' inconsistency and her father's punitiveness.

Unfortunately, Bert's development did not continue on its initial favorable course. His neurologic dysfunction included a true dyslexia, with sequential errors and reversals in both letters and numbers. As the demands for academic performance became more exacting with succeeding school years, his dyslexia became an increasing handicap. His speech, though improved, continued to be eccentric, and he began to show unproductive perseverative tendencies in his social activities, both of which created increasing isolation from his peer group. Simultaneously, his father, whose standards for intellectual performance and language use were perfectionist and rigid, became increasingly critical of Bert's school functioning and language use. By the time Bert was 10 years of age, he was actively avoiding much of his homework, had little social involvement with peers, and showed immature and inappropriate behavior when under stress.

A program of remedial instruction, parent guidance, and direct psychotherapy was instituted, with substantial improvement at first. However, Bert's father was unable to change his basically critical attitude toward his son, and the boy was also increasingly faced with the competitive challenge of his intellectually and socially successful younger sister. Furthermore, he began to exhibit not only a desirable persistence, but an increasingly irritating perseveration, which alienated him from his peers, and interfered with the productivity of his work functioning. He continued to show an outwardly cheerful and amiable manner, became involved in a number of useful community and civic projects, and by dint of dogged persistence managed to complete a course of professional training. Now in his late 20s, he has developed rigid moralistic standards and perseverative patterns. However, he has been able to achieve a junior position in his own professional field. He has also elaborated a defensive psychodynamic denial system, which has rendered several attempts at psychotherapy ineffective, has no social life outside of his many community dedications, has no sexual interests, but is content with his life and is self-supporting.

As unfavorable as Bert's life course had been up to recent years, even with his more severe neurologic dysfunction, he still has not suffered from the severe degree of psychopathology as has been evident in Barbara's case. This appears clearly related to the differences in coping ability and adaptive capacity for a handicapped youngster of easy temperament and high persistence as contrasted to difficult temperament and low persistence. Also, although both their fathers made excessive and rigid demands on them, it appeared evident that Bert's father was not as destructive in his behavior as was Barbara's father. Again, this appears to have resulted, in part at least, from the different parental response to a temperamentally easy youngster, as contrasted to a difficult child, and also the different response to hostile criticism of a temperamentally easy individual as opposed to a difficult one.

The additional stress imposed by difficult temperament on a handicapped child has also been indicated by our analysis of a mildly mentally retarded sample of 52 children, varying in age from 5 to 11 years, of middle-class background and living at home. Thirty-one of the 52 children were evaluated as having a behavior disorder on the basis of systematic clinical evaluation (Chess & Hassibi, 1970). Such a high incidence of behavior disorders in the mentally retarded corresponds to the figures from other reports (Philips & Williams, 1975). Temperament scores on the 52 children in our sample were obtained by item scoring of the parent interview data as in the NYLS. Each child was designated as having 0 to 5 signs of the difficult child, depending on whether he was above or below the median of the group in the five temperamental categories of irregularity, withdrawal reactions to new situations, slow adaptability, high intensity, and negative mood. Of the 5 children with 5 signs of the difficult child, all had a diagnosis of behavior disorder. Of the 10 children with 4 signs, 8, or 80%, had such a diagnosis. By contrast, of the 30 children with 0 to 2 signs (the temperamentally easy children), only 12, or 40%, suffered from a behavior disorder (Chess & Korn, 1979).

It is of interest that a comparison of this sample and another group with various physical handicaps resulting from congenital rubella with the NYLS sample did not show any striking differences in the incidence of the difficult child constellation (Thomas & Chess, 1977, Chapter 5). Hertzig and Mittleman (1984) have reported a similar negative finding in a comparison of 66 low-birth-weight children with the NYLS sample. However, within the low-birth-weight sample itself, those who exhibited evidence of central nervous system dysfunction or disorder were more likely to show the difficult child pattern than were those who were neurologically intact.

Thus, though further systematic studies of this issue are desirable, the available evidence suggests that physical handicap, inlcuding mental retardation, but excepting neurologic dysfunction, may not be a risk factor for the development of difficult temperament. It is rather that the simultaneous presence of a physical handicap and difficult temperament magnifies the stresses imposed on a child by the normal sequential demands of socialization and task mastery. But this does not mean that the prognosis in such cases is inevitably bleak. Even in the case of Barbara, cited above, different parental handling might have made for a highly significant change for the better in her developmental course. This is a tenable speculation, given her history of marked improvement in residential centers and severe relapses on visits home to her parents.

PERSISTENCE VERSUS PERSEVERATION

High persistence is a normal temperamental attribute, and, in many circumstances, a most desirable behavioral characteristic. Perseveration, as illustrated in the cases of Barbara and Bert above in this chapter, is

the consequence of neurologic dysfunction, or, at times, other psychopathology, and is never a desirable behavioral attribute. The serious
consequences of perseveration for both Barabara and Bert are typical of
the reports of parents with brain-damaged children of normal intelligence who have sought our professional help over the years. Whatever
their other concerns over their child's problems, these parents have
consistently echoed each other with the same complaint. "With the
other children, I expect them to say 'why can't I' and repeat this a few
times, but I know it will pass. But with Joey, it is clear it will go on
forever." Or, they will say, "This repeating over and over again drives
us all up a wall." And when forced to put a stop to such a youngster's
perseverative question or act, if the family had to get moving to some
other activity, they could predict the storm and even violence that
could result. If, as in Bert's case, the perseveration was accompained by
easy temperament, these might not be violent tantrums when the
youngster was forced to desist from a perseverative act. But even so, the
quiet repetitive insistence with oblivion to its effect on others, can still
be diastrous in its tendency to create social isolation and to interfere
with the youngster's effective academic or work functioning.

The clinical differentiation of persistence from perseveration has
important implications for diagnosis, treatment, and prognosis.
Though both persistent and the perseverative youngsters may show
similar strenuous objections to being diverted from activities in which
they are absorbed, the differential diagnosis between the two is usually
not difficult. The persistent child's activity is typically clearly and
specifically goal-directed on a level appropriate to his age and interests. The task is carried through sequentially to completion, at which
time the youngster becomes reasonably receptive to suggestions as to
what is appropriate for the next scheduled activity—mealtime, bedtime, homework, and so on. The perserverative child, on the other
hand, persists in an action interminably, no clear end-point to the
activity may be evident, and the attempt to turn his attention elsewhere
may be just as difficult after an hour as after 10 minutes. Even where
healthy persistence and pathologic perseveration are present in the
same individual, as in Bert's case, the distinction between the two is
also not difficult. When Bert plugged away doggedly at his demanding
academic subjects with a clear goal in mind this was evidence of his
persistent temperament. When he badgered his college roommate interminably to participate with him in donating blood or volunteering
time to a conservative project to the point where his roommate moved
out—and no one would move in with Bert—this was an example of his
pathologic perseveration.

For the highly persistent youngster who may be having difficulties because of this attribute, the prognosis is usually favorable. His parents and others can learn how to help him to schedule his activities so that they do not have to be prematurely interrupted, such as by mealtimes or a family excursion. The youngster can be taught that projects do not always have to be completed at one sitting. At the same time, a basis for healthy self-esteem can be built by the repeated experiences or completing challenging tasks successfully. And, as the child grows older, he can develop insight into the nature of the persistent pattern, learn to recognize the early warning signs of frustration when he is interrupted in an activity in which he is absorbed, and develop healthy coping mechanisms to short-circuit such reactions of frustration.

For the pathologically perseverative youngster, by contrast, even with concerned and cooperative parents, the prognosis is all too often unfavorable. Occasionally, some of the treatment strategies that are effective with the persistent child may help to some extent with the perseverative one. And sometimes, such youngsters may gain some insight, as they mature, into the nature of their difficulties. But, the basic difference as regards management and treatment is that the persistent youngster has the normal capacity for flexibility and adaptation in functioning which makes change and rechanneling of behavior possible, while the neurologic dysfunction that causes perseveration also creates rigidity instead of flexibility of behavior. As a result, the parents of a perseverative youngster have to rely on mechanical rules such as stating "You are only allowed to ask this question three times," or "You must stop whatever you are doing at dinnertime," with little hope that the child will learn to appreciate the rationale and value of such limits, no matter how often the issues were made. And even if the youngster gains some insight into the problem as he matures, he may have at best only limited success, even with professional help, in translating this insight into effective coping mechanisms to ameliorate the destructive aspects of the perseveration.

OTHER TEMPERAMENTAL ISSUES WITH THE HANDICAPPED CHILD

The nature of a special physical handicap and the special problems it creates for social functioning and task achievement may give special importance to one or another temperamental characteristic. Thus, for the child with athetosis, the struggle to achieve at best a modest degree of motor dexterity will be easier if the general activity level is low, and harder if the child is temperamentally highly active. In other words, the youngster's ability to control the abnormal muscular movements may be significantly affected by the general level of his motor activity.

The deaf individual has to be cautious in new situations where the inability to catch acoustic cues from the immediate environment may endanger his safety—an automobile coming from an unexpected direction, a warning shout from someone outside his vision, a sound of something falling or breaking. Such protective cautiousness may be enhanced if the subject's initial reactions to the new are intermediate between approach and withdrawal, and his responses are characterized by relatively low intensity and motor activity. If, however, the subject moves impulsively, due to quick positive responses to the new, and there are intense reactions with a high motor component, his safety may be endangered.

The blind child copes with the environment by mobilizing the other senses. If he has a low sensory threshold he will find it easier to absorb information from the environment through tactile, auditory, olfactory, temperature, and kinaesthesthic stimuli than if the threshhold to these stimuli is high.

There are only examples of a few of the possible temperament–organism interactions in handicapped children that may affect significantly their ability to cope with the demands and expectations of their environment. It is the clinician who can tease out the meaningful interactions in each case, and use this evaluation to formulate a program of management that will enhance the positive aspects of these youngsters' temperament, and mimimize its deleterious effect.

SUMMARY

The basic theme of this chapter is that specific temperamental characteristics may play an especially important role in a handicapped youngster's development. Temperament may exacerbate the special stresses such a youngster faces in coping effectively with his environment, or it may make possible an amelioration of these special stresses. Each case has to be individualized; the analysis of the dynamics of temperament–child interaction in each case will usually clarify for the clinician the optimal strategies for prevention and treatment.

Our emphasis has been on temperament, given the theme of this volume. However, the same issue is true of other functional factors—

each may exercise a greater influence on the handicapped child's development than would be the case for a nonhandicapped youngster. Thus, in our mentally retarded sample and in the profoundly deaf cogenital rubella group, the new and more complex peer group activities of adolescence have created difficulties in coping far beyond those faced by the NYLS population (Chess, 1980; Chess *et al.*, 1980). The more complex level of peer relationships and academic demand, the beginnings of active social relationships, the progressive change in parent–child relationships which characterize this new developmental stage were evident for all our populations, normal and handicapped. Except for the small minority with substantial behavior disorder, the NYLS group coped adequately with these new demands and expectations, and in many cases with little evidence of the traditionally described adolescent "storm" and "turmoil" (Chess & Thomas, 1984). For the physically handicapped or mentally retarded child, by contrast, the new demands and expectations or adolescence were typically highly stressful. Even where previous levels of adaptation in the community had been excellent, and where families were highly supportive, a deaf or retarded adolescent often could not cope successfully with the demands which were encountered at this new developmental level (Chess, 1980; Chess *et al.*, 1980).

Thus, temperament is only one of a number of functional variables that have special specificance for the handicapped child's adaptive level at various developmental stages. As with the nonhandicapped child, but more exquisitely so, the influence of specific temperamental attributes may be highly important in certain handicapped children, and at certain developmental stages, and of relatively minor significance in other cases or situations. No a priori judgment can be made, and it is the clinician's task to evaluate the relative contribution of all the possible functional variables to the dynamics of the developmental course in any individual child.

PART FOUR

Overview

CHAPTER 17

The Clinical Significance of Temperament

As we have emphasized throughout this volume, in no way do we propose a temperament theory of personality development or of clinical practice. A child, or adult's temperament is one of the many variables that shape the course of normal or deviant psychologic development. As the case vignettes in this volume have illustrated, in some cases temperament plays a highly significant role in the etiology and evaluation of a behavior disorder. In other instances, temperament has a modest influence on development, and in other individuals it is of relatively minor significance. And, in the individuals where temperament represents an important variable, the specific temperamental attribute or constellation that is of significance will vary from case to case.

Furthermore, it is never temperament by itself that is of etiologic significance. It is always the dynamics of the temperament–environment interaction—whether a goodness of fit or a poorness of fit—which is the crucial determinant of healthy or disturbed psychologic functions. (Here, of course, we are not considering those pathologic syndromes, such as autism or manic-depressive illness, in which some pattern of biologic dysfunction is of primary importance. Even in such syndromes, however, temperamental factors may sometimes operate to mitigate or exacerabate the severity of the symptoms.)

These formulations would appear to present the clinician with a formidable task. Any simplistic model that assumes a linear unidimensional relationship between some specific set of antecedent factors and the later psychopathologic outcome becomes inadequate in dealing with the individual–environmental process over time, or with the variations in the type and severity of the influence of any one variable from one case to another. The developmental psychologist Walter Mischel has put this issue well, pointing out that recent research gives us a view of:

> the person as so complex and multifaceted as to defy easy classification and comparison on any single or simple common dimension, as multiply influenced by a host of interacting determinants, as uniquely organized on the basis of prior experiences and future experiences and yet as rule-guided in systematic, potentially comprehensible ways that are open to study by the methods of science. It is an image that has moved a long way from the instinctual drive-reduction models, the static global traits, and the automatic stimulus–response bonds of traditional personality theories. It is an image that highlights the shortcomings of all simplistic theories that view behavior as the exclusive result of any narrow set of determinants, whether these are habits, traits, drives, reinforcers, constructs, instincts, or genes and whether they are exclusively inside or outside the person. (1977, p. 253)

The determination that the many aspects of temperament can be a significant part of the multifaceted and complex character of a person's psychologic functioning emphasizes Mischel's point that human personality defies "easy classification and comparison on any single or simple common dimension" (1977, p. 253). The burden of responsibility of the mental health professional, the pediatrician, the nurse, or the educator is increased by the necessity to identify the nature and significance of temperament within individual patients, clients, or students. But this burden is enormously lightened when the clinician can formulate and carry through an effective therapeutic strategy, once he or she has identified the poorness of fit between the person's temperament and the environment. By contrast, the clinician's burden is magnified when therapeutic intervention is ineffective because of failure to identify the significant role of temperament in any particular case.

THE GOODNESS OF FIT MODEL

Mischel emphasizes that the fact that though a person's psychologic organization is complex and multifaceted, and "multiply influenced by a host of interacting determinants," he or she is also "rule-guided in systematic, potentially comprehensive ways that are open to study by the methods of science" (1977, p. 253). We ourselves have found that the concept of goodness versus poorness of fit provides a useful approach that is "rule-guided in systematic potentially comprehensive ways that are open to study by the methods of science." A number of other investigators have also begun to find this formulation useful, though some prefer the term match vesus mismatch to goodness versus poorness of fit (Greenspan, 1981; Kagan, 1971; Murphy, 1981; Stern, 1977). We do not in the least propose that the goodness of fit model is the *only* useful formulation for the analysis of the complex multiple interacting factors that shape individual human development. Modifications of this model, or qualitatively different approaches will inevitably be generated in forthcoming decades by developmental psychologists and psychiatrists. The life-span perspective formulated by Baltes and associates (1980) is one such promising alternative, which in a number of ways is consistent with the goodness of fit model. In the life-span perspective, development is considered to be a lifelong process, and three sets of interacting influences are defined as determining the course of development: (1) normative age-graded influences, (2) normative history-graded (evolutionary) influences, and (3) nonnormative life events.

DIFFICULT TEMPERAMENT

We have conducted our discussion of temperament throughout this volume in terms of the categories and constellations that we ourselves have identified, defined, and rated. This has been so because we and others have found this particular systematic approach to temperament to have general applicability to many different types of populations, and to be of preventative and therapeutic values to clinicians in dealing with their patients, clients and students. A number of other schemes for defining and rating temperament have been proposed by some other investigators, either as modifications of our formulations or as qualitatively different approaches (see Porter & Collins, 1982). Several of these alternative schemes appear promising conceptually and potentially valuable practically. However, none of them have as yet demonstrated a degree of clinical usefulness sufficient for us to recommend them to the clinician as additions or modifications of our own formulations.

One current question under debate is the use of the term "difficult temperament." The term difficult temperament as we have used it came from our early identification of a specific pattern in children of biologic irregularity, withdrawal tendencies, slow adaptability, marked intensity of reactions, and relatively frequent negative mood. Children with all or most of these characteristics were especially difficult to manage for thier caretakers. However, some other investigators, such as Dr. Carey (Chapter 14) and Dr. Turecki (Turecki & Tonner, 1985) have pointed out that parents may find their children difficult because of a number of different temperamental attributes, and at different age-groups. Also, difficult temperament as we have defined it, may not make for difficulty of management for a caretaker in societies with markedly different child-care practices and attitudes from our own culture (Super & Harkness, 1981). All these considerations have merit, but we ourselves have found our formulations of difficult temperament to be decidedly useful clinically—in the diagnostic process, in discussions with parents, and in the formulation of effective preventative and therapeutic strategies. We presume the debate over the term "difficult temperament" will be resolved in one manner or another in the future. In the meantime, the clinical and research questions involved can remain clear if each clinical and research report indicates specifically the criteria the clinician or investigator are using for his or her designation of difficult temperament.

CONSISTENCY OF TEMPERAMENT OVER TIME

A number of the clinical vignettes detailed throughout this volume have included histories from the parents indicating consistency in the child's current temperament, at the time of clinical evaluation, with the child's behavioral characteristics at earlier age-periods. While in some cases, this might have reflected biased distortions in parental recall, in other cases we were impressed by the likelihood that the parents were giving accurate reports, especially when both parents agreed on the objective details of the child's past history. This consistency in temperament has also been evident, and sometimes strikingly so, in some of the anterospective records of the NYLS subjects.

However, statistical analyses of our NYLS temperament ratings, as well as reports from other centers, indicate only modest levels of consistency in temperament over time for a group of subjects as a whole (Porter & Collins, 1982; Thomas & Chess, 1977). Such a finding should not be surprising. All other psychological phenomena, such as intellectual competence, coping mechanisms, adoptive patterns, and value systems, can and do change over time in many individuals, sometimes dramatically. How could it be otherwise for temperament?

Maturational factors, neurophysiologic changes, and a host of environmental influences—all these may serve to produce continuity in temperament in some individuals and change in others. (This issue is discussed in greater detail in Appendix B.)

The issue of continuity and change is a major focus of interest for the research students of temperament. The elucidation of the factors responsible for consistency or change promises to add significantly to our knowledge of the dynamic processes in both healthy and deviant psychologic development. The clinician, on the other hand, is primarily concerned with the delineation of the individual's current temperament, and the nature of its influence on that person's problems in behavioral or academic functioning. To be able to trace the evolution of the problem backwards in time to its origin is valuable to the clinician, but not essential if the earlier data are confused or ambiguous.

THE FUTURE

Temperament studies are currently one of the major areas of research in developmental psychology and psychiatry. A number of research questions are actively being explored, of which a few can be mentioned: the dynamic processes of continuity and change; the theoretical conceptualization of the nature of temperament; the factors that shape the nature of temperamental characteristics in the young infants; and the identification of new functionally significant temperamental attributes. As these studies cystallize into definite formulations based on substantial bodies of relevant data, such changes or modifications in our present knowledge will undoubtedly have important practical as well as theoretical implications. These will undoubtedly enhance further the usefulness of the application of temperamental issues to clinical practice.

Temperamental
Categories and
Their Definitions

1. Activity level. The motor component present in a given child's functioning and the diurnal proportion of active and inactive periods. Protocol data on motility during bathing, eating, playing, dressing, and handling, as well as information concerning the sleep–wake cycle, reaching, crawling, and walking, are used in scoring this category.

Examples in infancy of statements indicating high activity are, "He moves a great deal in his sleep and must be re-covered several times each night," "She kicks and splashes so much in the bath that the floor must be mopped afterward," or "He has recently learned to turn over and now he does it constantly." Examples of statements indicating low activity would be, "In the morning I find him lying in the same place he was when he fell asleep," or "She can turn over but she doesn't do it much."

At toddler age, examples might be as follows for high activity: "When a friend from nursery school comes to visit, she immediately starts a game of running around wildly," or for low activity, "Given a choice of activities, he usually selects something quiet such as drawing or looking at a picture book."

In middle childhood, statements indicating high activity might be, "When he comes home from school he is outside immediately playing an active game," or "In the house she is constantly doing acrobatics—even while doing her homework. She is in constant motion." A statement indicating a low activity level might be, "Typically she gets involved with a tremendous jigsaw puzzle and sits quietly working at it for hours."

2. Rhythmicity (regularity). The predictability and/or unpredictability in time of any function. It can be analyzed in relation to the sleep–wake cycle, hunger, feeding pattern, and elimination schedule.

In infancy, statements illustrative of high regularity are, "Unless she is sick, her bowel movement comes predictably once a day immediately after her breakfast," or "Nap time never changes no matter where we are, and he sleeps from 2 to 2½ hours without fail." Examples of statements showing irregularity are, "I wouldn't know when to start toilet training since bowel movements come at any time and he has from 1 to 3 a day," or "At feedings, sometimes she drains the bottle but other times she is done after only 2 ounces or so."

In the toddler period, high rhythmicity would be exemplified by reports such as, "Her big meal is always at lunch time," while a statement indicating low rhythmicity would be, "Sometimes he falls asleep right after dinner and on other days he keeps going till 9 or 10 p.m.—there is no predicting."

In middle childhood, examples of statements of high regularity are, "He awakens like clockwork each morning; I never need to wake him for school," or "She comes in from play at the same time each day without being called; she says she feels hungry." A statement indicating irregularity might be, "If he hasn't finished his homework by bedtime, he just continues since he never gets sleepy at the same hour at night."

3. Approach or withdrawal. The nature of the initial response to a new stimulus, be it a new food, a new toy, or a new person. Approach responses are positive, whether displayed by mood expression (smiling, verbalizations, and the like) or motor activity (swallowing a new food, reaching for a new toy, active play, and so on). Withdrawal reactions are negative, whether displayed by mood expression (crying, fussing, grimacing, verbalizations, or the like) or motor activity (moving away, spitting new food out, pushing new toy away, and so forth).

Statements showing high approach in infancy: "He always smiles at a stranger," "She loves new toys," or "He is interested in tasting anything new we give him." High withdrawal would be illustrated by, "He ignores a new toy until it has been around for several days," and "When I introduce a new food, her first reaction is to spit it out."

In the toddler period, a statement illustrating high approach would be, "We went to her new play group yesterday; as always she plunged right in." High withdrawal in the same situation might be shown by, "We started a new play group 2 weeks ago. Although it meets 3 times a week, he remained on the side for the first whole week and only last week did he begin to participate in activities."

In later childhood, a statement of high approach might be, "He came home from his new school the first day talking as if everybody was his best friend and phoned one of his classmates immediately." A high-withdrawal illustration would be, "The class just started to learn fractions. As usual, she is all confused and is sure she will never learn. I reminded her that she always says that with a new subject but later she masters it well."

4. Adaptability. Responses to new or altered situations. One is not concerned with the nature of the initial responses, but with the ease with which they are modified in desired directions.

Illustrations in infancy of high adaptability are, "When he first was given cereal, he spit it out but it took only 2 or 3 times and he was eating it with gusto," or "She used to tell her new stuffed bear 'I don't like you' but after a few days she began to play with it and now it's her best friend." Low adaptability in infancy would be illustrated by, "Every time I put her into her snow suit she screams and struggles till we are outside—and that has been going on for 3 months."

At toddler age, high adaptability would be exemplified by, "She got her first tricycle and couldn't master it, called it 'stupid.' But then I noticed her practicing on it everyday and by a week she was out pedaling happily with her friends." A statement illustrating low adaptability would be, "It took him all fall to go contentedly to nursery school and each time he gets a cold and is out for several days, he becomes reluctant to go again."

In middle childhood, a statement of high adaptability might be, "He went to a tennis camp this summer. Although it was a totally new type of schedule and he felt uncomfortable at first, he became easily involved and felt comfortable within the first week." A low-adaptable child would be exemplified by, "She started a new school with a different way of teaching. Although it is now 3 months, she still gets confused and wants explanations in the old fashion."

5. Threshold of responsiveness. The intensity level of stimulation that is necessary to evoke a discernible response, irrespective of the specific form that the response may take, or the sensory modality affected. The behaviors utilized are those concerning reactions to sensory stimuli, environmental objects, and social contacts.

In infancy, statements illustrating low threshold would be, "If a door closes even softly, he startles and looks up," or "She loves fruit but if I put even a little cereal with it she won't eat it." Reports of high-threshold behavior are, "He can bang his head and raise a bump but he doesn't cry or change his behavior," or "I can't tell from her actions when she is wet or soiled, I have to check by looking."

At toddler age, examples of low threshold would be, "She likes her eggs scrambled one particular way; if they are a shade harder or softer she won't eat them," or "He complains about any pants if the waistband is the slightest bit tight." High-threshold examples might be, "She never complains of feeling cold even though she may be shivering and her lips are blue," or "Whether clothing texture is smooth or rough doesn't make any difference; he seems comfortable in every type."

In middle childhood, statements exemplifying low threshold are, "She is the first one in any group to notice an odor or feel a change in the room temperature," or "He is very alert to people's expressions and comments when I look tired." Examples of high threshold are, "He came home from playing soccer with a blistered heel and he hadn't noticed it or felt any discomfort," or "One of the lights went out while she was doing her homework and she didn't notice it, just went on with her work.'"

6. Intensity of reaction. The energy level of response, irrespective of its quality or direction.

Examples of high intensity in infancy are, "When she is hungry she cries loudly from the beginning—there is no mild fussing at all," or "If he hears music he bubbles with loud laughter and bounces in time to it." Examples of low intensity would be, "He had an ear infection and his eardrums were bulging but he behaved only slightly less frisky than usual and whimpered a bit," or "If he hears a loud noise he fusses but doesn't cry."

In the toddler period, statements indicating high intensity might be, "As soon as she has trouble with a puzzle she screams and throws the pieces," or "When I make his favorite dessert, he jumps with joy and runs shouting to tell his sister." Examples of low intensity are, "If another child takes her toy she grabs it back but doesn't cry," or "If his clothing is uncomfortable he tells me quietly while insisting that it be changed."

In middle childhood, illustrations of high intensity are, "They call him a sore loser because he yells that his opponent is a cheater, and he throws things around in anger," or "In the restaurant she couldn't get the food she wanted and screamed and made a huge fuss." Examples of low intensity might be, "She was taken to a musical show for her birthday. Although she had chosen it herself and told her friends about it, she was deadpan during the performance," or "I know he was very upset at failing the test, but outwardly he appeared only a little subdued."

7. *Quality of mood.* The amount of pleasant, joyful, and friendly behavior, as contrasted with unpleasant, crying, and unfriendly behavior.

In infancy, examples of negative mood might be, "Every time he sees food he doesn't like, he whines and fusses until I take it off the table," or "Each night when put to sleep he cries at least 5 or 10 minutes." Illustrations of positive mood are, "When he sees me take out his bottle of juice, he begins to smile and coo," or "If he is not laughing and smiling I know he's getting sick."

At the toddler period, examples of negative mood would be, "She typically comes home from nursery school full of complaints about the other children," or "At night he regularly feels cheated—for example, he wants one more story, and at no time does he go to bed pleasantly." Positive mood statements are, "He got new shoes and he ran around bubbling with pleasure and showing everyone he met," or "It's a pleasure to come home; she tells me all the nice things she did with smiles of enjoyment."

In middle childhood, statements showing negative mood might be, "School just started last week and he has already accumulated grievances about each teacher," or "We went shopping for new pants and shirts but she found something wrong with everything we looked at—there's no pleasing her." Positive mood would be exemplified by, "The class went on an excursion and her teacher commented on how cooperative and helpfully she behaved," or "He never objects to home chores, just takes out the garbage and does whatever he is asked with a smile."

8. *Distractibility.* The effectiveness of extraneous environmental stimuli in interfering with or in altering the direction of the ongoing behavior.

An example in infancy of high distractibility would be, "He likes to poke objects into the electric outlets but his attention can easily be shifted by offering a toy," or "If someone passes by while she is nursing, she not only looks but also stops sucking until the person has gone." Statements illustrating low distractibility would be, "She has learned to push a little table around the house and if it gets stuck she cannot be sidetracked but keeps trying," or "When he is hungry and it takes a while to get his food ready, it is not possible to get him involved in play—he just keeps crying until he is fed."

In the toddler period, high distractibility might be demonstrated by, "She's not a nagger. If she wants special cookies she sees in the supermarket she will ask once or twice, but then accept a substitute," or "His room is strewn with toys—he scarcely has begun one when his eye is caught by another and he keeps changing, forgetting to put anything back." Low distractibility would be shown by, "He got a new kind of interlocking blocks and we couldn't get him to leave them even when his best friend came to play," or "If she decides she wants to go out to play and it is raining, she will fuss and won't accept any substitute."

In middle childhood, statements of high distractibility would be, "His homework takes a long time as his attention repeatedly is side-tracked," or "She is constantly losing something, as she gets involved with something else and forgets it." Low distractibility might be shown by, "His friends ask him to come to play hockey but if he is making a model airplane, they can't pull him away," or "Once she starts reading a book, we can't get her attention until she gets to the end of a chapter."

9. *Attention span and persistence.* Two categories that are related. Attention span concerns the length of time a particular activity is pursued by the child. Persistence refers to the continuation of an activity in the face of obstacles to the maintenance of the activity direction.

In infancy examples of high persistence would be, "Even though we can get him sidetracked by a toy, as soon as we stop playing with him he returns to his own task of poking at the electric outlet," while long attention span would be illustrated by, "If I give her some magazines she will contentedly tear up paper for as long as a half hour." A statement indicating low persistence would be, "If the bead doesn't go on the string immediately, she gives up," while short attention span would be shown by, "Although she loves her teddy bear, she only plays with it for a few minutes at a time."

In the toddler period high persistence would be indicated by a statement such as, "If he is pushing his wagon about and it gets stuck he struggles and yells until it moves again or else he comes for help—he doesn't give up," while long attention span would be shown by, "She can be engrossed playing in the sandbox for almost an hour." A statement of low persistence would be, "He asked to be taught to draw a dog but lost interest after the first try," and this would also indicate short attention span.

In middle childhood, a statement illustrating high persistence and long attention would be, "She couldn't understand her grammar home-work at first but she stubbornly kept at it until she had mastered it even though it took 2 hours." Short attention span but high persistence would be illustrated by, "She wouldn't give up until she had learned her part in the play, but she worked at memorizing for only about 15 minutes at a time." A statement indicating short attention span and low persistence would be, "He decided to learn how to figure skate but after 5 minutes he gave up trying."

Three temperamental constellations of functional significance have been defined by qualitative analysis of the data and factor analysis. The first group is characterized by regularity, positive approach responses to new stimuli, high adaptability to change, and mild or moderately intense mood that is preponderantly positive. These children quickly develop regular sleep and feeding schedules, take to most new foods easily, smile at strangers, adapt easily to a new school, accept most frustration with little fuss, and accept the rules of new games with no trouble. Such a youngster is aptly called an easy child, and is usually a joy to his or her parents, pediatricians, and teachers. This group comprises about 40% of our NYLS sample.

In the toddler period, middle childhood, and adolescence such children are quickly at ease in a new school or with new people and are welcomed by others because they are good-natured and helpful. In response to the positive welcome they receive, their own sense of ease tends to be reinforced and they continue to welcome new experiences.

At the opposite end of the temperamental spectrum is the group with irregularity in biological functions, negative withdrawal responses to new stimuli, nonadaptability or slow adaptability to change, and intense mood expressions that are frequently negative. These children show irregular sleep and feeding schedules, slow acceptance of new foods, prolonged adjustment periods to new routines, people, or situations, and relatively frequent and loud periods of crying. Laughter, also, is characteristically loud. Frustration typically produces a violent tantrum. These are characteristics of the difficult child, and mothers and pediatricians find such youngsters troublesome indeed. This group comprisess about 10% of our NYLS sample.

Given sufficient time, these children do adapt well, especially if places and people and environmental circumstances remain constant. However, should there be a total change in surroundings and type of expectations in the developmental periods of toddler, middle childhood, and/or adolescence, the difficult child constellation is likely to come into evidence again.

The third noteworthy temperamental constellation is marked by a combination of negative responses of mild intensity to new stimuli with slow adaptability after repeated contact. In contrast to the difficult children, these youngsters are characterized by mild intensity of reactions, whether positive or negative, and by less tendency to show irregularity of biological functions. The negative mild responses to new stimuli can be seen in the first encounter with the bath, a new food, a stranger, a new place, or a new school situation. If given the opportunity to reexperience such new situations over time and without pressure, such a child gradually comes to show quiet and positive interest and involvement. A youngster with this characteristic sequence of response is referred to as the slow-to-warm-up child, an apt if inelegant designation. About 15% of our NYLS sample falls into this category.

These children, adolescents, and young adults are shy and need time to become comfortable in situations of new developmental demands. Their moderate or low intensity of mood expression may protect against stormy interactions, but under some circumstances in later childhood, adolescence, or adulthood may lead to the acceptance of a side-line position.

As can be seen from the above percentages, not all children fit into one of these three temperamental groups. This results from the varying and different combinations of temperamental traits that are manifested by individual children. Also, among those children who do fit one of these three patterns, there is a wide range in degree of manifestation. Some are extremely easy children in practically all situations; others are relatively easy and not always so. A few children are extremely difficult with all new situations and demands; others show only some of these characteristics and relatively mildly. For some children it is highly predictable that they will warm up slowly in any new situation; others warm up slowly with certain types of new stimuli or demands, but warm up quickly in others.

It should be emphasized that the various temperamental constellations all represent variations within normal limits. Any child may be easy, difficult, or slow-to-warm-up temperamentally, or may have a high or low activity level, distractibility, and low persistence or the opposite, or any other relatively extreme rating score in a sample of children for a specific temperamental attribute. However, such an amodal rating is not a criterion of psychopathology, but rather an indication of the wide range of behavioral styles exhibited by normal children.

In adolescence and adulthood also, temperamental traits may be present in varying combinations and may not fit into an easy-to-difficult spectrum.

Whether there has been continuity from infancy on or change in temperamental expression with the passage of years, the importance of temperamental individuality has to do with the interactions of that particular stage of life in the particular environment of that episode.

Consistency and Inconsistency of Temperament over Time

Theories of psychological development, whatever their bias, generally presume a linear predictable sequence from conception or birth onward. As Sameroff (1975) points out in his critical review of this concept, "Scientists with viewpoints biased toward either a maturational or an environmentalist position generally make an implicit assumption that behaviors necessarily build on each other to produce a continuity of functioning from conception to adulthood. The continuity seen in the physical identity of each individual is generalized to the psychological identity of each individual. Just as an individual retains the same body throughout the lifespan, so must he have the same mind."

The concepts of continuity and predictability take credence from the multitude of instances in which adults behave as they did in their earlier years, pursue the same interests and express the same values and goals, and resist vigorously attempts by others to change these behaviors and values. The IQ score is presumed to remain constant from early childhood on, and so are the psychodynamic machanisms the individual uses to cope with his environment. If linear continuity exists, then we can predict the course of behavioral development and know where and how to intercede to prevent behavior disorders in the future.

Reprinted by permission of the publisher from *Temperament and Development*, by A. Thomas and S. Chess, 1977, Chapter 12, New York: Brunner/Mazel.

Theories of development may take many forms: preformism on a hereditary and constitutional basis; predetermined stages of instinctual development in Freudian theory; a hierarchy of ideational-behavioral stages in Erikson's formulation; conditioned reflex patterns to avoid anxiety in behavior theory; or sociological theories such as the culture of poverty. But almost all agree in asserting that later behavior derives directly and predictably from childhood patterns.

Where a developmental concept, such as Piaget's, envisions successive stages which are qualitatively different, other theorists will assert that even in such instances the character of functioning at a new stage is determined by the nature of functioning at the preceding stage. This commitment to the continuity–predictability model is well articulated by Bronson (1974): "Along with some others, I see our apparent inability to make empirical predictions about later personality from the early years as so much against good sense, common observation, and the thrust of all developmental theories that I can take it only as an indictment of established paradigms and methods rather than as evidence of a developmental reality."

As we originally began to observe clinically and impressionistically the phenomenon of temperament, we were struck by the many dramatic evidences of continuity in individuals we knew, sometimes from early childhood to adulthood. It was tempting to generalize from these instances to the concept that an adult's temperamental characteristics could be predicted from a knowledge of his behavior style in early childhood. However, such a formulation would be completely at variance with our fundamental commitment to an interactionist viewpoint, in which individual behavioral development is conceived as a constantly evolving and changing process of organism–environment interaction.

All other psychological phenomena, such as intellectual competence, coping mechanisms, adaptive patterns, and value systems, can and do change over time. How could it be otherwise for temperament? Perhaps our inability to predict accurately from earlier behavior does reflect a "developmental reality" and not just "an indictment of established paradigms and methods" (Bronson, 1974). Perhaps the continuity that is so frequently observed results not from consistency in the psychological attribute per se, but from consistency in the environment–organism interaction. Thus, Bloom (1964) states that intelligence loses its plasticity after about 4 years of age. However, he makes this point: "Our research suggests that although the environment may have its greatest effect on individuals in the first year or so that they are within it, its effect is stabilized and reinforced only when the environment is relatively constant over a period of time."

The NYLS has provided the opportunity to examine a number of issues with regard to continuity or discontinuity in psychological development. The middle childhood period has been studied in relation to Freud's concept of a sexual latency period which was expanded by others to an all-encompassing concept denoting the absence of change during this age-period. As Shaw (1966) commented, the term came to suggest "that nothing really important is happening and that the child is simply waiting for puberty to begin." Our own findings in the NYLS indicated clearly that the middle childhood period is one of continued development and psychologic change (Thomas & Chess, 1962). We would suggest that the label "latency" is a confusing and inappropriate way to designate and characterize children between the ages of 6 and 12, and that the term be abandoned.

The problem of prediction from early to later childhood and adolescence is also highlighted by the cases of behavior disorder in the NYLS (Thomas & Chess, 1976). Of 42 clinical cases diagnosed in the childhood period and then followed into adolescence, 19 recovered, 5 improved, 3 were unchanged, 8 became mildly or moderately worse, and 7 became markedly worse. In a number of the cases the clinical course could be related to specific factors, such as the effectiveness of parent guidance and the overall nature of the parent–child relationship. In other instances, however, the reasons for favorable outcome are not obvious, despite the extensive longitudinal data available in each case. In addition, 5 new cases have thus far been identified in the adolescent period. Here, again, our review of the anterospective longitudinal data, while still incomplete, has as yet not revealed any specific characteristics of the 5 cases or their families in early childhood which could have been predictive of the development of pathology.

CONSISTENCY OF TEMPERAMENT OVER TIME: METHODOLOGICAL PROBLEMS

In considering the data on the consistency of temperament over time, certain methodological problems should first be mentioned. A number of the difficulties in attempting to predict later psychological development from infancy data have been discussed by Rutter (1970). These include: (1) the amount of development still to occur, that is, the fact that most of psychological development takes place after early infancy;

(2) modifiability of psychological development by the child's subsequent experience; (3) effects of intrauterine environment on the characteristics of the young infant, and disappearance of these effects over time; (4) the effects of differing rates of maturation, which may make for wide variations in different children in levels of correlation between infancy and later measures; and (5) differences in the function being tested in infancy and maturity, so that a test in infancy may not measure the same attribute as a test in later childhood or adult life.

With regard to temperament scores, Rutter points up several specific methodological problems, such as the reliance on adjectives parents use in describing their children's behavior, the possibility of selective bias in determining which episodes of behavior the parent or other observer reports, and the problem of separating the content from the style of behavior. Most important, he feels, is the effect that the changing context of the child's behavior might have on the behavioral ratings.

This last problem raised by Rutter bears on a knotty issue in all developmental research. A specific characteristic may have significant continuity in an individual or a group from one age period to another. Yet the changing context of the child's behavior and the emergence of new forms of behavior at later age-stage levels of development may give the same characteristic very different forms of expression. Kagan (1971), in his consideration of this issue, has used the term "homotypic continuity" to refer to stabilities over time in the same response and "heterotypic continuity" to refer "to stabilities between two classes of responses that are manifestly different, but theoretically related." He points out that even if this behavioral phenomenon itself may remain stable over time, it may still be the expression of different motives, standards, and expectancies.

The problem, therefore, is one of determining when dissimilar behavior over time reflects the same characteristic—whether it be temperament, motivation, cognition, values and standards, or psychopathology—and when the same behavior reflects different characteristics at different age-periods. As regards temperament specifically, the behavioral criteria for any temperamental trait must necessarily change over time as the child's psychological functioning develops and evolves. What remains consistent over time is the *definitional identity* of the characteristic (a term suggested by our coworker, Dr. Sam Korn). Thus, a 2-year-old may have loud temper tantrums, and at 18 years of age be described as "hot tempered." Both behaviors, though phenomenologically different, will fit the definition of intensity of mood. Or a 2-month-old may show his withdrawal responses by the first reactions to the bath and a new food, and a 10-year-old by his first reactions to a new peer group or academic subject.

Definitional identity over time, of course, is not self-evident. It involves theoretical concepts of the developmental process, and investigators with different theoretical frameworks will disagree as to whether specific behaviors at different age-periods reflect the same psychological characteristic or not. The validity and heuristic value of any theoretical concept, as well as the internal consistency of its application to specific behavioral phenomena, are then evaluated according to traditional scientific methods.

In addition to these issues raised by Rutter, several other methodological problems regarding the determination of consistency over time have been apparent in the NYLS. A child's characteristic expression of temperament may be blurred at any specific age-period by routinization of functioning. Thus, an infant who shows marked withdrawal reactions to the bath, new foods, and new people may, a year or 2 later, show positive responses to these same stimuli because of repeated exposure and final adaptation. If, at that time he experiences few new situations and stimuli, the withdrawal reaction may not be evident. Adaptation and routinization of activities may, in the same way, blur the expression of other temperamental traits, such as irregularity, slow adaptability, and negative mood expression. Limitation of opportunity for physical activity may lead to frequent restless movements which may be interpreted as high activity or even hyperactivity. The procedures for quantitative scores necessarily rely on routine judgments and scoring approaches which can preclude the identification of meaningful subtleties in the developmental course of individual children. Specific single items of behavior may sometimes be significant in indicating temperamental consistency from one age-period to another, but quantitative scoring methods can hardly give proper weight to the importance of such functionally significant items.

Finally, the issue of consistency of temperament over time cannot be studied globally. One or several temperamental traits may show striking continuity from one specific age-period to another and the other attributes may not. At other age-periods the reverse may be true: the originally consistent traits may not show the correlations, whereas other attributes may now do so. The factors affecting the identification of continuity over time are so complex and variable as to create all kinds of permutations in the patterns of correlations.

CONSISTENCY OF TEMPERAMENT OVER TIME: QUANTITATIVE ANALYSIS

As indicated above, the factors which may make for inconsistency of temperament over time or for the blurring of patterns of consistency which may exist are especially likely to influence the quantitative data analysis. The NYLS quantitative temperament scores for the first 5 years of life were utilized to calculate interyear correlations for the nine categories. The scores for an individual child were pooled for each year. Product–moment correlations were calculated based on these pooled weighted scores for years 1 to 5. The correlations are presented in Table B-1.

As can be seen from Table B-1, there are significant correlations from one year to the next for all categories except approach/withdrawal, distractibility, and persistence. As the time span for the comparison is increased, from 1 year to 2, 3, or 4 years, the number of significant correlations decreases. The number of significant correlations is greatest for the categories of activity level and adaptability.

Approach/withdrawal, distractibility, and persistence, the 3 categories with the least interyear correlations, are also the 3 categories with skewed distribution curves of the group-weighted scores for each of the first 5 years. The other 6 categories, with higher interyear correlations, all approximate normal distribution curves. This suggests that a lack of sufficient differentiation of the subjects by the quantitative scores for approach/withdrawal, distractibility, and persistence may be at least partially responsible for the low level of interyear correlations.

The dwindling in significant correlations over longer time periods may be due to the cumulative effect of the methodological problems discussed above, to change in the expression of temperament over time, or both. It would be of interest to analyze quantitatively the consistency of temperament over time in individual children. It might be that certain children show marked consistency and others show marked inconsistency. These variations might be correlated with specific environmental influences or events. The coding of data in the NYLS would make such an analysis feasible, but thus far such a project has not been undertaken.

McDevitt (1976a) has recently reported a longitudinal assessment of continuity in temperamental characteristics from infancy to early childhood. The sample consisted of 187 children from primarily white middle-class families. The Carey questionnaire was administered to

TABLE B-1. Interyear Correlations for Each of the 9 Categories (N = 100-110)

CATEGORY	1-2	1-3	1-4	1-5	2-3	2-4	2-5	3-4	3-5	4-5
Activity	.30[a]	.21[a]	.26[a]	.16	.30[a]	.31[a]	.23[a]	.26[a]	.29[a]	.31[a]
Rhythmicity	.44[a]	.39[a]	.21[a]	.15	.32[a]	.03	.07	.10	.09	.37[a]
Adaptability	.38[a]	.22[a]	.18	.07	.46[a]	.37[a]	.25[a]	.54[a]	.33[a]	.51[a]
Approach/withdrawal	.07	.13	.01	−.03	.11	.14	.06	.30[a]	.07	.33[a]
Threshold	.39[a]	.36[a]	.14	.21[a]	.25[a]	−.03	.09	.18	.19	.11
Intensity	.47[a]	.17	.02	.10	.28[a]	.01	.13	.30[a]	.14	.32[a]
Mood	.45[a]	.25[a]	.10	.08	.18	.06	.16	.28[a]	.11	.25[a]
Distractibility	−.05	.13	−.12	.12	.15	.05	−.06	.12	.37[a]	.14
Persistence	.11	.04	.01	.09	.38[a]	.23[a]	.16	.24[a]	.28[a]	.13

[a]Correlation is significant beyond the .05 level of confidence for respective N (N varies due to cases with no scored items in particular category for a given year).

the mothers when the children were between 4 and 8 months of age, and the Behavioral Style Questionnaire developed by McDevitt and Carey was administered when the children were between 3 and 7 years of age. Quantitative analysis showed that activity level, adaptability, threshold, and intensity were stable for children of both sexes up to 5 years. Rhythmicity was stable for girls, mood for boys. At 5 to 7 years activity level and mood were stable, but only for boys. At each age interval, easy, slow-to-warm-up and difficult temperament types were obtained by cluster analysis, with a significant degree of consistency of cluster assignment from infancy to 5 years. From infancy to 5 to 7 years, there was little cluster stability. McDevitt takes the position that "temperamental characteristics are influential in personality and behavior throughout development and that periods of instability are reflective of concurrent developmental changes in behavioral competence or major changes in social environment. . . . It is the theoretical definition of the constructs which remains stable" (McDevitt, 1976b).

CONSISTENCY OF TEMPERAMENT OVER TIME: QUALITATIVE ANALYSIS

As the children in the NYLS have been followed from early infancy through adolescence, a number of qualitative longitudinal studies of the children have been done. These analyses have provided information on a number of issues: responses to environmental events and stresses in the preschool years (Thomas, Birch, Chess, & Robbins, 1961), adaptive patterns in the preschool child (Hertzig, Chess, Birch, & Thomas, 1962), development in middle childhood (Thomas & Chess, 1972), temperament and school functioning and learning (Chess, Thomas, & Cameron, 1976b), temperament and behavior disorders (Thomas, Chess, & Birch, 1968), sexual patterns in adolescence (Chess, Thomas, & Cameron, 1976a), and the evolution of behavior disorders into adolescence (Thomas & Chess, 1976). These qualitative studies also make it possible to trace the consistency of temperamental characteristics in individual children over time.

In general, five patterns can be defined: (1) clear-cut consistency; (2) consistency in some aspects of temperament at one period and in other aspects at other times; (3) distortion of the expression of temperament by other factors, such as psychodynamic patterns; (4) consistency in temperament but qualitative change in temperament–environment interaction; and (5) change in a conspicuous temperamental trait. Any individual child may show a combination of several of these five possibilities, that is, consistency over time with one or several temperamental traits, distortion in another, change in several others, etc.

These five patterns will be illustrated by brief vignettes from the longitudinal data.

Consistency over Time

Karen's responses to new situations and new people were typical of the slow-to-warm-up child in infancy and childhood. No problems developed because her parents understood and accepted her behavioral patterns and gave her enough time to adapt to new situations in an unpressured way. One incident of interest occurred when the nursery school had a special program for the parents. When Karen came in with her mother and saw the congregation of strange adults, she climbed on her mother's lap, stayed there all evening, and refused to join her group. As the mother described it, "All the other parents were looking at me, and I knew they were mentally criticizing me for encouraging my daughter's clinging and dependency." Fortunately for Karen, her mother was amused by the experience, and not threatened by these derogatory judgments of other parents.

Karen, now 16 years old, has pursued this same developmental course throughout. She has responded "warily" (as her mother puts it) to almost all new situations—a change of school, a new summer group program, a new curriculum. However, this initial slow-to-warm-up reaction has never created avoidance or permanent withdrawal from stimulating situations and experiences. A new mathematics course was difficult and distressing at first, but she persisted and now plans to take an elective course next year. Karen still asks her mother to call a new doctor or dentist for the first appointment, but then takes over all the subsequent arrangements. She has many friends and interests and has become one of the student activity leaders. She is assertive and appropriately independent for her age, with no evidence of excessive dependency on her parents or others.

Dorothy's temperamental pattern was characterized by frequent negative reactions of mild intensity, a high degree of persistence, and a relatively low activity level. These characteristics were difficult for her parents to understand and accept. They themselves were both intense, positive, and energetic people. Dorothy tended to express frustration by whining and fussing—behaviors which irritated her parents considerably. However, once the parents gained insight into Dorothy's normal behavioral style, they were able to make allowance for her slow movements and accept her pattern of expression.

In the middle childhood years Dorothy's persistence became a major asset in mastering academic demands. Though she lacked a superior IQ level, her ability to plug away at tasks resulted in a high level of academic achievement and a sense of confidence in her scholastic abilities. She also made friends slowly but successfully. In the early adolescent years, however, she again came into conflict with her mother. Her father had died suddenly, a younger sister had developed serious behavioral problems, and the mother was highly pressured by her need to work full-time, maintain the family, and cope with the younger sister's difficulties. The tension in the family increased Dorothy's negative reactions, her mother was now impatient with them because of her own burdens, and frequent antagonistic mother–child interactions developed. However, these never evolved into any significant behavior disorder at home and Dorothy's academic and social functioning outside the home continued satisfactorily.

Dorothy was accepted into an excellent college away from home and did well in the beginning. By the end of the first year, however, she began to be progressively unhappy over her social functioning, dropped out of college after the first semester of the second year and asked for psychiatric consultation with one of us (A.T.). In this interview Dorothy reported increasing dissatisfaction with her peer social relationships, both male and female. She made friends slowly, as always, but this did not disturb her. What did concern her was her difficulty in "opening up" to her friends, in reciprocating their confidences and expressions of positive feeling. This one-sided interchange caused her relationships to drift, with eventual withdrawal and isolation on her part. Her academic work was no problem. In this area she was self-confident and could easily concentrate and work hard, as always.

Psychiatric evaluation showed no evidence of a major mental illness. Dorothy's facial expression was serious, even gloomy, though she did smile brightly though briefly at intervals. Her concerns were expressed in a low, even voice, though she was thoughtful and focused intently on the issues that bothered her. Her major temperamental characteristics were clearly unchanged from childhood: mild negative mood expressions and persistence. Her low activity level was reflected in the sedentary nature of her interests. While it was probable that these temperamental characteristics were playing a major role in the development of her current behavior problems, analytic psychotherapy, which was arranged, was required to define the interplay of temperament with other possible etiological influences.

Consistency in Some Aspects of Temperament at One Period and Other Aspects at Other Times

Carl requested a discussion with one of us (S. C.) after his first term in college because of feelings of depression and inability to cope with the academic and social situation at college. He had made virtually no friends and found studying difficult, experiences he could not recall ever having had before. He had done well academically in high school, had many friends, found school enjoyable, and had a wide range of interests, including the piano. In the interview he was alert, articulate, and in very good contact. He did not appear depressed, but rather bewildered at what was happening, exclaiming, "This just isn't me!"

The anterospective longitudinal data showed that in earlier life Carl had been one of our most extreme difficult child temperamental types, with intense, negative reactions to new situations and slow adaptability only after many exposures. This was true whether it was the first bath or first solid foods in infancy, the beginning of nursery school and elementary school, first birthday parties, or the first shopping trip. Each experience evoked stormy responses, with loud crying and struggling to get away. However, his parents learned to anticipate Carl's reactions, knew that if they were patient, presented only one or a few new situations at a time, and gave him the opportunity for repeated exposure, Carl would finally adapt positively. Furthermore, once he adapted, his intensity of responses gave him a zestful enthusiastic involvement, just as it gave his initial negative reactions a loud and stormy character. His parents became clear that the difficulties in raising Carl were due to his temperament and not to their being "bad parents." The father even looked on his son's shrieking and turmoil as a sign of "lustiness." As a result of this positive parent–child interaction, Carl never became a behavior problem even though difficult children as a group are significantly at risk for disturbed development.

In his later childhood and high school years Carl met very few radically new situations. He lived in the same community and went through the neighborhood school with the same schoolmates and friends. Academic progression was gradual and new subjects were not introduced abruptly. He had sufficient time to adapt to new demands, and generally became enthusiastically involved with a number of activities. As a result, he developed an appropriate positive and self-confident self-image. He played the piano and spoke with animated zest of his pleasure in this activity. He was asked in the interview, "Do you remember what happened when you first started piano lessons?" He thought for a moment and a startled expression came over his face. He described how he had asked his mother if he could take lessons, and she said yes—but she insisted on one condition, that he stick to the lessons for 6 months, no matter how he felt, and then, if he wanted, he could give them up. He agreed, started, and began by "hating it." But he stuck to the bargain and 6 months later his mother asked if he wanted to quit. His answer was, "Are you crazy? I love it!"

When Carl went off to college away from home, however, he was suddenly confronted with a whole series of new situations—strange surroundings, an entirely new peer group, new types of faculty approaches, school schedules, and curriculum, and a complex relationship with a girl student with whom he was living. Again, as with the many new adaptive demands of early childhood, his temperamental responses of withdrawal and intense negative reactions were expressed. Other possible reasons for his difficulties were explored—dependency needs for his parents, sexual conflict, anxiety over academic demands, peer competition—but no evidence of any of these was elicited.

Only the one discussion was necessary with Carl, and consisted primarily in clarifying for him his temperamental pattern and the techniques he could use for adaptation. Actually, Carl had already begun to take these steps on his own—cutting the number of new subjects, disciplining himself to study each subject daily for a specific time, attenuating his involvement with the girl, and making a point of attending peer social group activities, no matter how uncomfortable he felt. By the end of the academic year his difficulties had disappeared and his subsequent functioning has been on the previous positive level. He was told that similar negative reactions to new experiences might occur in the future. His response was, "That's all right. I know how to handle them now."

Carl's behavior showed a number of dramatic shifts over the years, from early childhood to middle childhood and early adolescence, to the onset of college life and then to his subsequent adaptation at college. But these behavioral changes did not constitute change in his temperamental pattern. The phenomenon of shifts in behavioral patterns over time even though underlying psychodynamic patterns remain consistent is well recognized. The same phenomenon can occur with temperament.

Distortion of the Expression of Temperament over Time

Norman was seen at age 17 by one of us (S. C.), who had followed him since age four and a half because of persistent behavior disturbance. At age 17 he had already dropped out of two colleges in one year, and was planning to go abroad for a work–study program. He was in good contact, but dejected and depressed. He was extraordinarily self-derogatory, said he couldn't finish anything he started, was lazy, and didn't know what he wanted to do. "My father doesn't respect me, and let's face it, why should he." He talked of "hoping to find myself" in a vague, unplanned way.

Norman had always been a highly distractible child with a short attention span. Intelligent and pleasant, the youngest in his class throughout his school years due to birth date, he started his academic career with good mastery. However, at home his parents were impatient and critical of him even in the preschool years because of his quick shifts of attention, dawdling at bedtime, and apparent "forgetfulness." By his fifth year he showed various reactive symptoms such as sleeping difficulties, nocturnal enuresis, poor eating habits, and nail-tearing. Year by year his academic standing slipped. His father, a hard-driving, very persistent professional man, became increasingly hypercritical and derogatory of Norman. The father equated the boy's short attention span and distractibility with irresponsibility, lack of character, and lack of will-power. He used these terms openly to the boy and stated that he "disliked" his son. The mother grew to understand the issue, but no discussion with the father as to the normalcy of his son's temperament and the impossibility of the boy's living up to his standards of concentrated hard work succeeded in altering the father's attitude. He remained convinced that Norman had an irresponsible character and was headed for future failure—indeed a self-fulfilling prophecy. There were several times when the boy tried to comply with his father's standards and made himself sit still with his homework for long periods of time. This only resulted in generalized tension and multiple tics and Norman could not sustain this effort so dissonant with his temperament—another proof to himself and his father of his failure. Direct psychotherapy was arranged in early adolescence, but Norman entered this with a passive, defeated attitude and the effort was unsuccessful. His subsequent development was all too predictable.

In Norman's case the dissonance between parental standards and demands and his temperamental characteristics led to psychodynamic patterns which then distorted, but did not change, temperament qualitatively. The acceptance of his father's derogatory and hypercritical value judgments on himself led to increasing drifting, shifting quickly from one vague plan to another, grasping at straws—all in all, a caricature of his temperamental characteristics of distractibility and short attention span.

Consistency in Temperament, but Qualitative Change in Temperament–Environment Interaction

Nancy, when seen in the routinely scheduled interview at age 17, was bright, alert and lively. She was involved in a number of activities that interested her, and reported an active social life, good school functioning, and a pleasant relationship with her parents. She had no symptoms of psychological disturbances. Nancy's report of positive functioning was confirmed in the separate interview with her parents. They did describe her as "hot-headed," but did not consider this a problem.

It would have been very difficult to predict this favorable development into adolescence in Nancy's early years. Like Carl, she was a difficult child temperamentally from early infancy onward. But unlike Carl's parents, Nancy's parents responded to her intensity, irregularity in biological functions, negative reactions, and slow adaptability so as to produce extreme stress and difficulty in development in the youngster. The father was highly critical of her behavior, rigid in his expectations for quick positive adaptation, and punitive when Nancy did not respond to his demands. The mother was intimidated by both husband and daughter and vacillating and anxious in her handling of her child. By the age of 6 Nancy developed explosive anger outbursts, fear of the dark, thumb-sucking, hair-pulling, and poor peer group relationships. Her symptoms and clinical findings were severe enough to warrant the diagnosis of neurotic behavior disorder, moderately severe. Psychotherapy was instituted with some improvement. But the dramatic change occurred when in the fourth and fifth grades Nancy showed evidence of musical and dramatic talent. This brought increasingly favorable attention and praise from teachers and other parents. This talent also ranked high in her parents' own hierarchy of desirable attributes. Nancy's father now began to see his daughter's intense and explosive personality, not as a sign of a "rotten kid" as heretofore, but as evidence of a budding artist. She was now a child he could be proud of, and he could afford to make allowances for her "artistic" temperament. With this view of Nancy and her temperament the mother was also able to relax and relate positively to her daughter. Nancy was permitted to adapt at her own pace, the positive aspects of her temperament came into evidence, and her self-image improved progressively. By adolescence all evidence of her neurotic symptomatology and functioning had disappeared and she was considered as recovered from her neurotic disorder.

Change in a Conspicuous Temperamental Trait over Time

David, when seen in the direct interview at age 17 years, was obese and conspicuously apathetic and lethargic. He reported little interest or involvement in any kind of outside activities. The time-related interview with his parents confirmed this observation of David as a very low-active adolescent.

In his early years David had been consistently one of the most motorically active children in our study sample. He was always in motion, with a cheerful and friendly manner. However, David's home environment was not a happy one, but marked by constant discord and destructive competition between his parents. They repeatedly preached to David and others what a superior child he was (David did indeed have a superior IQ), and that any difficulties he had in school were due to poor teaching. As time went on David's school performance deteriorated, as did his other activities. The parents held the school and teachers entirely responsible for their son's growing school failure, and over time David internalized his parents' almost paranoid-like projection of blame. Motivation dwindled, any critical self-evaluation was entirely absent, and disinterest and apathy became progressively dominant features of his overall functioning. With these attitudes it was no surprise that resistance to psychotherapy was complete.

In David's case, temperament did not appear to play an influential role in the ontogenesis of his behavior disorder. Furthermore, a conspicuous temperamental characteristic of his early years, high activity level, was no longer in evidence by adolescence. On the contrary, he was apathetic and sluggish and showed a strikingly low activity level. The inertia and inactivity appeared to be psychodynamically determined.

In our original analysis of David's development, we conceived of the possibility that his temperamental attribute of high activity level might not have been changed but only "submerged" by the psychodynamic influences on his behavior. However, temperament is a phenomenologic description of behavioral style at any particular point in time. Whatever the findings are at any time, whether high or low activity level, persistence or nonpersistence, etc., and whatever changes may occur, the designation of temperament is based on those findings. In that sense, the concept of "submersion" of a temperamental trait is inapplicable.

DISCUSSION

In the above vignettes, the data and findings have of necessity been selectively culled and reported from the enormous amount of longitudinal information available on each youngster. In each case, however, the essential facts regarding child psychopathology, parental attitudes and practices, and special environmental events available in our records have been sketched in. Of course, it is always possible that, even with the mass of data accumulated on each child, significant data have been missed at one point or another in the developmental course from infancy to adolescence. This is one of the inevitable contingencies of any behavioral research and a special hazard of an anterospective longitudinal study.

From the quantitative interyear correlations of temperament for years 1 to 5, and from the qualitatively derived vignettes, it is clear that temperament does not necessarily follow a consistent, linear course. Discontinuities over time are certainly to some extent the result of the methodological problems in data collection and analysis. Much more important, however, are the functional, dynamic reasons which determine continuity or discontinuity over time.

Temperament is a phenomenologic term in which the categorization of any individual is derived from the constellation of behaviors exhibited at any one age-period. These behaviors are the result of all the influences, past and present, which shape and modify these behaviors in a constantly evolving interactive process. Consistency of a temperamental trait or constellation in an individual over time, therefore, may require stability in these interactional forces, such as environmental influences, motivations and abilities. The vignettes reported above illustrate some of the vicissitudes of temperament over time as one expression of the dynamics of the organism–environment interactional process.

In Carl's case, the difficult child pattern was strikingly and consistently in evidence in early childhood in the response to the demands for adaptation to one new situation and expectation after another—the bath, new foods, new people, nursery school, etc. There were withdrawal reactions to the new, irregular biological functions, intense negative reactions to the new with much screaming, and slow adaptation. With patient, consistent, and understanding parents and no special new situations to overwhelm him, Carl finally made the necessary adaptations to become a smoothly functioning, relaxed, and happy child. He was then largely indistinguishable from the child who started with an easy temperament, except that Carl's positive mood expressions were enthusiastic and lusty—definitely an asset. An occasional special new situation, such as learning to play the piano, again evoked temperamental expressions of initial withdrawal, intense negative mood, and slow adaptation. Otherwise, the middle childhood period was serene, with successful progressive mastery of gradually evolving social and academic expectations and opportunities, and proportional development of self-confidence and a positive self-image. It would be inaccurate to say that the difficult temperament was "repressed" or "latent" during this period, and use the occasional short-lived expression of his earlier childhood characteristics as evidence of some "return of the unconscious." Rather, it should be said that at any period the observable temperamental characteristics were the expression of his actual temperament at that time. Any difference from a previous time would be the consequence of modification by the evolving organism–environment interactional process. A temporary change to difficult temperament we would interpret as an actual change due to special environmental influences, not an activation of temperamental characteristics existing in some latent form. Continuity from one period to another was indicated by similarity in temperamental responses at different periods, given the same interactional dynamics. Another youngster, with a different temperamental potential, would, of course, have responded differently to the new.

However, continuity is not identity. Carl's distressing behavioral manifestations in the first year of college were similar to the difficult temperamental reactions in infancy, but not identical. His psychological structure was different at 18 years from 1 year of age in self-image, self-awareness, self-assurance born out of a succession of successful mastery experiences, and in the repertoire of adaptive techniques available to him. As a result, the expression of temperament was different and the sequence of coping activity was also different.

In Karen, Dorothy, and Norman, consistency in temperament over time was clearly evident. But this did not mean an identical developmental course for all three. In Karen's case, the environment was uniformly favorable at all times, with smooth, positive progression through childhood and adolescence. For Dorothy, the environment was basically positive, though with periods—in early childhood and the beginning college years—in which excessively stressful demands were made which were dissonant with her temperamental potential. As a result, relatively mild behavior disorders developed at these dissonant interactional periods.

In Norman's case, the environment was consistently unfavorable and dissonant with his temperamental capacities, and served to exaggerate and distort these temperamental traits in a pathological direction. In David's case, the organism–environment interactional process was also pathogenic, but was of such a nature as to change rather than distort a major temperamental trait.

Nancy illustrates most dramatically the difficulty in predicting developmental sequences. An unanticipated emergence of a special talent transformed the basic character of the organism–environment interaction. In other instances, a similar degree of change might occur from an unpredictable change in the environment or some other new emerging feature in the child's own characteristics.

Continuity and predictability can thus not be assumed for a specific attribute or pattern of the child, whether it be temperament, intellectual functioning, motivational attributes, or psychodynamic defenses. What is predictable is the process of organism–environment interaction. Consistency in development will come from continuity over time in the organism and significant features of the environment. Discontinuity will result from changes in one or the other which make for modification and change in development.

References

Allport, G. W. (1961). European and American theories of personality. In H. P. David & H. Von Bracken (Eds.), *Perspectives in personality theory* (pp. 3-24). New York: Basic Books.

American Psychiatric Association. (1968). *Diagnostic and statistical manual of mental disorders* (2nd ed.). Washington, DC: Author.

American Psychiatric Association. (1980). *Diagnostic and statistical manual of mental disorders* (3rd ed.). Washington, DC: Author.

Arnold, L. E. (Ed.). (1978). *Helping parents help their children.* New York: Brunner/Mazel.

Baltes, P. B., Reese, H. W., & Lipsitt, L. P. (1980). Life-span developmental psychology. *Annual Review of Psychology, 31,* 65-110.

Bates, J. E. (1980). The concept of difficult temperament. *Merrill–Palmer Quarterly, 26,* 299-319.

Bloom, B. S. (1964). *Stability and change in human characteristics.* New York: John Wiley & Sons.

Blosser, C. (1979). Avoiding potential behavior problems in children. *Pediatric Nursing, 5,* 11-15.

Bronson, W. C. (1974). Mother-toddler interaction: A perspective on studying the development of competence. *Merrill–Palmer Quarterly, 20,* 275-301.

Brown, J. B. (1977). Infant temperament: A clue to childbearing for parents and nurses. *American Journal of Maternal Child Nursing, 2,* 228-232.

Brown, M. S., & Murphy, M. A. (Eds.). (1981). *Ambulatory pediatrics for nurses* (2nd ed.). New York: McGraw-Hill.

Bruch, H. (1954). Parent education, or the illusion of omnipotence. *American Journal of Orthopsychiatry, 24,* 723-732.

Burks, J., & Rubenstein, M. (1979). *Temperament styles in adult interaction.* New York: Brunner/Mazel.

Burks, J., & Rubenstein, M. (1985, October). *Clinical implications of temperamental differences.* Paper presented at the Third Annual St. Louis Conference on Infants and Preschoolers, St. Louis, MO.

Cameron, J., & Rice, D. (in press). Developing anticipatory guidance programs based on early assessment of infant temperament. *Journal of Pediatric Psychology.*

Carey, W. B. (1974). Night wakening and temperament in infancy. *Journal of Pediatrics, 84,* 756-758.

Carey, W. B. (1981). The importance of temperament-environment interactions for child health and development. In M. Lewis & L. Rosenblum, (Eds.), *The uncommon child* (pp. 31-55). New York: Plenum Press.

Carey, W. B. (1982). Clinical use of temperament data in pediatrics. In R. Porter & G. Collins (Eds.), *Ciba Foundation Symposium 89: Temperamental differences in infants and young children* (pp. 191-202). London: Pitman.

Carey, W. B. (1984a). "Colic"—Primary excessive crying as an infant-environment interaction. *Pediatric Clinics of North America, 31*(5), 993-1005.

Carey, W. B. (1984b, November). *The continuing confusion of attention deficit disorder and temperament.* Paper presented at symposium on Temperament Interactions in the Educational Process, St. Louis, MO.

Carey, W. B. (1985a). Interactions of temperament and clinical conditions. In M. Wolraich & D. Routh (Eds.), *Advances in developmental and behavioral pediatrics* (Vol. 6, pp. 83-115). Greenwich, CT: JAI Press.

Carey, W. B. (1985b). Temperament and increased weight gain in infants. *Journal of Developmental and Behavioral Pedatrics, 6*, 128-131.

Carey, W. B. (1986). Clinical interactions of temperament: Transitions from infancy to childhood. In R. Plomin & J. Dunn (Eds.), *The study of temperament: Changes, continuities & challenges* (pp. 151-162). Hillsdale, NJ: Erlbaum.

Carey, W. B., & Levine, M. D. (1983). Comprehensive diagnostic formulation, in M. D. Levine, W. B. Carey, A. C. Crocker, & R. T. Gross (Eds.), *Developmental-behavioral pediatrics* (pp. 1036-1040). Philadelphia: W. B. Saunders.

Carey, W. B., & McDevitt, S. C. (1978). Stability and change in individual temperament diagnoses from infancy to early childhood. *Journal of the American Academy of Child Psychiatry, 17*, 331-337.

Carey, W. B., & McDevitt, S. C. (1980). Minimal brain dysfunction and hyperkinesis: A clinical viewpoint. *American Journal of Diseases of Children, 134*, 926-929.

Carey, W. B., McDevitt, S. C., & Baker, D. (1979). Differentiating minimal brain dysfunction and temperament. *Developmental Medicine and Child Neurology, 21*, 765-772.

Chess, S. (1964). Mal de mère. *American Journal of Orthopsychiatry, 34*, 613-614.

Chess, S. (1980). The mildly mentally retarded child in the community: Success versus failure. In S. B. Sells, R. Crandall, M. Roff, J. S. Strauss, & W. Pollin (Eds.), *Human functioning in longitudinal perspective* (pp. 91-102). Baltimore: Williams & Wilkins.

Chess, S., Fernandez, P., & Korn, S. (1980). The handicapped child and his family: Consonance and dissonance. *Journal of the American Academy Child Psychiatry, 19*, 56-67.

Chess, S., & Hassibi, M. (1970). Behavior deviations in mentally retarded children. *Journal of the American Academy of Child Psychiatry, 9*, 282-297.

Chess, S., & Korn, S. (1970). Temperament and behavior disorders in mentally retarded children. *Archives of General Psychiatry, 23*, 122-130.

Chess, S., & Thomas, A. (1982). Infant bonding: Mystique and reality. *American Journal of Orthopsychiatry, 52*, 213-222.

Chess, S., & Thomas, A. (1984). *Origins and evolution of behavior disorders: Infancy to early adult life.* New York: Brunner/Mazel.

Chess, S., Thomas, A., & Cameron, M. (1976a, March). *Sexual attitudes and behavior patterns in a middle class adolescent population.* Paper presented at the meeting of the American Orthopsychiatric Association.

Chess, S., Thomas, A., & Cameron, M. (1976b). Temperament: Its significance for early schooling. *New York University Educational Quarterly, 73*, 24-29.

Chow, M., Durand, B., Feldman, M., & Mills M. (1984). *Handbook of pediatric primary care.* New York: John Wiley & Sons.

Clements, S. D. (1966). *Minimal brain dysfunction in children.* Washington, DC: Government Printing Office.

Coleman, J. C. (1978). Current contradictions in adolescent theory. *Journal of Youth and Adolescence, 7*(1), 1-11.

DeVries, M. W. (1984). Temperament and infant mortality among the Masaiob East Africa. *American Journal of Psychiatry, 141*, 1189-1194.

Dubos, R. (1965). *Man adapting.* New Haven: Yale University Press.

Dworkin, P. H. (1983). Pediatric role definition. In M. D. Levine, W. B. Carey, A. C. Crocker, & R. T. Gross (Eds.), *Developmental-behavioral pediatrics* (pp. 1022-1035). Philadelphia: W. B. Saunders.

Engel, G. L. (1977). The need for a new medical model: A challenge for biomedicine. *Science, 196,* 129-135.

Erikson, E. (1963). *Childhood and society* (2nd ed.). New York: W. W. Norton.

Erikson, E. (1968). *Identity, youth and crisis.* New York: W. W. Norton.

Erikson, K. (1976). *Everything in its path.* New York: Simon & Schuster.

Forehand, R. I., & McMahon, R. J. (1981). *Helping the noncompliant child: A clinicians' guide to parent training.* New York: Guilford Press.

Freud, A. (1960). The child guidance clinic as a center of prophylaxis and enlightenment. In J. Weinreb (Ed.), *Recent developments in psychoanalytic child therapy* (pp. 25-38). New York: International Universities Press.

Freud, A. (1965). *Normality and pathology in childhood: Assessments of development.* New York: International Universities Press.

Freud, S. (1924). *Collected papers* (Vol. 2). London: Hogarth.

Gordon, E. M., & Thomas, A. (1967). Children's behavioral style and the teacher's appraisal of their intelligence. *Journal of School Psychology, 5,* 292-300.

Gould, R. L. (1972). The phases of adult life: A study of developmental psychology. *American Journal of Psychiatry, 129,* 521-531.

Gough, J. W. (1973). *John Locke's political philosophy.* Oxford: Oxford University.

Greenspan, S. I. (1981). *Psychopathology and adaptation in infancy and early childhood,* New York: International Universities Press.

Heagerty, M., Glass, G., King, H., & Manly, M. (1980). *Child health: Basics for primary care.* New York: Appleton-Century-Crofts.

Hertzig, M, Chess, S., Birch, H. G., & Thomas, A. (1962). Methodology of a study of adaptive functions of the pre-school child. *Journal of the American Academy of Child Psychiatry, 2,* 236-245.

Hertzig, M., & Mittelman, M. (1984). Temperament in low birthweight children. *Merrill-Palmer Quarterly, 30,* 201-212.

Hymovich, D. (1982). *Nursing of children—a family centered guide for study.* Philadelphia: W. B. Saunders.

Jersild, A. T. (1968). *Child psychology.* Englewood Cliffs, NJ: Prentice-Hall.

Kagan, J. (1971). *Change and continuity in infancy.* New York: John Wiley & Sons.

Kagan, J. (1984). *The nature of the child.* New York: Basic Books.

Katsura, H., & Millor, G. K. (1978). The difficult child in day care—a nursing challenge. *American Journal of Maternal Child Nursing, 3,* 166-170.

Keogh, B. K. (1982). Children's temperament and teacher decisions. In R. Porter & G. Collins (Eds.), *Ciba Foundation Symposium 89: Temperamental differences in infants and young children* (pp. 267-278). London: Pitman.

Keogh, B. K. (1984, November). *The influence of temperament and the educational experiences of at-risk and handicapped children.* Paper presented at symposium on Temperament Interaction in the Educational Process, St. Louis, MO.

Korn, S. J., & Gannon, S. (1983). Temperament, cultural variation and behavior disorder in preschool children. *Child Psychiatry and Human Development, 13,* 203-212.

Lerner, R. M., & Busch-Rossnagel, N. (Eds.). (1981). *Individuals as producers of their development.* New York: Academic Press.

Levinson, D. J. (1978). *The seasons of a man's life.* New York: Knopf.

Marmor, J. (1983). Systems thinking in psychiatry: Some theoretical and clinical implications. *American Journal of Psychiatry, 140,* 833-838.

Martin, R. P., Nagle, R., & Paget, K. (1983). Relationships between temperament and classroom behavior, teacher attitudes, and academic achievement. *Journal of Psychoeducational Assessment, 1,* 377-386.

McDevitt, S. C. (1976a). *A longitudinal assessment of continuity and stability in temper-*

amental characteristics from infancy to early childhood. Unpublished doctoral dissertation, Temple University, Philadelphia.

McDevitt, S. C. (1976b). Personal communication.

McDevitt, S. C., & Carey, W. B. (1981). Stability of ratings versus perceptions of temperament from early infancy to 1–3 years. *American Journal of Orthopsychiatry, 51,* 342–345.

Mercer, R. T. (1981). A theoretical framework for studying factors that impact on the maternal role. *Nursing Research, 30,* 73–77.

Mercer, R. T. (in press). Predictors of maternal role attainment at one year post birth. *Western Journal of Nursing Research.*

Millor, G. K. (1981). A theoretical framework for nursing research in child abuse and neglect. *Nursing Research, 30,* 78–83.

Millor, G. K. (1984, May). *Children's temperaments and maternal childbearing behaviors in abusive and non-abusive families.* Paper presented at the annual meeting, Western Society for Research in Nursing, San Francisco.

Mischel, W. (1977). On the future of personality measurement. *American Psychologist, 32,* 246–254.

Moller, J. S. (1983). Relationship between temperament and development in preschool children. *Research in Nursing and Health, 6,* 25–32.

Murphy, L. B. (1981). Explorations in child personality. In A. I. Rabin, J. Aronoff, A. M. Barclay, & R. A. Zucker (Eds.), *Further explorations in personality* (pp. 161–195). New York: John Wiley & Sons.

Murphy, L. B., & Moriarty, A. E. (1976). *Vulnerability, coping and growth.* New Haven: Yale University Press.

Neugarten, B. L. (1979). Time, age, and the life cycle. *American Journal of Psychiatry, 136,* 887–894.

Offer, D., & Offer, J. (1975). *From teenage to young manhood.* New York: Basic Books.

Philips, I., & Williams, N. (1975). Psychopathology of mental retardation: A study of 100 mentally retarded children. *American Journal of Psychiatry, 132,* 1265–1271.

Porter, R., & Collins, G. (Eds.). (1982). *Ciba Foundation Symposium 89: Temperamental differences in infants and young children.* London: Pitman.

Pullis, M., & Cadwell, J. (1982). The influence of children's temperament characteristics on teacher's decisions strategies. *American Educational Research Journal, 19,* 165–181.

Roberts, F. B. (1983). Infant behavior and the transition of parenthood. *Nursing Research, 32,* 213–217.

Rose, A. M. (1955). Mental health and mental disorder. New York: W. W. Norton.

Rubenstien, R. A., & Brown, R. T. (1984). An evaluation of the validity of the diagnostic category of attention deficit disorder. *American Journal of Orthopsychiatry, 54,* 398–414.

Rutter, M. (1970). Psychological development: Predictions from infancy. *Journal of Child Psychiatry and Psychology, 11,* 49–62.

Rutter, M. (1979). *Changing youth in a changing society.* London: Nuffield Provincial Hospital Trust.

Rutter, M. (1980). Introduction. In M. Rutter (Ed.), *Scientific foundations of developmental psychiatry* (pp. 1–7). London: Heinemann.

Rutter, M. (1982). Temperament: Concepts, issues, and problems. In R. Porter & G. Collins (Eds.), *Ciba Foundation Symposium 89: Temperamental differences in infants and young children* (pp. 1–16). London: Pitman.

Rutter, M. (1983). Introduction: Concepts of brain dysfunction syndromes. In M. Rutter (Ed.), *Developmental neuropsychiatry* (pp. 1–11). New York: Guilford Press.

Sameroff, A. J. (1975). Early influences on development: Fact or fancy? *Merrill-Palmer Quarterly, 21,* 275–301.

Scarr, S. (1984). *Mother care/other care*. New York: Basic Books.

Schmitt, B. D. (1983). Pediatric developmental-behavioral counseling. In M. Levine, W. B. Carey, A. C. Crocker, & R. T. Gross (Eds.), *Developmental-behavioral pediatrics* (pp. 1043–1057). Philadelphia: W. B. Saunders.

Shaw, C. R. (1966). *The psychiatric disorders of childhood*. New York: Appleton-Century-Crofts.

Shaywitz, S. E., & Shaywitz, B. A. (1984). Evaluation and treatment of children with attention deficit disorders. *Pediatrics in Review, 6*, 99–109.

Smith, R. J., & Steindler, E. M. (1983). The impact of difficult patients upon treaters: Consequences and remedies. *Bulletin of the Menninger Clinic, 47*, 107–116.

Stein, S. P., Holzman, S., Karasu, T. B., & Charles, E. S. (1978). Mid-adult development and psychopathology. *American Journal of Psychiatry, 135*, 676–681.

Stern, D. (1977). *The first relationship*. Cambridge, MA: Harvard University Press.

Stevenson, J., & Graham, P. (1982). Temperament: A consideration of concepts and methods. In R. Porter & G. Collins (Eds.), *Ciba Foundation Symposium 89: Temperamental differences in infants and young children* (pp. 36–46). London: Pitman.

Super, C. M., & Harkness, S. (1981). Figure, ground and gestalt: The cultural context of the active individual. In R. M. Lerner & N. A. Busch-Rossnagel (Eds.), *Individuals as producers of their development* (pp. 69–86). New York: Academic Press.

Tackett, J. J. M., & Hansberger, M. (Eds.). (1980). *Family-centered care of children and adolescents: Nursing concepts in child health*. Philadelphia: W. B. Saunders.

Terr, L. C. (1981). Psychic trauma in children: Observations following the Chowchilla school-bus kidnapping. *American Journal of Psychiatry, 138*, 14–19.

Thomas, A. (1981). Current trends in developmental theory. *American Journal of Orthopsychiatry, 51*, 580–609.

Thomas, A., Birch, H. G., Chess, S., & Robbins, L. C. (1961). Individuality in responses of children to similar environmental situations. *American Journal of Psychiatry, 117*, 434–441.

Thomas, A., & Chess, S. (1957). An approach to the study of sources of individual differences in child behavior. *Journal of Clinical and Experimental Psychopathology and Quarterly Review of Psychiatry and Neurology, 18*, 347–357.

Thomas, A., & Chess, S. (1972). Development in middle childhood. *Seminars in Psychiatry, 4*, 331–341.

Thomas, A., & Chess, S. (1976). Evolution of behavior disorders into adolescence. *American Journal of Psychiatry, 133*, 5.

Thomas, A., & Chess, S. (1977). *Temperament and development*. New York: Brunner/Mazel.

Thomas, A., & Chess, S. (1980). *Dynamics of psychological development*. New York: Brunner/Mazel.

Thomas, A., & Chess, S. (1981). The role of temperament in the contributions of individuals to their development. In R. M. Lerner & N. A. Busch-Rossnagel (Eds.), *Individuals as producers of their development* (pp. 231–254). New York: Academic Press.

Thomas, A., Chess, S., & Birch, H. G. (1968). *Temperament and behavior disorders in children*. New York: New York University Press.

Thomas, A., Chess, S., & Korn, S. J. (1982). The reality of difficult temperament. *Merrill-Palmer Quarterly, 28*, 1–20.

Thomas, A., Chess, S., Sillen, J., & Mendez, O. (1974). Cross-cultural study of behavior in children with special vulnerabilities to stress. In D. Ricks, A. Thomas, & M. Roff (Eds.), *Life history research in psychopathology* (Vol. 3, pp. 53–67). Minneapolis: University of Minnesota Press.

Turecki, S., & Tonner, L. (1985). *The difficult child*. New York: Bantam.

Vaillant, G. E. (1977). *Adaptation to life.* Boston: Little, Brown.

Vaillant, G. E., & Vaillant, C. O. (1981). Natural history of male psychological health. X. Work as a predictor of positive mental health. *American Journal of Psychiatry, 138,* 1433–1440.

Ventura, J. N. (1982). Parent coping behaviors, parent functioning, and infant temperament characteristics. *Nursing Research, 31,* 269–273.

Werner, E. E., & Smith, R. S. (1982). *Vulnerable but invincible.* New York: McGraw-Hill.

Whaley, L. F., & Wong, D. L. (1983). *Nursing care of infants and children.* St. Louis: C. V. Mosby.

Wicoff, J. S. (1983, December 1). Personal communication.

Index